Job Quality in an Era of Flexibility

Experiences in a European context

Edited by Tommy Isidorsson
and Julia Kubisa

Routledge
Taylor & Francis Group
LONDON AND NEW YORK

First published 2019 by Routledge

2 Park Square, Milton Park, Abingdon, Oxon, OX14 4RN
605 Third Avenue, New York, NY 10017

Routledge is an imprint of the Taylor & Francis Group, an informa business

First issued in paperback 2020

British Library Cataloguing-in-Publication Data
A catalogue record for this book is available from the British Library

Library of Congress Cataloging-in-Publication Data
Names: Isidorsson, Tommy, editor. | Kubisa, Julia, 1979– editor.
Title: Job quality in an era of flexibility : experiences in a European context / edited by Tommy Isidorsson and Julia Kubisa.
Description: 1 Edition. | New York : Routledge, 2019. | Series: Routledge studies in employment relations | Includes bibliographical references and index.
Identifiers: LCCN 2018024364 | ISBN 9781138561595 (alk. paper)
Subjects: LCSH: Quality of work life. | Job satisfaction.
Classification: LCC HD6955 .J633 2019 | DDC 331.25/6—dc23
LC record available at https://lccn.loc.gov/2018024364

ISBN: 978-1-138-56159-5 (hbk)
ISBN: 978-0-367-73352-0 (pbk)

Typeset in Sabon
by Apex CoVantage, LLC

This book is an initiative that evolved out of the activities of the Marie Curie 'ChangingEmployment' programme 317321, led by Professor Paul Stewart, University of Strathclyde. Theme 3 of the programme: 'Employee Wellbeing and Work Life Quality' on which this book is based, was led by Dr Tommy Isidorsson, University of Gothenburg together with postdoc Dr Julia Kubisa, University of Gothenburg.

ChangingEmployment SEVENTH FRAMEWORK PROGRAMME MARIE CURIE ACTIONS

Job Quality in an Era of Flexibility

This is the era of flexibility. Under constant pressure to be adaptable, organizations increasingly adopt employment practices such as zero-hours contracts, the casualization of the workforce and the use of temporary and agency labour. These flexible practices are central to debates about the changing nature of job quality and its causes, trends and consequences.

Arguing that job quality is central to understanding contemporary work, this book explores the internal and external pressures for flexibility in workplaces, professions and sectors and how this pressure shapes workers' experiences of job quality. By studying job quality dynamics via case studies from organizations and occupations in the UK, Poland, Belgium and Sweden, the volumes illustrates the diversity of practices and experiences, as well as market pressures and institutional arrangements which effect working lives. Finally, the editors propose a policy debate on the new concept "flexiquality" – a combination of flexibility and job quality that can be beneficial for both management and workers.

By providing a comparative international reference on job quality, flexible working arrangements, and managerial strategies, this wide-ranging volume will be of interest to all scholars of work place studies, HRM and the sociology of work.

Tommy Isidorsson is Associate Professor, Work Science, University of Gothenburg, Sweden and Member and Supervisor at ChangingEmployment Marie Curie ITN. His main interest has been how firms and organisations adapt to changes in demand, i.e. the different strategies utilised for handling changes in production volume including working-time flexibility, functional flexibility and numerical flexibility. His interest in numerical flexibility includes several studies on agency workers focusing on mechanisms that influence the development of these strategies for flexibility and their consequences on a societal level, workplace level and individual level. He is the author of many publications on temporary agency workers.

Julia Kubisa, Marie Curie Experienced Researcher, Post-doc at University of Gothenburg, Sweden, Assistant Professor at the Institute of Sociology, University of Warsaw, Poland. For her PhD she researched women's activation in Polish trade unions, focusing on the position of nurses and midwives in the Polish healthcare system and their patterns of protest, the impact of healthcare system reform on working conditions and trade unions' activities. Her research interests are in the field of the sociology of work, including the gendered division of labour, labour relations in transforming economies and new patterns of job quality.

Routledge Studies in Employment Relations
Series editors: Rick Delbridge and Edmund Heery
Cardiff Business School

Aspects of the employment relationship are central to numerous courses at both undergraduate and postgraduate level. Drawing insights from industrial relations, human resource management and industrial sociology, this series provides an alternative source of research-based materials and texts, reviewing key developments in employment research.

Books published in this series are works of high academic merit, drawn from a wide range of academic studies in the social sciences.

Employment Relations in the Hospitality and Tourism Industries
Rosemary Lucas

Reward Management (**second edition**)
A critical text
Edited by Geoff White and Janet Druker

Latest in the Routledge Research in Employment Relations series

Management in the Airline Industry
Geraint Harvey

Towards a European Labour Identity
The case of the European Works Council
Edited by Michael Whittal, Herman Knudsen and Fred Huijgen

The Internet of People, Things and Services
Workplace transformations
Edited by Claire A. Simmers and Murugan Anandarajan

Job Quality in an Era of Flexibility
Experiences in a European context
Edited by Tommy Isidorsson and Julia Kubisa

For more information about this series, please visit: www.routledge.com

Contents

Acknowledgements

We are very much indebted to our contributors, both for their expertise and their valuable feedback and collaboration during the entire process of writing the book. Dragoş Adăscăliţei, Stephen Bouquin, Kristina Håkansson, Pedro Mendonca, Kirsty Newsome, Dora Scholarios, Pille Strauss-Raats and Justyna Zielińska, in particular, offered advice and extensive comments at various stages of the project. The usual disclaimers about responsibility apply.

This book is an initiative that evolved out of the activities of the Marie Curie 'ChangingEmployment' programme 317321, led by Professor Paul Stewart, University of Strathclyde. We thank Paul Stewart for the support of the project. Theme 3 of the programme: 'Employee Wellbeing and Work Life Quality', on which this book is based, was led by Dr Tommy Isidorsson, University of Gothenburg together with postdoc Dr Julia Kubisa, University of Gothenburg.

Contributors

Dragoş Adăscăliţei PhD, Lecturer in Human Resource Management and Employment Relations at the Management School, University of Sheffield, United Kingdom Marie Curie Early Stage Researcher at ChangingEmployment Marie Curie ITN

Stephen Bouquin Professor at Centre Pierre Naville, Department of Sociology, Université d'Evry Val d'Essonnes, France. Member and Supervisor at ChangingEmployment Marie Curie ITN Member and Supervisor at ChangingEmployment Marie Curie ITN

Nadja Doerflinger PhD, post-doctoral researcher at the Centre for Sociological Research, KU Leuven, Belgium

Kristina Håkansson Professor at the Department of Sociology and Work Science, University of Gothenburg, Sweden Member and Supervisor at ChangingEmployment Marie Curie ITN

Hannah Hesselgreaves Lecturer at the Institute of Health and Wellbeing, University of Glasgow, Scotland Senior Research Associate

Tommy Isidorsson Associate professor, Department of Sociology and Work Science, University of Gothenburg, Sweden Member and Supervisor at ChangingEmployment Marie Curie ITN

Julia Kubisa PhD, assistant professor at the Institute of Sociology, University of Warsaw, Poland. Marie Curie Experienced Researcher ChangingEmployment Marie Curie ITN

Pedro Mendonca PhD, Lecturer HRM/OB Nottingham Business School Nottingham Trent University Marie Curie Early Stage Researcher at ChangingEmployment Marie Curie ITN

Sian Moore Professor in Employment Relations and Human Resource Management and Director Work, Employment and Research Unit, University of Greenwich, UK.

Kirsty Newsome Professor of Employment Relations and Associate Dean Research, Sheffield University Management School, UK Member and Supervisor at ChangingEmployment Marie Curie ITN

Raymond Pratt Scottish Women's Institutes, Scotland

Valeria Pulignano Professor of Sociology of Work and Industrial Relations, KU Leuven, Belgium Member and Supervisor at ChangingEmployment Marie Curie ITN

Cilla Ross Vice Principal of Education and Research, Co-operative College Member and Supervisor at ChangingEmployment Marie Curie ITN

Dora Scholarios Professor of Work Psychology, Department of Human Resource Management, University of Strathclyde, Glasgow, Scotland Member and Supervisor at ChangingEmployment Marie Curie ITN

Pille Strauss-Raats PhD student at the Department of Sociology and Work Science, University of Gothenburg, Sweden Marie Curie Early Stage Researcher at ChangingEmployment Marie Curie ITN

Federico Vegetti PhD, Post-doctoral researcher, Central European University, Budapest, Hungary

Justyna Zielińska PhD student at the Institute of Sociology, University of Warsaw, Poland

Figures and tables

Figures

Tables

1 Job quality in an era of flexibility

Introduction

Julia Kubisa and Pedro Mendonca

Throughout the most part of the last 20 years, flexibility has been viewed as a defining feature of relations in the labour and economic markets. The challenges of a globalising economy, the race for lower costs of production and the pressure to limit public spending have created a constant need to answer and to adapt to changes – by companies in the private sector and by public enterprises. This brought a prevalence of 'no long term' relationships, a short-term perspective and acceptance of risk that have become perceived as a norm in an everyday life shaped by the managerial discourse.

What about the working lives? While flexibility is increasingly recognised as inevitable, its drawbacks have been pointed out within the debate on the rise of a precarious class and diminishing social securities for workers (Standing, 2009, 2011, 2014). There is increasing consensus that the European attempt to balance the flexibility for employers by state protection of social security and lifelong learning for workers under the name of flexicurity has brought an unbalanced development of flexibility in comparison to securities (Burroni and Keune, 2011). In this context, it is relevant to ask what are the consequences for the everyday experiences of workers in their jobs? What is happening to forms of contracts, working time arrangements, autonomy or social work environment? In times of a constant need for change – what is happening to job quality?

The overarching aim for the volume is not only to describe how but also to explain *why* job quality is affected or influenced by different strategies for flexibility. Placed within the context of job quality debates in European policies in the period of post-crises labour market deregulation, the edited volume aims to illustrate how the pursuit for job quality within the setting of flexibility shapes the working conditions in occupations, at workplaces and in sectors in chosen European countries. At the same time, the volume is concerned with exploring the workers' experiences and the ways in which they are able to reshape and recast the quality of their own jobs by regulating the employers' behaviour. The authors within this volume show a far more complex picture of how job quality is shaped, experienced and regulated, when compared to macroeconomic research dominating the research field of job quality in Europe. Overall, the volume presents the recent quantitative and qualitative research in the field of job quality and flexibility conducted by the members of the 7th Framework Programme, Marie Curie Initial Training Network, *ChangingEmployment*.

The order of this chapter is as follows. It starts with an overview on debates on job quality in order to grasp its multi-dimensional character. Then in broad lines it presents what is happening to job quality in an era of flexibility. This is followed by a theoretical framework with conceptualisations of flexibility and the index of job quality that will serve as point of reference for the research presented in the volume. The last sections are dedicated to introducing the European context for the research presented in the volume and the structure of the following chapters.

Understanding job quality

Job quality had been central to the EU's employment strategy in the beginning of the 2000s. It was claimed that job quality, and not only job creation, contributes to economic sustainability, social cohesion and individual well-being (European Commission, 2001; European Commission, 2002). The 'more and better jobs' agenda aspired by the European Union would allow its members to endure competition from low-wage countries and compete in a knowledge-based and highly skilled economy. This aspiration has been consequently followed up with renewed European employment strategies aimed at smart, sustainable and inclusive growth that included commitment to fostering high levels of employment and productivity (Hurley, Fernández-Macías and Storrie, 2013).

However, the 2008 financial crisis shifted emphasis from quality to quantity of jobs, in order to fight the increasing unemployment (Muñoz de Bustillo, Fernández-Macías, Esteve and Antón, 2009). During and after the crisis, there was a significant shift towards more aggressive flexible labour market policies. As Meardi (2014) argues, the once distinctive European 'social model' was replaced by a financial focus, fiscal retrenchment, and policies rooted on providing employers with higher flexibility leverage to face economic downturns. However, the emphasis on flexibilisation that this model advocates has led to researchers identifying an aggravated trend towards labour market dualisation, where lower-quality jobs with little job security and fewer skill requirements became more common (Eurofound, 2012; Gallie, 2013). This has been accompanied by increasing problems of economic inequalities, growing labour market insecurity, decreasing levels of social integration and lower levels of general quality of working life (Dieckhoff and Gallie 2007; Burroni and Keune, 2011; Eurofound, 2012; Gallie, 2013; Holman and McClelland, 2011).

The centrality of job quality in the political agenda in the context of dismantling the European social model has made it the aim of considerable scrutiny from regulatory organisations and academics, working to understand its causes, trends and consequences (Appelbaum, Bernhardt and Murnane,

2003; Coats, 2009; Gallie, 2007, 2013; Green, 2006, 2013; Holman, 2013; Warhurst, Carre, Findlay and Tilly, 2012; Clark, 2005; European Commission, 2001; Grimshaw and Rubery, 2005). Yet the nature and components of job quality are still debated. Analyses tend to focus on a number of dimensions of what might comprise job quality, typically highlighting the importance of pay and skills (Clark, 2005). However, many researchers have drawn emphasis to its other potential components, such as job security, training and development, work organisation, task discretion, employee voice, job satisfaction, working time and work-life balance (Green, 2006; Gallie, 2007, 2013; Coats, 2009; Kalleberg, 2011). The European Commission has identified ten job quality dimensions, including both subjective and objective elements: intrinsic job quality; skills, lifelong learning and career development; gender equality; health and safety at work; inclusion and access to labour market; work organisation and work-life balance; flexibility and security; social dialogue and worker involvement; diversity and non-discrimination; and work performance (Kelliher and Anderson, 2008). It thus emerges that job quality can be understood as multi-dimensional, though the precise definition and the full understanding of the interconnections between its components are yet to be clear and consensual (Muñoz de Bustillo, Fernández-Macías, Antón and Esteve, 2011; Carré, Findlay, Tilly and Warhurst, 2012).

One of the most challenging aspects in political economy is to understand how economies can contribute to creating more good quality jobs in different sectors and at different skill levels within the labour market despite employers' effort to use flexibility. Progress is likely to be limited without addressing job quality through a multi-dimensional and multilevel approach (Muñoz de Bustillo et al., 2011). As Muñoz de Bustillo et al. (2011, p. 457) argue 'jobs do not exist in a vacuum, but in a social context in which there are public and private institutions like a welfare state and the family'. Thus, jobs, and consequently individuals, are influenced by the context in which they are embedded, meaning that a comprehensive examination of job quality involves looking at different sectoral and institutional country contexts, as well as the perspectives of social actors, such as managers, workers and trade unions. The examination of these perspectives may help to better assess and understand the ways in which job quality is shaped in an era of flexibility; whether job quality under flexible working practices differs in different organisational, sectoral and national settings; and, finally, what are the workers' experiences of job quality and strategies to improve or maintain the quality of their own jobs.

Both quantitative and qualitative studies have contributed significantly to the understanding of trends, drivers and experiences of job quality in existing research. On the one hand, there are those studies analysing job quality through European – or nationwide – datasets at the 'macro' level in order to track and understand changes in job quality over time. These macroeconomic studies argue that organisations are embedded in institutional frameworks that shape job quality outcomes (Gallie, 2013; Green, 2006; Muñoz de Bustillo et al., 2009) and tend to focus on the impact of static measures such as employment protection legislation on labour market indicators such as the rate of unemployment (Howell and Rehm, 2009) or underemployment (Bell and Blanchflower, 2010).

On the other hand, job quality has also been analysed on 'micro' or workplace levels. These studies aim to investigate job quality through the lenses of specific types of workplace regimes (Taylor, Hyman, Mulvey and Bain, 2002; Thompson, 1989; Thompson and Warhurst, 1998). Both approaches have strengths and weaknesses. Although the first provides the analysis of job quality with clear measures and representative datasets, it may leave what is happening in the workplace as a 'black box' and fall short in connecting directly with the concrete work experience of workers (Sengupta, Edwards and Tsai, 2009). The second approach provides strong accounts of the context in which job quality is analysed, allowing for a finely detailed picture of workplace regimes and workers' experiences. At the same time, it is limited in conceptualising and measuring job quality, as well as identifying the wider politico economic factors that shape jobs at the workplace level (Sengupta et al., 2009). This volume contributes to job quality debates by exploring how institutional factors feed into the organizational level for a more complete picture as well as exploring additional drivers, such as market forces.

As Muñoz de Bustillo et al. (2009, 2011) point out, the standard analysis of the labour market usually focuses on quantity: the number of jobs and the employment or unemployment rates. However, jobs differ – they can be 'good' or 'bad' and each of those characteristics is multi-dimensional and dependent on the sectoral and national context (Kalleberg, Reskin and Hudson, 2000; McGovern, Smeaton and Hill, 2004; Gallie, 2013; Grimshaw and Lehndorff, 2010). Although there is established evidence that job quality outcomes vary between countries (Gallie, 2013; Eurofound, 2012), there is also increasing literature stressing the role of sectoral and organisational factors in the variation of job quality outcomes (Crouch, Schröder and Voelzkow, 2009; Lloyd and Payne, 2016), providing critical information on the segmented differences in working life experiences. Additionally, Muñoz de Bustillo et al. (2009, 2011) underline it is crucial to study job quality in times of crisis, when policy priorities are shifted towards job quantity and fighting unemployment. They point out that monitoring job quality is important as it allows to see the dynamics of change within the context of crisis – whether that would be destruction of worst jobs, or overall improvement. As Doogan (2009) frames it, knowledge about the quantity and quality of jobs, and the job structure enables better understanding of deep changes that we are facing as societies – such as globalisation or technological change.

The era of flexibility and its impact on job quality

Flexibility has become the driving concept behind the restructuring of work (Bradley, Erickson, Stephenson, and Polity, 2000). Currently, flexibility is presented as a solution that helps to bear the pressures of contemporary markets. The customers who seek for new niche products, the increasing globalised competition and the fact that 'change' is the only phenomenon we can be sure about – this all creates a context in which flexibility solutions are seen as inevitable. While the concept is commonly used in the public discourse, it is also value-saturated and surprisingly undefined (Engstrand, 2007). Flexibility is generally seen as beneficial and positive, even though this kind of argumentation comes from the managerial discourse that conflates the interests of employers and workers under a common goal. As an example, employment flexibility is associated with personal choice and freedom, and opportunity for personal regeneration (Handy, 1995).

The flexibility that is advised and promoted is mostly organization-oriented, just as it was described over 30 years ago in Atkinson's model of 'flexible firm' (Atkinson, 1984),promoted by managerial theorists (Womack, Jones and Roos, 1990) and still a firm point of reference for management debates. The model presents several types of flexibility. The functional flexibility means quick and smooth redeployment of employees between activities and tasks, along with changes of products and production methods. The numerical flexibility can be external or internal and stands for an increase or decrease of the number of employees according to a company's needs, including working hours, which loosens the contractual relationship between manager and worker. This is supported by financial flexibility that is based on new pay and remuneration systems such as assessment-based pay and a cost-cutting approach, and on organisational flexibility that relates to the suppleness of the organisation of a corporation (Atkinson, 1984; Atkinson and Meager, 1986; Womack et al., 1990; Furåker, Håkansson and Karlsson, 2012).

As flexibility became a subject of critical debate within the sociology of work and political economy, it was pointed out that it must be linked with factors such as economic pressures, an unstable market, technological change, privatisation, high unemployment, decline in the power of trade unions, deregulation of the employment relations and weakening of social benefits (Ladipo and Wilkinson, 2002). A crucial change in the economy and labour market composition happened when flexible labour was moved from the peripheries of Fordist production to the core post-Fordist capital accumulation, along with the development of the service sector (Hardt and Negri, 2000). That points to a direct connection between flexibility and uncertainty, instability, vulnerability and insecurity, which is a result of the transfer of risks from states and businesses to workers, their families and communities (Hewinson, 2016). The incorporation of flexible labour practices into global production networks can be viewed as a coercive process that engages in competition from both supplier firms and the states. The strategies of the latter to show their ability to provide a flexible investment environment include not only tax benefits, but first and foremost the provision of disciplined, cheap or skilled workers.

Companies use flexibility to adjust to supply and demand of the external labour market. They can take up distancing strategies, like the use of temporary work agencies, self-employment of former employees or subcontracting. They can use functional flexibility by introducing multi-skilled employees and group organisation or they can take advantage of internal and external numerical flexibility by using different working time and contract arrangements – part-time, temporary work and agency work workers (Furåker et al., 2012; Hudson, 2002).

The rise of zero-hour contracts has brought into research focus the issue of flexible working time arrangements – a form of flexibility once overlooked. Rubery, Ward, Grimshaw and Beynon (2005) and more recently Wood (2016) have suggested that working time flexibility may represent a new regulation within the employment relationship. Some researchers have linked this type of flexibility as beneficial to the employee, providing opportunity to choose their own working hours (Guest, 2002). Contrastingly, others have argued that it is more common to find flexible working time practices that are detrimental for employees' job quality experience and undermine workers' coping arrangements while benefiting employers (Wood, 2016; Håkansson and Isidorsson, 2003).

Financial flexibility creates a variety of employment solutions in terms of forms of contracts that are not necessarily clear for workers. It involves knowledge and risk taking on the side of workers, which poses problems in the context of decreasing trade union membership or difficulties in access to legal advisory (Pollert, 2007). Heery and Salmon (2000) argue that the current employment relationship stems from an 'age of insecurity'. They suggest that the economic risk is being transferred increasingly from employers to employees through ever-more contingent employment practices. This trend comes from the shift of a dominant pattern in which internal labour markets protected workers from market forces, to a new employment relationship where pressures from markets are brought inside the organisation and used to mediate the relationship between workers and management (Heery and Salmon, 2000). The ever-increasing flexibility practices adopted by firms, either to take advantage of institutional arrangements or as responses to market derivatives, have been central within the debates of the changing nature of job quality (Kalleberg, 2011). Many accounts argue that critical to this debate is the prolific use of flexible forms of contracts (Kalleberg, 2011; Huws, 2011).

Research studies looking to understand increasing levels of contingent labour have focused on how its use is facilitating numerical flexibility at a firm level (Caroli, Gautié, Lloyd, Lamanthe and James, 2010; Kalleberg, 2011). It is argued that in order to respond to fluctuations on market demand and to keep labour costs low, firms employ individuals with low levels of job security (Kalleberg, 2011). Atkinson (1984) argues that firms tend to differentiate three groups of employees in order to cope with market fluctuations. The first group comprises multi-skilled core-workers whose roles and skills make them indispensable for the firm and are therefore typically given a full-time permanent contract. The first peripheral group provides numerical flexibility via atypical employment such as fixed-term contracts. In the second peripheral group the workforce is not employed at the user-firm but they perform their work there, consisting of temporary agency workers, outsourced and subcontracted workforce (Atkinson, 1984). Similarly, Kalleberg (2003) differentiates between standard and non-standard employment, with standard work arrangements entailing regular full-time jobs with a single employer. Kalleberg (2003) argues that employees with such contracts are regarded as key for the running of the business and are well integrated into the organization, whereas workers with non-standard employment are located in the organisation's periphery, experiencing temporary and/or part-time work. Both theories are united by the argument that firms rely on a core full-time group of workers who are fundamental for the successful running of the business, and a peripheral group of contingent workers that are functionally used to adjust to market fluctuations.

Researchers have emphasised the negative consequences of job insecurity for employees' physical and mental health as it can lead to psychological distress (De Cuyper and De Witte, 2007; Vander Elst, Van den Broeck, De Witte and De Cuyper, 2012). More recently, Vander Elst, Van Den Broeck, De Cuyper and De Witte (2014) have found that job insecurity is related to lower organisational commitment, individual performance and to higher levels of poor general health. Moreover, Taylor (2013) argues that such flexible dynamics lead to fear of losing jobs, which forces individuals to comply with increasingly demanding managerial mechanisms. Relating to the unpredictability of working time, it has been found that short notice changes interfere with workers' ability to manage personal duties and responsibilities, resulting in family-life related disruptions. Rubery et al. (2005), Findlay, Kalleberg and Warhurst (2013) and Carré et al. (2012) have highlighted the importance of working time to the work-life balance.

Theoretical approach – conceptualisation of flexibility and job quality

For the purpose of this volume we look at the theories that conceptualise flexibility in terms of contradistinctions at the level of labour market and organisations and take the stakeholders' perspectives into account. We understand it as a necessary tool that will help grasp the ambiguity of flexibility and the variety of its consequences for job quality. For the purpose of better understanding the changes in job quality, we will present the multidimensional index that combines work quality and employment quality.

First, we move to those debates on the character of flexibility which are focused on the difference or variety of interests of employees and employers (Furåker, Håkansson and Karlsson, 2007; Wood, 2016; Kalleberg, 2011; Henly, Luke Shaefer and Waxman, 2006; Mccrate, 2013).

The question 'flexibility for whom?' can be elaborated in the analysis of the benefits that flexible arrangements bring to the parties of the labour process. On the basis of a flexibility literature review Karlsson (2007) distinguishes between *having* flexibility and *being* flexible, which means that it is always one side setting the conditions of flexibility and the other that has to be flexible to adjust. The author suggests that flexibility is a managerial term, therefore it is worth analysing whom it benefits most – for whom it is good and for whom it is bad. There are four possible answers: it is good both for employers and workers; good for the employers but bad for workers; bad for both parties; bad for employers but good for workers.

The first of these options, good for both employers and workers, is rooted in the management literature and the flexible specialisation approach as presented by Piore and Sabel (1984). It is a somewhat abstract model of thinking about working life and workplaces as constantly changing, benefiting both parties. Companies can adapt to fast-changing markets, and workers are offered more empowerment in multi-dimensional work teams in which they do not train – they educate themselves. Karlsson points out that this rosy picture has found little empirical proof.

In terms of the second answer, Karlsson shows that it is usually taken for granted that flexibility is good for employers. The flexible work organisation was supposed to give more autonomy and responsibility to the workers. In exchange workers should benefit from wider power and responsibility, but the extent is not uniform for all employees. In work teams an employee has lots of responsibility, is broadly skilled, experiences job rotation and gets involved in problem-solving groups. Karlsson emphasises that empirical evidence shows that downsizing that happens nowadays in companies has hit employees hard and given rise to looser connections so there is no inclination for employee training but a sharp decline in job security. The flexibility in the form of teams often results in moving pressures from management into the teams themselves. Therefore, it seems that as the first answer is the theory, the second answer is the practice.

There can also be a third answer, stating that flexibility may adversely affect both parties. The bad flexibility, as described by Karlsson, produces lose-lose outcomes experienced both by employees in form of greater risk, longer hours and increased workloads and stress and by employers, as it generates low levels of morale and commitment amongst employees, which in turn impacts on individual performance and organisational productivity. Karlsson points out that flexicurity is often presented as a way to avoid those negative consequences. However, the flexicurity debate usually increases acceptance for flexibility and warnings against too much flexibility are scarce.

However, in his view it is very difficult to point out a situation of the fourth option, when flexibility is bad for employers but good for employees. Karslsson admits that such cases are scarce and can be found in companies that maintain cases of 'family friendly' working time arrangements that are positive for workers but not regarded as such by the managers.

The second framework that we find useful in understanding flexibility and its impact on job quality is based on opposition to stability (Jonsson, 2007), and in consequence – on four models of reaction – flexibility, stability, instability and inflexibility, based on an exchange-relation perspective. Building on a general definition of flexibility as the ability to respond effectively to changing circumstances (Mandelbaum, 1978), Jonsson shows that flexibility should be analysed in two separate dimensions – in terms of 'changing circumstances' and in terms of 'response' to them, involving a change in state or activity. The 'effective' response implies that it is desirable in relation to the changing circumstances. In an employment relation flexibility and stability are based on the variability of employer and employee contributions and the desirability of this variability. Employees contribute work, while employers contribute compensation or remuneration for this work. As both sides can view the contribution differently, what is seen as flexibility by one side can be seen as instability by the other, with flexibility understood as desirable variability and variability that is not desirable is not considered flexibility.

The companies need some points of stability to develop flexibility in other areas. As the 'reengineering' approach failure proved, even in times of constant change, a certain dose of stability is needed. It is thus crucial to ask 'who is flexible for whom?' (Jonsson, 2007, p. 36) – employees can be flexible for their own needs and purposes or for the needs of employer. The typology of flexibility and stability is based on several dimensions: employment stability and employment flexibility; working time; workplace; work; and remuneration. The research underlines that in many cases flexibility is treated as an inherent property rather than the one which is relative to a particular point of view; flexibility is always 'flexibility for somebody'. Variable working time can be made to suit employees' need to fit their work around care obligations or the employer's need to increase workforce at times of higher demands. In terms of flexible payment the salary paid to employees may vary in time to be lower to serve economic needs of the employer while resulting in economic instability for employees. Flexibility from a labour market perspective and flexibility from the perspective of individual labour market participants are clearly empirically related but do not necessarily coincide.

For the purpose of understanding the impact of flexibility on job quality, job quality itself has to be analysed in terms of its different dimensions. In this volume we follow several dimensions of the index of job quality elaborated by Muñoz de Bustillo et al. (2009) as a starting point to study relations between flexibility practices and dimensions of job quality. The index elaborated for the EU by Muñoz de Bustillo et al. combines dimensions of work quality and employment quality, along with those that belong to both categories, enabling it to show the multi-dimensional and interconnected character of job quality. Employment quality relates to the contractual relationship between employer and employee – wage, type of contract, working hours, distribution of working hours and social benefits. Work quality is related to the material characteristics of a task and the environment within which it is performed – temperature, noise, physical effort, speed, autonomy, risk of accidents and social work environment. Additionally, there are two dimensions that relate both to employment and to work quality – participation and skill development (on-the-job training and formal training).

The idea behind the index of separate dimensions that are interconnected will help in understanding the unevenness and ambiguity of the impact of flexibility and at the same time – to have a better grasp of the situation within the organisational 'black box'.

Experiences of job quality in a European context

The edited volume presents a European multilevel analysis of changes in job security and employability, and an analysis of discourses on job quality in European policies. This is followed by a set of case studies on organisations and occupations in the UK, Poland, Belgium and Sweden. The choice of countries and workplaces shows the diversity of practices and experiences within the European Union. The book relates to the effects of the 2008 crisis and post-crisis contexts, such as the weakening emphasis on job quality and focus on the quantitative aspect of job creation in European policies, precarious work being legitimised by higher rates of unemployment, and the rise of flexible employment arrangements. This collection of cases, accompanied by a European overview, goes beyond the static discussions about institutional arrangements at a country level and shows how job quality is shaped within organisations and workplaces, by management, workers and trade unions.

This volume focuses on the situation in the chosen sectors, as well as the organisational strategies and the individual level – workers' perceptions of job quality and its impact on their social networks, as well as their capacities to shape the job quality dimensions in forms of organised and individual strategies. Understanding job quality at the organisation level is complex, with a variety of pressures that can be pointed out as its shapers. First, there is the national institutional arrangement to provide a basis for employment arrangements and working conditions, the influence of social partners and the outcomes of social dialogue in the form of collective agreements. Additionally, there are market pressures on the national and transnational levels, along with financial pressures.

The authors study job quality dynamics in the old and new sectors, bringing in experiences in manufacturing and various services. By using the general 'flexibility for whom?' question and looking for examples of flexibility and instability, the authors of this volume seek to show the impact of flexibility on job quality.

Structure of the volume

The edited volume consists of twelve individual chapters in four sections.

The second section presents an overview of the changes in European labour markets and provides a context to the following sections.

In Chapter 2 Stephen Bouquin looks at job quality in the European policy discourse to understand what happened to the concept of job quality after the crisis and how the job quality aspect was replaced by the quantitative approach of job creation. The European policy frameworks do mobilise a lot of themes, notions and concepts that are used in social sciences. Quality of work is one of these. He proposes to analyse how the theme 'quality of work' appeared in the European policy discourse: when, how and by which definitions it was used since the early 2000s. He develops a lexicometrical analysis applied on a corpus of official documents produced by EU institutions. In a second section, he focuses on the discussions between policy makers and eventually, social scientists, on how this multifaceted issue can be achieved in practice. In Chapter 3 Dragoş Adăscăliţei and Federico Vegetti use a multilevel analysis to investigate the crisis-induced labour market reforms and their implications for job quality and employability in Europe. The economic and financial crisis that started in 2008 has been the most severe economic downturn that the European Union (EU) has faced since its creation. Importantly, the crisis has been correlated with a wave of labour market reforms that introduced significant changes to the rights that employees have both individually and collectively. What have been the implications of the crisis-induced labour market reforms for the quality and security of jobs in Europe? Has deregulation affected workers' perceptions of job security? And was the crisis experienced similarly across Europe? This chapter seeks to answer these questions by analysing the effects of the economic crisis and labour market deregulation on job security in the EU. To do so, the chapter uses data from the European Social Survey collected in 2004 (wave 2) and 2010 (wave 5), to test whether perceptions of job security and employability have changed in response to deregulatory labour market reforms. Using a multilevel estimation strategy, the chapter finds that the crisis-induced labour market reforms have not negatively impacted workers' perceptions of job security. Instead, unemployment levels and the generosity of active labour market policies (ALMPs) are the only significant predictors of self-perceptions about job security. Furthermore, we find that self-perceived employability is negatively affected by unemployment rates and positively correlated with GDP growth.

This is followed by a third section with eight cases in four European countries presenting changes in job quality at an organisational level, in selected occupations, in public and private sector, manufacturing and services, and in the context of various flexibility arrangements. The chapters focus on job quality understood as the combination of employment quality and work quality, illustrating how the different dimensions of job quality are intertwined with their dynamic nature (Muñoz de Bustillo et al., 2009). Flexibility practices can impact changes in one or more dimensions of job quality, while certain aspects remain unaffected. The case studies enable the development of 'the view from below' by focusing on workplaces and occupations and showing what happens to working lives' experiences under various flexibility practices.

In Chapter 4 Dora Scholarios, Hannah Hesselgreaves and Raymond Pratt examine the quality of working time within a public sector context – the police service – where demands for operational efficiency create pressures for employer-centred flexibility in shift patterns and schedules. The focus is on one particular aspect of shift working – unpredictable start and finish times – which leads to cumulative intensity in working time over a shift pattern. The authors consider the effects of unpredictable working time on individual officers, with a focus on work-life conflict, perceived stress, health behaviour (alcohol consumption, sleep disturbance, sickness absence) and symptoms (digestive and cardiovascular problems). The study allows reflection on the wider implications of how the quality of working time is changing – significantly, through an erosion of employee control over working time – to meet strategic requirements for flexible scheduling. This pattern applies across a range of front-line occupations, with important potential consequences for employee well-being and health.

In Chapter 5 Kirsty Newsome, Sian Moore and Cilla Ross explore the impact of supply chain capitalism on the quality of work of parcel delivery workers in the UK. This research evidence highlights the fierce competitive and contractual pressures faced by parcel delivery organisations. It considers how these supply pressures impact on the labour process of delivery workers through cost savings and the capacity of ICT in integrating the supply chain and monitoring the movement of products to the consumer. The chapter also investigates how ICT impacts on the nature of parcel delivery work in a variety of ways. This includes a consideration of the role of ICT in removing worker discretion and monitoring worker movement and activity, as well as invading the porosity of the working day and intensifying work effort. The research evidence highlights the use of ICT as a performance management tool with the capacity to monitor the activity of remote workers. The research also explores the growing pressures on working time for parcel delivery workers, revealing how 'chasing time' is increasingly part of the working day. However, the evidence also highlights the role of trade union organisations in mediating some of the excesses of these ICT systems. In theoretical terms the chapter wishes to contribute to growing debates on the impact of supply chain pressures on job quality.

In Chapter 6 Julia Kubisa aims to unpack and show the consequences of changes to forms of contracts in the healthcare sector in Poland, by framing them in the debate on job quality and flexibility. In the last 10 years new forms of contracts that are not regulated by the Labour Code were introduced in the sector and presented as a form of flexibility in healthcare management. The author discusses whom this kind of flexibility serves – employers, employees, both or neither. The influence of flexibility on other dimensions of job quality is discussed, and the relation between job quality and the quality of care provided by nurses is analysed. The chapter focuses on the dynamics of job quality, showing the impact of flexibility arrangements introduced by management and the nurses' agency – in that case, collective actions performed by a trade union. The author discusses how nurses link job quality with the quality of care in their union agenda, by framing a combination of low wages and low staffing as low job quality that negatively impacts quality of care.

In Chapter 7 Justyna Zielińska explores the character of strategies of workers regarding job quality in call centres in Poland in the conditions of highly flexible management practices. The chapter discusses the potential impact on job quality of workers in workplaces with high turnover and low access to skill development, on the basis of qualitative research. The work in a call centre is organised with high intensification of work, pressure on 'efficiency', standardisation of work, managing by constant control ('disciplinary glance') and stress. Work and employment is also characterised by high flexibility (especially numerical and functional) and a striving for cost reduction, as well as performing emotional labour. The chapter examines job quality in call centres by looking at work pressures. The author analyses the strategies of workers in the conditions of a workplace that is designed to provide temporary employment – to what extent they try to impact their job quality and in which cases they choose the 'exit' option.

In Chapter 8, Voice and Employment Quality for Temporary Agency Workers in Sweden and Belgium, the researchers Kristina Håkansson, Valeria Pulignano, Tommy Isidorsson and Nadja Doerflinger aim at explaining how institutional settings interplay with employment quality for temporary agency workers. The focus for the study is how national and sectoral regulation on employment and representation influences job security for temporary agency workers at the workplace level, thereby contributing to shaping those workers' employment quality.

By comparing two similar Belgian and Swedish workplaces, the chapter assesses how different social arrangements for Temporary Agency Workers, including both regulatory settings at the national level and the collective practices of representation and voice of agency work at local levels, can explain agency workers' experience of job security. The chapter shows that national regulations and collective structures for representation shape the unions' possibilities to represent agency workers and their general approaches towards Temporary Agency Workers. Hence, the findings add to the understanding of the conditions contributing to job insecurity and representation insecurity for agency workers. The results also show that a strong representation structure at the client organisation and inclusive attitudes towards agency workers are prerequisites, but are not sufficient to guarantee security. This chapter indicates that national regulation granting agency workers on assignment access to collective voice in the client organisation is crucial for job security. Thus, this chapter illustrates the multi-dimensionality of job quality by showing how job security and representation security are intertwined.

In Chapter 9 Pedro Mendonca examines the role of labour in regulating and shaping job quality, through a case study of a bottling hall belonging to a Scottish spirits manufacturer in the UK. It explores how the drive towards flexibility – reflected in the casualisation of labour – impacts on workers' job quality experience. It examines whether such flexible practices hinder the union's role in shaping and regulating job quality on the shop floor. By analysing the dynamics happening on the company level, this chapter addresses job quality as a contested outcome of the power relation between employer and employee. The author engages in the debate on the validity of core (a full-time group of workers who are fundamental to the successful running of the business) and periphery (contingent workers who are functionally used to adjusting to market fluctuations), and on the use of flexibility for employers and employees. This was found to deeply affect workers' job quality, not only in terms of stress and work-life balance, but also in work intensity and work pressures. Data revealed that the union was not able to improve job quality experiences, and it actually deepened the segregation and segmentation of certain groups of workers. This was related to the lack of institutional and, in some way, associational power.

In Chapter 10 Kristina Håkansson and Tommy Isidorsson discuss job quality in terms of job security and employability in workplaces using temporary agency workers. The general picture from previous research is that temporary agency workers have lower job quality due to a more insecure position compared to workers in other types of employment relations. Most studies are done in contexts where the agency workers have temporary contracts lasting for the time of the assignment or lack the rights to pay in-between assignments. This study fills this gap and investigates job security and employability for temporary agency workers when their working conditions are equal to that of user firm employees. The aim is to elucidate and explain how job quality expressed as job security and employability is perceived in workplaces using temporary agency workers. We have selected a 'best case' situation involving temporary agency workers who share the same work tasks as user firm employees and who are highly integrated within the work organisation. Their analysis shows no difference concerning perceived employability between temporary agency workers and user firm employees. However, they differ in job security. The most important explanation for temporary agency workers' lack of job security is the lack of skill development offered by their employer, i.e. the temporary work agency.

In Chapter 11 Pille Strauss-Raats presents a cross-national comparative case study and investigates the social aspects of job quality, operationalised through measures of social integration, support and participation among blue-collar employees at two comparable production sites of one high-performance multinational company in Sweden and Poland. Contextualising employee survey findings from permanent direct-hired, temporary direct-hired and temporary agency workers in national regulatory regimes and organisational as well as trade union practices, the study looks into how the use of atypical work contracts affects the social dimension of job quality for all employee groups. Results show that within the regulatory context that facilitates integration of agency workforce within user firm there was also full social integration with no contract differences in perceived support after controlling for other job characteristics. However, in the context of restricted short-term TAW that induced employer segregation practice of flexible workforce, agency workers reported higher support levels when compared to user employees. The chapter illustrates how individual-level job quality is shaped by organizational choices within the frames of their wider regulatory contexts and sheds light on how social support as a critical dimension of job quality is intertwined with other job characteristics within the particular context of TAW but also points to potential unintended consequences of flexibility practices within user firms.

In section four, Chapter 12, which is the concluding chapter, Tommy Isidorsson and Julia Kubisa strive to take the job quality research further by asking what are the broader themes coming out of the chapters that show how different dimensions of job quality and their interrelations are affected by flexibility practices. They discuss the context of macro changes in market pressures and consequences of deregulation, deepening segmentation within organisations and segregation of workers, the variety of outcomes of flexibility of the working time, the weakening of collective voice and the importance of participation as a component of job quality. The authors discuss possibilities to broaden the debate on job quality on the basis of the research presented in the volume. One suggestion presented in the final chapter for researchers as well as social partners is to include the role of the client in the discussion on the mechanisms of shaping job quality. Another suggestion is to start a debate on the conditions in which flexibility practices will not deteriorate job quality and will become beneficial both for management and workers.

References

Appelbaum, E., Bernhardt, A. and Murnane, R. (2003). *Low-Wage America: How Employers Are Reshaping Opportunity in the Workplace*. New York, NY: Russell Sage Foundation.

Atkinson, J. (1984). *Flexibility, Uncertainty and Manpower Management*. IMS Report No. 89. Brighton: Institute of Manpower Studies.

Atkinson, J. and Meager, N. (1986). *Changing Working Patterns: How Companies Achieve Flexibility to Meet New Needs*. London: Institute of Manpower Studies, National Economic Development Office.

Bell, D. N. F. and Blanchflower, D. G. (2010). Recession and unemployment in the OECD unemployment crisis (Focus). *CESifo Forum: A Quarterly Journal on*

European Economic Issues (a joint initiative of Ludwig-Maximilians-Universität and the Ifo Institute), 11(1), pp. 14–22.
Bradley, H., Erickson, M., Stephenson, C. and Polity, S. W. (2000). *Myths at Work*. Cambridge: Polity.
Burroni, K. (2011). Flexicurity: A conceptual critique. *European Journal of Industrial Relations March*, 17(1), pp. 75–91.
Caroli, E., Gautié, J., Lloyd, C., Lamanthe, A. and James, S. (2010). Delivering flexibility: Contrasting patterns in the French and the UK food processing industry. *British Journal of Industrial Relations*, 48(2), pp. 284–309.
Carré, F., Findlay, P., Tilly, C. and Warhurst, C. (2012). Job quality: Scenarios, analysis and interventions. In Warhurst, C., Carre, F., Findlay, P. and Tilly, C. (Eds.) *Are Bad Jobs Inevitable? Trends, Determinants and Responses to Job Quality in the Twenty First Century*. Basingstoke: Palgrave Macmillan, pp. 2–22.
Clark, A. (2005). What makes a good job? Evidence from OECD Countries. In Bazen, S., Lucifora, C. and Salvedra, W. (Eds.) *Job Quality and Employer Behaviours*. Basingstoke: Palgrave Macmillan, pp. 11–30.
Coats, D. (2009). The sunlit uplands or bleak house? Just how good are today's workplaces? In Bolton, S. and Houlihan, M. (Eds.) *Work Matters: Critical Reflections on Contemporary Work*. Basingstoke: Palgrave Macmillan, pp. 21–37.
Crouch, C., Schröder, M. and Voelzkow, H. (2009). Regional and sectoral varieties of Capitalism. *Economy and Society*, 38(4), pp. 654–678.
De Cuyper, N. and De Witte, H. (2007). Job insecurity in temporary versus permanent workers: Associations with attitudes, well-being, and behaviour. *Work & Stress*, 21(1), pp. 65–84.
Dieckhoff, M. and Gallie, D. (2007). The renewed Lisbon Strategy and social exclusion policy. *Industrial Relations Journal*, 38(6), pp. 480–502.
Doogan, K. (2009). *New Capitalism?: The Transformation of Work*. Cambridge: Polity.
Engstrand, Å. K. (2007). Flexibility's new clothe: A historical perspective on the public discussion in Sweden. In Furåker, B., Håkansson, K. and Karlsson, J. Ch. (Eds.) *Flexibility and Stability in Working Life*. Basingstoke: Palgrave Macmillan.
Eurofound. (2012). *Trends in Job Quality in Europe*. Luxembourg: Publication Office of European Union.
European Commission. (2001). *Employment and Social Policy: A Framework Investing in Quality*. Communication From the Commission to the European Parliament, the Economic and Social Committee and the Committee of the Regions, COM (2001) 313.
European Commission. (2002). *The 2002 Broad Economic Policy Guidelines*. http://ec.europa.eu/economy_finance/publications/pages/publication7642_en.pdf
Findlay, P., Kalleberg, A. L. and Warhurst, Ch. (2013). The challenge of job quality. *Human Relations*, 66(4), pp. 441–451.
Furåker, B., Håkansson, K. and Karlsson, J. Ch. (2007). *Flexibility and Stability in Working Life*. Basingstoke: Palgrave Macmillan.
Furåker, B., Håkansson, K. and Karlsson, J. Ch. (Eds.) (2012). *Commitment to Work and Job Satisfaction: Studies of Work Orientations*. New York, NY: Routledge.
Gallie, D. (Ed.) (2007). *Employment Regimes and the Quality of Work*. Oxford: Oxford University Press, pp. 1–33.
Gallie, D. (Ed.) (2013). *Economic Crisis, Quality of Work, and Social Integration: The European Experience*. Oxford: Oxford University Press.

Green, F. (2006). *Demanding Work: The Paradox of Job Quality in the Affluent Economy*. Princeton, NJ: Princeton University Press.

Green, F. (2013). *Is Britain Such a Bad Place to Work? The Level and Dispersion of Job Quality in Comparative European Perspective*. Research Paper No. 40. London: Centre for Learning and Life Chances in Knowledge Economies and Societies. Available at: www.llakes.org.

Grimshaw, D. and Lehndorff, S. (2010). Anchors for job quality: Sectoral systems of employment in the European context. *Work Organisation, Labour and Globalisation*, 4(1), pp. 24–40.

Grimshaw, D. and Rubery, J. (2005). Inter-capital relations and the network organisation: Redefining the work and employment nexus. *Cambridge Journal of Economics*, 29(6), pp. 1027–1051.

Guest, D. (2002, June). Perspectives on the study of work-life balance. *Social Science Information*, 41(2), pp. 255–280.

Håkansson, K. and Isidorsson, T. (2003). Flexible times: Dynamics and consequences of company strategies for flexibility. In Flemming, D. and Thörnqvist, C. (Eds.) *Nordic Management-Labour Relations and Internationalization: Converging and Diverging Tendencies*. Copenhagen: Nordic Council of Ministers.

Handy Ch. (1995). *The Empty Raincoat: Making Sense of the Future*. London: Arrow.

Hardt, M. and Negri, A. (2000). *Empire*. Cambridge, MA: Harvard University Press.

Heery, E. and Salmon, J. (2000). *The Insecure Workforce*. London: Routledge.

Henly, J., Luke Shaefer, H. and Waxman, E. (2006). Nonstandard work schedules: Employer- and employee-driven flexibility in retail jobs. *Social Service Review*, 80(4), pp. 609–634.

Hewinson, K. (2016). Precarious work. In Edgell, S., Gottfried, H. and Granter, E. (Eds.) *Handbook of Sociology of Work and Employment*. Los Angeles, CA, London, New Delhi, Singapore and Washington, DC: Sage Publications.

Holman, D. (2013). Job types and job quality in Europe. *Human Relations*, 66(4), pp. 475–502.

Holman, D. and McClelland, C. R. (2011). *Job Quality in Growing and Declining Economic Sectors of the EU*. Report No. SSH-CT-2009-244597, Manchester.

Howell, D. R. and Rehm, M. (2009). Unemployment compensation and high European unemployment: A reassessment with new benefit indicators. *Oxford Review of Economic Policy*, 25(1), pp. 60–93.

Hudson, M. (2002). Flexibility and the reorganisation of work. In Burchell, B., Ladipo, D. and Wilkinson, F. (Eds.) *Job Insecurity and Work Intensification*. Routledge.

Hurley, J., Fernández-Macías, E. and Storrie, D. (2013). *Employment Polarisation and Job Quality in the Crisis: European Jobs Monitor 2013*. Dublin: Eurofound.

Huws, U. (2011). Passing the buck: Corporate restructuring and the casualisation of employment. *Work Organisation, Labour and Globalisation*, 5(1), pp. 1–9.

Jonsson, D. (2007). Flexibility, stability and related concepts. In Furåker, B., Håkansson, K. and Karlsson, J. Ch. (Eds.) *Flexibility and Stability in Working Life*. Basingstoke: Palgrave Macmillan.

Kalleberg, A. L. (2003). Flexible firms and labor market segmentation. *Work and Occupations*, 30(2), pp. 154–175.

Kalleberg, A. L. (2011). *Good Jobs, Bad Jobs: The Rise of Polarized and Precarious Employment Systems in the United States, 1970 to 2000s*. New York, NY: Russell Sage Foundation.

Kalleberg, A. L., Reskin, B. F. and Hudson, K. (2000). Bad jobs in America: Standard and nonstandard employment relations and job quality in the United States. *American Sociological Review*, 65, pp. 256–278.

Karlsson, J. (2007). For whom is flexibility good and bad? An overview. In Furåker, B., Håkansson, K. and Karlsson, J. Ch. (Eds.) *Flexibility and Stability in Working Life*. Basingstoke: Palgrave Macmillan.

Kelliher, C. and Anderson, D. (2008). Doing more with less? Flexible working practices and the intensification of work. *Human Relations*, 63, pp. 83–106.

Ladipo, D. and Wilkinson, F. (2002). More pressure, less protection. In Burchell, B., Ladipo, D. and Wilkinson, F. (Eds.) *Job Insecurity and Work Intensification*. London: Routledge.

Lloyd, C. and Payne, J. (2016). *Skills in the Age of Over-Qualification Comparing Service Sector Work in Europe*. Oxford: Oxford University Press.

Mandelbaum, M. (1978). *Flexibility in Decision Making: An Exploration and Unification*. Toronto: Department of Industrial Engineering, University of Toronto.

Mccrate, E. (2013). Employer-oriented schedule flexibility, gender and family care. In Figart, D. M. and Warnecke, T. L. (Eds.) *Handbook of Research on Gender and Economic Life*. Cheltenham: Edward Elgar Publishing, pp. 273–289.

McGovern, P., Smeaton, D. and Hill, S. (2004). Bad jobs in Britain: Nonstandard employment and job quality. *Work and Occupations*, 31(2), pp. 225–249.

Meardi, G. (2014). The (claimed) growing irrelevance of employment relations. *Journal of Industrial Relations*, 56(4), pp. 594–605.

Muñoz de Bustillo, R. M., Fernández-Macías, E., Antón, J.-I. and Esteve, F. (2011). E pluribus unum? A critical survey of job quality indicators. *Socio-Economic Review*, 9, pp. 447–475.

Muñoz de Bustillo, R. M., Fernández-Macías, E., Esteve, F. and Antón, J. I. (2009). *Indicators of Job Quality in the European Union*. Employment and Social Affairs. Brussels: European Parliament.

Piore, M. J. and Ch. F. Sabel. (1984). *The Second Industrial Divide: Possibilities for Prosperity*. New York, NY: Basic Books.

Pollert, A. (2007). Britain's flexible labour force: New barriers to individual employment rights. In Furåker, B., Håkansson, K. and Karlsson, J. Ch. (Eds.) *Flexibility and Stability in Working Life*. Basingstoke: Palgrave Macmillan.

Rubery, J., Ward, K., Grimshaw, D. and Beynon, H. (2005). Working time, industrial relations and the employment relationship. *Time & Society*, 14(1), pp. 89–111.

Sengupta, S., Edwards, P. K. and Tsai, Ch-J. (2009). The good, the bad and the ordinary. *Work and Occupations*, 36(1), pp. 26–55.

Standing, G. (2009). *Work After Globalization: Building Occupational Citizenship*. Cheltenham: Edward Elgar Publishing.

Standing, G. (2011). *The Precariat: The New Dangerous Class*. London: Bloomsbury Academic.

Standing, G. (2014). *A Precariat Charter: From Denizens to Citizens*. London: Bloomsbury Academic.

Taylor, P. (2013). *Performance Management and the New Workplace Tyranny: A Report for the Scottish Trades Union Congress*. Scottish Trades Union Congress. http://www.stuc.org.uk/files/Document%20download/Workplace%20tyranny/STUC%20Performance%20Management%20Executive%20Summary%20final.pdf

Taylor, P., Hyman, J., Mulvey, G. and Bain, P. (2002). Work organisation, control and the experience of work in call centres. *Work, Employment and Society*, 17(3), pp. 435–458.

Thompson, P. (1989). *The Nature of Work: An Introduction to Debates on the Labour Process*. London: Palgrave Macmillan.

Thompson, P. and Warhurst, Ch. (1998). *Workplaces of the Future*. Basingstoke: Palgrave Macmillan.

Vander Elst, T., Van Den Broeck, A., De Cuyper, N. and De Witte, H. (2014). On the reciprocal relationship between job insecurity and employee well-being: Mediation by perceived control? *Journal of Occupational and Organizational Psychology*, 87(4), pp. 671–693.

Vander Elst, T., Van den Broeck, A., De Witte, H. and De Cuyper, N. (2012). The mediating role of frustration of psychological needs in the relationship between job insecurity and work-related well-being. *Work & Stress*, 26(3), pp. 252–271.

Warhurst, Ch., Carre, F., Findlay, P. and Tilly, Ch. (2012). *Are Bad Jobs Inevitable? Trends, Determinants and Responses to Job Quality in the Twenty First Century*. Basingstoke: Palgrave Macmillan.

Womack, J. P., Jones, D. T. and Roos, D. (1990). *The Machine That Changed the World*. New York, NY: Palgrave Macmillan.

Wood, A. J. (2016). Flexible scheduling, degradation of job quality and barriers to collective voice. *Human Relations*, 69(10), pp. 1989–2010.

2 Job quality in Europe

Stephen Bouquin

Introduction

In this chapter, we will take a close look at the issue of 'job quality' as an element of the public discourse part of the employment policies elaborated on the European level. We will first of all present the context in which the theme of job quality and other similar themes emerged. Job quality but also 'quality of work', 'decent work' and precarisation are relatively recent topics in the literature. On the level of public policies, we wanted to analyse the emergence of this vocabulary as part of a broader discourse on the problems of employment and social exclusion. In order to do that we have chosen to apply a lexicographical discourse analysis. We measured between 1995 and 2015 the frequency of notions, concepts and lexical expressions linked to the broader theme of employment and developed some elements of explanations linked to the socio-economical context as well as the evolution of discourse in general. We conclude with reflections about the different causes that may help us to understand why work and employment is nowadays often associated with a lack of quality, growing stress and a well-being that is under threat for a significant section of the labour force.

Recognising 'job quality' as an issue in itself

In the 1990s and millennium years, several datasets showed that an increase in employment by numbers tends to go hand in hand, sometimes with some delay, with an improvement regarding the quality of work (Eurofound, 2008; Amossé and Kalugina, 2013). Attention to job quality began to emerge in the early 2000s when it was referenced in several conclusions of European Council meetings. On a policy level, the *European Employment Strategy* (*EES*) explicitly mentioned the double aim of restoring competiveness and enhancing social cohesion. At the summit of Brussels (Laeken) in 2001, a resolution was adopted regarding social cohesion, stating the following criteria:

- intrinsic quality of work
- lifelong learning and career development

- gender balance and equal opportunities
- health and safety
- flexibility and job security
- degree of openness achieved upon the labour market
- work organisation and work-life balance
- social dialogue and involvement /participation of employees
- diversity and non-discrimination
- economic performance and productivity.

Some of these criteria were critically discussed (Bellal and Bouquin, 2002) notably because 'social cohesion' combined both objective and subjective dimensions. Also, the preconditions of this 'social cohesion' were quite unclear. In some documents job quality was understood as directly linked to productivity, because the mainstream approach considers it as dependent upon an added value produced by labouring activity. The more productivity work generates, the better job one tends to have. Increasing productivity would therefore lead to higher quality of work. However, critical approaches acknowledged that increasing productivity can also be achieved through intensification of work which translates itself into exhaustion and stress.

Other institutions and organisations started during the late 1990s to develop their own definitions. The *European Foundation for the Improvement of Working Conditions,*[1] also called the *Dublin Foundation*, elaborated a framework around four criteria:

- career and job security
- development of competencies, skills
- health and well-being
- work-life balance.

In a similar way, the International Labour Office started to work out a framework around 'decent work'. Labour sociologists (Dahl, Nesheim and Olsen, 2009) reflected upon this variety of definitions and dimensions regarding the measurement of quality of work, taking into account income (wages), job security, working conditions and job satisfaction. The European Foundation is responsible for collecting and analysing the data of the European working conditions survey. Using data going back to the early 1990s, this survey made it possible to conduct a longitudinal comparative analysis. One of the observations it helped to make was to understand the evolution between 1995 and 2005 as quite paradoxical. As was underlined by Green (2006), job satisfaction was declining while job opportunities were growing. Normally, following traditional neoclassical models, more job vacancies or job opportunities are expected to give employees the capacity to negotiate better work settings and higher wages and therefore improve their 'job satisfaction'. But this was far from being the case. In France, the labour economists Jennifer Bué and Thomas Coutrot (2004) showed that lowering job satisfactions were linked with heavier workloads, intensification and less autonomy while the risks associated with job-loss were still high, even if the employment crisis was somehow fading away. Precariousness was increasing in France, even when unemployment was reduced. Following the analysis of Bué and Coutrot (2004), the improving working conditions had also a higher cost for employers, exceeding the return in terms of productivity while hard or 'bad jobs' performed better. The paradox is therefore clearly explained: even with less unemployment/more job opportunities, job satisfaction was undermined by harder working conditions, stress and so on. Employers are able to deal with low job satisfaction because the employee turnover is high, which means that the exhausted ones are replaced by 'new and fresh' employees. The conclusion was obvious: job quality and quantity of work do not necessarily go hand in hand, and the first is probably determined by a wide range of variables. Of course, these conclusions were not shared among all in the community of labour sociologists. For those following a more neoclassical approach, job quality remains a dependant variable more or less directly determined by functioning of the labour market.

Nevertheless, empirical research (Davoine, 2006) showed that those countries with the best performance regarding job creation were also those having higher quality of work. The *European Households Panel* data shows that positive job transitions still exist: after having started as a minus for 25-year-olds in casual jobs and without much job security, most of these youngsters succeed in finding better working situations after a period of time, i.e. improving the quality of their work. This trend depends, of course, upon their skills and behaviour. Other research showed that the most dynamic sectors in terms of job creation were also the ones with the best working conditions.

On a more general level, we can say that the issue of job quality certainly arose because more analysis took into account the tendency of precariousness, although this phenomenon is sometimes limited to particular sections of the workforce such as the youth, migrants, women and the semi- or unskilled labour force. Still, even skilled categories such as technicians, engineers or white-collar employees face heavier workloads and a decrease in work autonomy. Therefore, even reporting above average quality of work is not necessarily sufficient to find expression in high job satisfaction.

We saw that quality of work was subject to various and conflicting definitions. The variety regarding outcomes of research made it even more complicated to leave behind the wrong definitions. Drawing upon research from the early 2000s Bustillo (2009) and Lehndorf (2015), proposed a renewed framework with five dimensions:

- work organisation (characteristics of the employee job)
- wages and payment system (processes through which workers remunerated or incentivised their jobs)

- security and flexibility (security of tenure or being employed and of retaining sources of income when ill or unemployed; flexibility refers to working practices that enable organisations to respond to change, and for workers to balance their work and life)
- skills and development (requirements of workers to develop skills within their jobs, the training opportunities they have and the career opportunities open to them)
- representation and voice (features of jobs that allow workers to speak up about work-related issues of importance to them, with reference to opportunities for participation, involvement and representation).

According to these authors, each dimension contains several indicators. For example, work organisation includes job design characteristics (e.g. job discretion, ergonomics, social support and so on) as well as team design characteristics (autonomous work groups, participation in offline and online teams). Following their scheme, high-quality jobs will feature more work and employment-related factors that promote positive outcomes for the employee. Still, a high-quality job can lose some of its key characteristics: more routine, less interesting tasks, and less autonomy, despite high pay and high job security. Finding a way to measure changes among these indicators, and the impact of these changes upon satisfaction is a difficult task. A subjectivist approach, one that is actor-centred, will focus upon issues that determine the extent to which a job fulfils employee preferences and can give way to job satisfaction. The objectivist approach pays more attention to structural aspects and simply collects data about situations in order to bring into perspective how circumstances are changing on a short- or middle-term basis. It is very important to measure the extent to which wages, working time and work autonomy, are stable, improving or going backwards. Last but not least, the fifth criterion regarding the possibility for employees to be represented and to 'voice' demands is an important change in comparison with former definitions of 'job quality'. Being or not being represented can give way to change or show that lower job quality is correlated with the absence of for example trade unions.

These various definitions stimulated debate around how these multiple dimensions could be articulated in order to build an index with some weighted dimensions, since some are likely to have a relatively greater effect upon well-being than others. For example, one can say that job discretion and autonomy counts more than variance in training. However, some authors (Green, 2006; Tangian, 2007) refused to weight these dimensions because there is no reliable information about how to analyse them. Some sections of the labour force will consider certain dimensions more important than others. The social trajectories of individuals play an important role. Coming from the countryside or from a lower social status will lead an individual to regard low quality jobs differently, just as young people may consider such jobs temporary. Interviews showed that not all indicators contribute to the same extent, so the overall result will be falsified or less robust. It is also important to show that jobs or functions or professions see their quality of work going upwards or downwards. For that reason, researchers of the European Trade Union Institute Leschke and Watt, 2008) decided to work out the Job Quality Index (JQI) as an aggregated or single index that summarises overall level of job quality. The JQI is based upon information that can be found in the European Working Conditions Survey (EWCS), so longitudinal analysis is possible.

It is interesting to observe how the existence of the JQI has helped the scientific community to engage into research about the impact of 'the great recession'. Janine Leschke, Andrew Watt and Mairéad Finn (2012) were among the first researchers ready to compare the JQI before and after the crisis. A comparison between data from the European survey of 2005 and 2010 (Leschke, Watt and Finn, 2012) was carried out with two hypotheses: (1) the bargaining power of unions is lost because higher unemployment will tend to impose lowering working conditions upon employees who have little other options than to accept; and (2) the social composition of the labour force is changed since the crisis leads to the shedding of low productivity ('bad jobs') while the remaining jobs are more productive. The bargaining power and the composition hypotheses do not exclude each other as well, as it is possible that both neutralise each other on an aggregate level. In their research Leschke, Watt and Finn (2012) conclude that the severity of the crisis and low job quality are correlated, but they cannot precisely demonstrate how this correlation operates.

Discourse analysis of the European Employment Guidelines

How has the public discourse produced by EU institutions regarding quality of employment or job quality changed over the last 20 years? In order to answer this question, we have chosen to develop a lexicometric analysis applied upon a stable corpse of documents such as the annual 'Guidelines for the Employment Policies of the Member States'. These annual documents are part of the 'European Employment Strategy' that dates back to the late 1990s when the EU undertook to establish a set of common objectives and targets regarding employment policies. Of course, since employment policies as such remain mainly a national domain, the role played by the EU is to produce orientations or 'guidelines'. We must also not forget that documents such as the Guidelines are elaborated through consultation of several institutions or assemblies (European Commission, Parliament, Economic and Social Committee). Officially, the main aim of this European Employment Strategy is to favour the creation of more and better jobs throughout the EU. This official aim is now a constitutive part of the Europe 2020 growth strategy that is implemented through the European semester, an annual process promoting close policy coordination among EU Member States and EU Institutions.[2]

Since these Guidelines are based upon European and national statistical reports about the labour market as well as discussions that are being held on a regular basis in the European parliament as well as in the economic and social committee of the EU (with the presence of social partners), we can consider these documents as the major benchmark of how employment policies are phrased and conceptualised. It therefore delivers us important insights on how employment issues are dealt with and to what extent shifts in the political and economic situations may contribute to a different understanding of what is at stake.

First of all, we present an overview of the different lexical expressions related to employment policies produced by the Guidelines for Employment that do play the function of recommendations of national policies. The 'corpus' upon which we applied our analysis contains documents that are published by an official institution and published in the 'Official Journal' of the European Union' which can be found on the Eura-lex website, both under certified as open source of html-format.

Methodological note

From a methodological viewpoint, a lexicometric analysis is mainly mobilised by political scientists that want to study discourses and base themselves upon objective criteria. In France, a major contribution to this approach was made by Didier Demazière and Karl Van Meter (Demazière, Brossaud, Trabal and Van Meter, 2006). Most of the software programs make it possible to measure frequency of words, concepts or lexical expressions, on a synchronical and diachronical way. There exist different software programs (Alceste, Prospero, Lexico3, Weblex, Hyperbase), but one can also craft such an analysis in an artisanal way. For our research, we have chosen the most basic approach that counts among the established corpus and per document the frequency of lexical expressions. We did not go into an analysis of the lexical fields because of a risk of anachronism. We have selected the lexical expressions after a close reading of all these documents in order to select a first list of wordings, notions and expressions that are linked to or express a policy in itself. We did not take into account general expressions such as 'employment' or 'unemployment' because their significations are basically descriptive. We selected all expressions that are closely linked to policies as a way of dealing with the issues of unemployment and employment: 'employability', 'adaptability', 'labour market reforms', 'flexible/flexibility', 'lifelong learning', 'equal opportunities', 'labour market efficiency', 'training' as well as 'job quality' or 'quality of employment'.

At a second stage, we decided to make an analytical distinction between lexical expressions because all express the same views upon the issue of employment. Some of these lexical expressions are closer to an employee-centred approach which means that their implicit aim is to improve job quality or to enhance capacities or opportunities to be employed by way of developing skills through training and learning. Employability is clearly directed towards employees willing to enhance their position upon the labour market. Other lexical expressions are more into an employer-centred approach through lowering labour costs which is expected to facilitate employers to create more jobs. The same can be told about 'adaptability' since it means changing behaviour and personal profile to match more easily HR requirements. Developing 'entrepreneurship' among employed or unemployed persons is of the same kind, since it means favouring employees becoming 'self-employed' and starting a business by themselves. Parallel to the employer-centred approach we can also distinguish a more specific 'workfarist' approach, which is based upon positive and negative incentives (Jessop, 1993; Gallie, 2009; Bellal and Bouquin, 2002). Historically the policy of workfare was introduced by James Charles Ever in the USA during the 1970s and it refers to coercive measures in order to bring unemployed persons to accept easier jobs that do not correspond to their skills or preferences and sometimes also the obligation to work in order to receive benefits.

We tried to measure separately as much as possible the frequency of 'employee-friendly' and 'employer-friendly' notions. The rationale behind this choice is based upon the assumption that lexical expressions and language in general – especially regarding social issues which may mobilise conflicting issues – are never completely neutral but express also to a certain degree a certain perspective and agenda. This assumption is based upon our own research regarding social policies and employment policies conducted under the 4th framework TSER-program (Bouquin et al., 2002; Bouquin, 2004) and the recent actualisation of our research on this issue (Bouquin, 2017). Especially when discourses are produced by a 'technostructure' and political institutions, many wordings do have a content that goes beyond the simple semantical level. All methodological and theoretical foundations of lexicometric analysis are based upon this knowledge (Van Meter, 2006; Labbé and Labbé, 2013).

Results

Our quantitative and qualitative analysis has led us to produce an overview of frequency of all these lexical expressions. It helps to draw a chronological mapping of the wordings and gives insight in the balancing nature of these official documents. Of course, this overview gives an indication of how official recommendations are being formulated and it first of all reflects an evolution about '*the ways of understanding and dealing with the issue*'. It is also important to mention that we did not produce a complete measurement of the ideological framing of employment policies. The first and most important reason why we can't deliver such hard-sounding evidence is the fact that the same lexical expressions are sometimes used in different ways. Second, they may also be mobilised more frequently to give the final documents a balanced content in order to obtain acceptance through a complex procedure of governance that involves the representatives of national governments, the European Commission, social partners and even to a certain extent civil society.

Table 2.1 Overview of frequency of lexical expressions

years	*Employee-centred*	*Employer-centred*
1995	3	7
1996	3	8
1997	6	25
1998	19	22
1999	19	18
2000	10	12
2001	36	28
2002	41	27
2003	38	33
2004	38	33
2005	54	20
2006	54	20
2007	54	20
2008	52	18
2009	52	18
2010	31	22
2011	31	22
2012	31	22
2013	31	22
2014	31	22
2015	31	22
2016	31	22

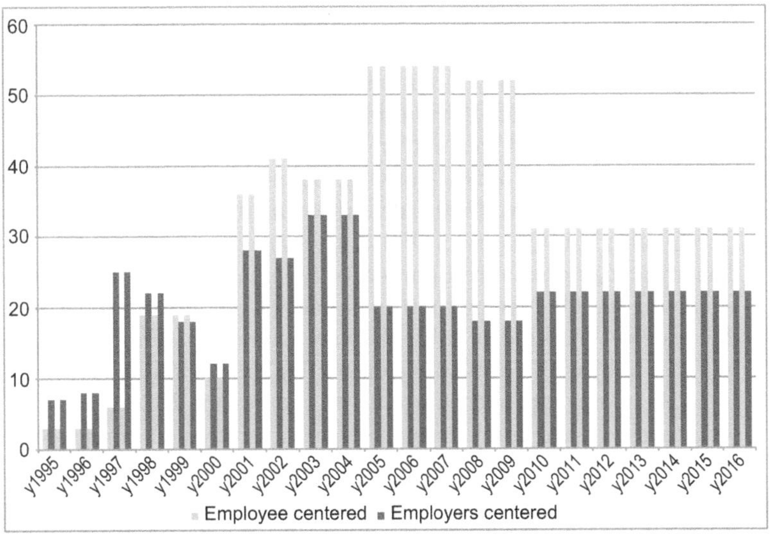

Figure 2.1 Frequency of quoting 'employer-centred' and 'employee-centred' lexical expressions in the EU-Employment Guidelines

From year 1995 up to 2016. Vertical axis means #/Horizontal refers to calendar years. Own calculations

When we integrate the collected data into a chart, during the last 20 years we can observe four distinct eras.

- The first era started in 1995 and ended in 1999. It corresponds to a period when Employment Guidelines were recently conceived and all notions did express in more or less explicit way a concern about the social problem of unemployment. To a certain extent, we can see the pro-market or employer-centred expressions losing in numbers and frequency.
- Then a second era started in 2000. It corresponds to the adoption of the Lisbon Strategy (spring 2000) which focussed upon increasing the employment rate. This means the enlargement of the labour market by integrating more people in the age of work as well as specific categories such as youngsters, women, elder employees. But, this policy was applied in a context where some EU member states were still facing high unemployment figures. In such a context, increasing the employment or activity rate can also have a negative impact upon job quality for example, since 'bringing more people to the labour market ' is not the same as 'increasing vacancies' or 'creating jobs'. It can also mean, through more frequent transitions between employment and unemployment, a higher flexible labour market with more precarity. Nevertheless, the active labour market policies go hand in hand with policies focussing upon enhancing employability (therefore enforcing more autonomy towards the employer) but also a larger recognition of qualitative aspects of employment. The official goal remains 'full employment' even if this aim can be understood in different ways, i.e. as a result of a dynamic labour market and/or the result of direct employment policies.
- A third era starts in 2005 and continues up to 2009. It brings to the forefront a higher frequency of employee-centred lexical expressions in comparison with employer-centred ones. We counted around 50 employee-centred notions which is quite more than the 20 for employer-centred expressions. And for the first time in 2005, the notion of 'Job Quality' appeared as such in a clear-cut way. Before, we have had wordings like 'more and better jobs' (2001) or improving job quality (2003), but now 'Job Quality' or 'Quality of Work' are starting to be mentioned as such. This means an official recognition of the issue of not only creating jobs or having people leaving their unemployed condition but also tackling the issue of 'the kind of jobs' they are exercising. This way of dealing with the subject remains stable even after the beginning of the crisis.
- In 2010, a new approach started with the Europe 2020 horizon. Firstly, we observe in the Guidelines a higher integration of employee-centred and employer-centred expressions. This is mirrored in a combined approach tackling the crisis both on supply-side as well as on demand-side of the labour market. Secondly, the agenda of the Employment Guidelines starts to be more closely linked with the macro-economic

> dimensions of EU policies. Indeed, they are part of the Europe 2020 strategy. The concrete consequence of this 'integrated approach' can be observed from the case 2012. From that year on, the European Package is the institutional 'platform' for a new stream of measures regarding the euro-zone and becomes a source of policies with much more constraints. So there is now a tool of governance that integrates macro-economic issues (balance-sheet of the budget, no deficit, spending review) with employment policies on the other hand. At the same time, the Employment Guidelines are maintained and if we observe that 'job quality' is still an issue frequently quoted, we must also recognise that it does not have much impact on the real existing policies. Notions such as 'flexicurity' (which combines flexibility and security and can be linked more with the Scandinavian model) are almost abandoned. If 'Quality of work' and 'Job quality' do occur a few times, the general rationale is one that focusses upon the supply-side from a pro-employers perspective. Even if this is not clearly measurable through a quantitative lexicometric analysis, we see clearly that the Employment Guidelines, although they still do exist, are losing a bit of importance. They are now renewed upon a pluri-annual basis and inside the Eurozone the 'policy mix' is more closely knit to satisfy the expectations of the employers.

As we can understand from an analysis of official documents, the 'Employment package' (launched April 2012) is a set of policy documents looking into how EU employment policies intersect with a number of other policy areas in support of smart, sustainable and inclusive growth. It identifies the EU's biggest job potential areas and the most effective ways for EU countries to create more jobs. Measures are proposed in a wide range of areas, including supporting job creation by encouraging labour demand, targeting subsidies to foster recruitments and reducing the tax on labour while ensuring fiscal sustainability, promoting and supporting self-employment, social enterprises and business start-ups, transforming informal or undeclared work into regular employment, boosting 'take home' pay, modernising wage-setting systems to align wages with productivity developments and fostering job creation. This new EU governance tool overlaps to a large extent with the former Employment Guidelines.

Although they combine as before a certain balance regarding key words and lexical expressions and even if they do expose their willingness for job creation, they pretend first of all to restore 'the dynamics of labour markets' through encouraging companies' internal flexibility. Still the guidelines express the need to protect jobs in crisis times, to encourage decent and sustainable wages, make job transitions pay, reduce the labour market segmentation between those in precarious employment and those on more stable employment, anticipate economic restructuring, develop lifelong learning and active labour market policies, and deliver youth opportunities and the youth employment package. In fact, much energy is devoted to the project of moving towards a European labour market by removing legal and practical obstacles to the free movement of workers and enhancing the matching of jobs and job-seekers across borders.

All these policy objectives do contain to a certain degree the wordings and the analytical expressions that can be found in academic literature. This fact alone means that scientific (academic research) should engage in more interdisciplinary debates, inviting political scientists to debate with economists, sociologists and vice versa. This would provide the basis for deeper knowledge with more reflexivity both for the scientific community as well as for civil society. From the viewpoint of policymakers, the objectives they pursue are linked to the belief that 'better functioning' or 'performance' of labour markets will deliver by itself relief and improve quality of working lives. Therefore, we should acknowledge that they remain almost blind regarding the real social dynamics of labour markets such as segmentation, exclusion, downscaling of social standards regarding wages, health and safety or more generally working conditions, especially when there is a shortage of job vacancies regarding the real existing supply of labour. The fact that such an imbalance has a negative effect upon wages, working conditions, health and safety and well-being is ignored in recent research (Bustillo, 2009). Leschke, Watt and Finn (2012) demonstrate that all dimensions of Job Quality are closely linked and that the presence of 'voice' and 'representation' condition to a large extent job quality. As a consequence, the issue of developing – through coordination, legal regulation, soft law or social dialogue – minimal standards regarding the quality of work or job quality is nowadays fading away in the European official discourse.

Conclusion

Om the one hand, we observed that there is a growing interest regarding the issue of job quality, although it took almost 10 years to be a visible issue in official European documents. Our lexicometric analysis demonstrated that since 2003 the notion of job quality (or quality of work) is more and more often used to tackle the issue of objective and subjective well-being at work. Researchers did succeed in identifying the most important criteria to assess job quality all around the labour market. At the same time, we observed a lot of negative evolutions. First of all, we can observe that new technologies and skill-biased technological change (GPS, more surveillance and control) can have negative impact upon well-being and the quality of work. Some tasks are becoming more complex but many others are becoming more standardised and will be automated sooner or later. In the meanwhile, the approach of lowering labour costs may put a brake on this evolution and maintain mainly 'boring' jobs. Secondly, competition between firms is intensifying, especially among outsourced activities and subcontractors and since the competition for obtaining a contract or an order is not always taking place on a common playfield with common social standards, this can lead to dilution and downsizing of the standards of 'good work'. Marketisation and lean production with their permanent cost pressures do reduce the possibilities for improving job quality. Thirdly, declining union influence has had negative effect upon job quality. Organising the labour force and giving voice to the social demands of the employees is less easy nowadays. Still, according to analysts of employment regimes (Gallie, 2009, 2013) or industrial relations (Warhurst, Carre, Findlay and Tilly, 2012; Plasman and Ryckx, 2011), unions always have a mitigating impact regarding the negative effects of competition, privatisation and marketisation as well as organisational changes. Improving job quality should give way to better organised and more effective action. Without agency, we can only expect that a better labour market situation will help employees to react through a strategy of exit or (clandestine) voice.

Notes

1 https://europa.eu/european-union/about-eu/agencies/eurofound_en
2 In particular, the implementation of the EES – supported by the work of the Employment committee – involves the following four steps of the European Semester: (1) Employment guidelines are common priorities and targets for employment policies proposed by the Commission, agreed by national governments and adopted by the EU Council. (2) The Joint employment report (JER) is based on (a) the assessment of the employment situation in Europe (b) the implementation of the Employment Guidelines and (c) an assessment of the Scoreboard of key employment and social indicators. It is published by Commission and adopted by the EU Council. (3) National Reform Programmes (NRPs) are submitted by national governments and analysed by the Commission for compliance with Europe 2020. (4) Based on the assessment of the NRPs, the Commission publishes a series of Country reports, analysing Member States' economic policies and issues Country-specific recommendations.

Bibliography

Amossé, T. and Kalugina, E. (2013). Qualité du travail et dynamique de l'emploi en Europe pendant la crise (2005–2010). In Spieser, C. (Ed.) *L'emploi en temps de crise. Trajectoires individuelles, négociations collectives et action publique*. CEE-éditions. Wolters Kluwer.

Bellal, S. and Bouquin, S. (2002). Vers une redéfinition des logiques de droits collectifs incarnés par le travail et son statut: les droits à l'emploi et les droits sociaux à l'épreuve de l'Etat social actif. *Année sociale*, pp. 264–285.

Bouquin, S. (2004). *Lutte contre la pauvreté. L'Europe vue d'en bas, Chômage et précarité en Europe. Entretien réalisé avec Stephen Bouquin*. Bruxelles: La Lettre Mensuelle socio-économique du Conseil Central de l'Economie, n°89.

Bouquin, S., Gray, A., Lévy, C. et al. (2002). *Minimas sociaux en Europe*. Rapport final l'Europe vue d'en bas. 4Th TSER Program, 278p.

Bouquin (2017), L'employabilité ou comment l'érosion de la norme d'emploi conduit à la dissolution de la relation salariale, pp. 189–200; in Glaymann D., Moatty F., Tiffon G., Durand JP. (2017), *Le piège de l'employabilité*. Critique d'une notion au regard de ses usages sociaux, PURennes, 256p.

Bué, J. and Coutrot, Th. (2004). *Conditions de travail: les enseignemenst de 20 ans d'enquête*. Toulouse: Octarès.
Burroni, L. and Keune, M. (2011, March). Flexicurity: A conceptual critique. *European Journal of Industrial Relations*, 17(1), pp. 75–91.
Bustillo, R. (dir) (2009). *Indicators of Job Quality in the European Union*. Directorate General for Internal Policies. Policy Department A: Economic and Scientific Policy Employment and Social Affairs. IP/A/EMPL/ST/2008–09. Available at: www.europarl.europa.eu/thinktank/en/document.html?reference=IPOL-EMPL_ET(2009)429972; www.europarl.europa.eu/RegData/etudes/etudes/join/2009/429972/IPOL-EMPL_ET(2009)429972_EN.pdf
Carre, F., Findlay, P., Tilly, C. and Warhurst, C. (2012). Job quality: Scenarios, analysis and interventions. In Warhurst, C., Carre, F., Findlay, P. and Tilly, C. (Eds.) *Are Bad Jobs Inevitable? Trends, Determinants and Responses to Job Quality in the Twenty First Century*. Basingstoke: Palgrave Macmillan, pp. 2–22.
Clark, A. (2005). What makes a good job? Evidence from OECD countries. In Bazen, S., Lucifora, C. and Salvedra, W. (Eds.) *Job Quality and Employer Behaviors*. Basingstoke: Palgrave Macmillan, pp. 11–30.
Dahl, S.-A., Nesheim, T. and Olsen, K. (2009). Quality of work: Concept and measurement. In Guillen, A.-M. and Dahl, S.-A. (Eds.) *Quality of Work in the European Union: Concept, Data and Debates From a Transnational Perspective*. Brussels: Peter Lang.
Davoine, L. (2006). *Are Quantity and Quality of Jobs Correlated? Using, Interpreting and Discussing the Laeken Indicators*. Centre d'Etudes de l'emploi, Documents de travail n°59.
Davoine, L. and Ehrel, C. (2006). *Monitoring Employment Quality in Europe: European Employment Strategy Indicators and Beyond*. Document de travail CEE n66.
Demazière, D., Brossaud, Cl., Trabal, P. and Van Meter, K. (2006). *Analyse textuelles en sociologie: Logiciels, méthodes, usages, Presses universitaires de Rennes. « Didact Méthodes »*, Rennes, 219p.
Eurofound. (2008). *Annual Report 2008*. Available at: www.eurofound.europa.eu/sites/default/files/ef_publication/field_ef_document/ef0907en_0.pdf.
Eurofound. (2012). *Trends in Job Quality in Europe*. Luxembourg: Publications Office of the European Union.
European Commission. (2001). *Employment and Social Policy: A Framework Investing in Quality*. Communication From the Commission to the European Parliament, the Economic and Social Committee and the Committee of the Regions, COM (2001) 313.
Gallie, D. (Ed.) (2009). *Employment Regimes and the Quality of Work*. Oxford: Oxford University Press, pp. 1–33.
Gallie, D. (Ed.) (2013). *Economic Crisis, Quality of Work, and Social Integration: The European Experience*. Oxford: Oxford University Press.
Green, F. (2004, Fall). Work intensification, discretion and the decline in well-being at work. *Eastern Economic Journal*, 30(4), pp. 615–625.
Green, F. (2006). *Demanding Work: The Paradox of Job Quality in the Affluent Economy*. Princeton, NJ: Princeton University Press.
Guillen, A.-M. and Dahl, S.-A. (Eds.) (2009). *Quality of Work in the European Union, Concept, Data and Debates From a Transnational Perspective*. Brussels: Peter Lang.
Holman, D. (2013). Job types and job quality in Europe. *Human Relations*, 66(4), pp. 475–502.

Jessop, B. (1993). Toward a Schumpeterian welfare state? Preliminary remarks on post-Fordist political economy. *Studies in Political Economy*, 40(1).
Labbé, D. and Labbé, C. (2013). *Lexicométrie: quels outils pour les sciences humaines et sociales?* Guyancourt, France: Usages de la lexicométrie en sociologie. Available at: https://hal.archives-ouvertes.fr/hal-00834039/document.
Lapido, D. and Wilkinson, F. (2002). More pressure, less protection. In Burchell, B., Lapido, D. and Wilkinson, F. (Eds.) *Job Insecurity and Work Intensification*. London: Routledge.
Lehndorff, S. (2015). Institutional anchors for job quality – the case of industrial relations. In Holtgrewe, Urusla, Ramioul, et Monique and Kirov, Vassil (Eds.) *Hard Work in New Jobs: The Quality of Work and Life in European Growth Sector*. Houndmills, Palgrave Macmillan, pp. 101–112.
Leschke, J. and Watt, A. (2008). *Job Quality in Europe*. ETUI Working Paper. Available at: www.etui.org/Publications2/Working-Papers/Putting-a-number-on-job-quality
Leschke, J., Watt, A. and Finn, M. (2012). *Job Quality in the Crisis: An Update of the Job Quality Index (JQI)*. ETUI Working Paper 2012, 51p. www.etui.org/.../12+WP+2012+07+EN+WEB+version.pdf
Plasman, R. and Ryckx, F. (2001). Collective bargaining and poverty: A cross-national perspective. *European Journal of Industrial Relations* [online]. Available at: http://journals.sagepub.com/doi/abs/10.1177/095968010172005.
Spieser, C. (2013). *L'emploi en temps de crise. Trajectoires individuelles, négociations collectives et action publique*. CEE-éditions. Wolters Kluwer.
Tangian, A. (2007). *Is Work in Europe Decent? A Study Based on the 4th Survey of Working Conditions 2005*. Düsseldorf: Institute for Economic and Social Sciences WSI.
Warhurst, Ch., Carre, F., Findlay, P. and Tilly, Ch. (2012). *Are Bad Jobs Inevitable?* Basingstoke: Palgrave Macmillan.

3 Deregulation, job security and employability during the Great Recession

A multilevel analysis

Dragoș Adăscăliței and Federico Vegetti

Introduction

The economic crisis that began in 2008 has created important labour market imbalances in many European Union (EU) member states. The steady decline in average unemployment levels witnessed across the EU by 2008 was suddenly cancelled, with average unemployment levels reaching 10.9 percent in the first quarter of 2013. This figure hid a large variation between EU member states: whereas Greece and Spain reached unprecedented levels of unemployment in 2013 of 27.5 percent and 26.1 percent respectively, in Germany the unemployment level stood at 5.2 percent in the same year. Even more, unemployment levels among disadvantaged labour market groups such as young workers have been much higher, in some cases being double or more than double the unemployment rate for all age groups.

In order to respond to the unemployment malaise, both the European Commission as well as national member states have searched for labour market policies that could assist the unemployed and mitigate the impact that the crisis had on national labour markets. At the supranational level, the Commission has advocated for a *flexicurity* approach to address unemployment, arguing that "flexicurity policies are the best instrument to modernise labour markets: they must be revisited and adapted to the post-crisis context, in order to accelerate the pace of reform, reduce labour market segmentation, support gender equality and make transitions pay" (European Commission, 2010, p. 2). In view of this recommendation, the majority of the EU member states have implemented extensive labour market reforms that sought to adjust their labour markets to the post-crisis economic realities. However, while these measures aimed at deregulating national labour markets by promoting the use of temporary and part-time contracts, introducing more flexible regulations for hiring and firing as well as giving employers the upper hand in setting working conditions, they generally did not follow up with improving security for workers. As a result, the economic crisis has triggered a wave of labour market reforms that have decreased the job security that employees used to enjoy prior to 2008.

This chapter examines the crisis-driven developments and seeks to explain what were the effects of the crisis-driven surge in unemployment and subsequent labour market reforms on job security and employability. It starts by describing the post-crisis labour market reforms that have been implemented in most of the EU member states. It shows that deregulatory labour market reforms have been the norm in fighting unemployment around Europe but that the effects of these reforms are hardly visible. Rather than reducing unemployment across the EU, these reforms have generally led to more precarious labour market conditions evidenced by increases in the number of temporary and part-time workers. In a second step, the chapter analyses the impact of unemployment and labour market reforms on workers' perceptions about job security and employability. Using data from two waves of the European Social Survey (ESS) that contain information on workers' well-being before and after the crisis (2004 and 2010), it shows that self-perceptions about job security are primarily influenced by unemployment levels. Employment protection legislation (EPL) for temporary contracts also seems to impact self-perceptions about job security but the estimated effect is less robust. Furthermore, the chapter shows that, at the individual level, workers in a temporary contract as well as young workers and foreigners perceive their job as being less secure. In comparison, public sector employment, as well as union membership, has a positive impact on job security. By comparison, we find that self-perceptions about employability are negatively influenced only by GDP levels: the higher the economic growth, the more likely that people will feel more secure about their prospects of finding another job.

Institutional changes and labour market trends after the crisis

The structural unemployment crisis that affected Europe during the 1980s reinforced the belief that labour markets in the old continent are too "rigid" and thus incapable of generating sufficient jobs (Blanchard, 2006). This belief implied that in order to solve the unemployment problem, labour markets had to be reformed, primarily by decreasing employment protection regulation for workers on permanent contracts and ensuring numerical flexibility by promoting atypical forms of work. In practice, the consensus around the need to adjust labour markets led to different policy solutions across Europe, depending on the institutional architecture of each country. In Mediterranean countries, reforms targeted primarily young workers while preserving the system of protections that the core labour force used to enjoy. This solution generated a dualist employment regime in which employment rights created substantial labour market segmentation between younger and older worker cohorts (Cutuli and Guetto, 2013). By comparison, Scandinavian countries opted for deregulation but also for compensating workers through generous safety nets and reintegrating them rapidly into the labour markets by investing in active labour market policies (ALMPs). This compromise generated inclusive employment regimes in which all workers enjoyed similar levels of protection while national labour markets remained flexible enough in order to adjust to fluctuations in supply and demand. Denmark became the poster child of this *flexicurity* approach which was later embraced and heavily promoted by the EU. Finally, the United Kingdom and Ireland chose to let market forces determine employment outcomes by opting for emphasising minimal employment protection and linking employee benefits to their marginal productivity, thus giving rise to a market-driven employment regime (Gallie, 2013).

Viewed from this employment regime perspective, the recent economic crisis has continued the cycle of deregulation that began during the 1970s employment crisis. Not only has the crisis accelerated the deregulatory trends that were already in place many EU countries, but it has also enforced even more the old views according to which labour markets are still too rigid to respond to swings in unemployment levels. Against this background, it is not surprising that the policy solutions that were used by governments in order to respond to the crisis have primarily focused on scaling back protection in the hope that, in the medium term, unemployment will decline. However, compared with the 1980s, the recent crisis has triggered much swifter labour market reforms that were passed by governments during very short time spans and that were oftentimes accompanied by changes in collective bargaining systems. These reforms have especially affected Mediterranean and Eastern European countries, where the crisis has hit the hardest but also where the majority of workers were already affected by low levels of employment protection.

As Figure 3.1 shows, there is a significant heterogeneity between countries' reactions to the crisis in terms of the size and direction of employment protection legislation (EPL) reforms. In general, Nordic and Continental countries have preserved their pre-crisis levels of protection both for regular and temporary contracts. Most of the EPL reforms introduced in these countries concerned the use of agency work. In this respect, Denmark, Finland and Sweden have moved towards implementing the EU temporary agency work directive (2008/104/EC) which aims to set some minimum standards for workers on these types of contracts. Part of the EU's flexicurity approach, the directive secures only minimal rights for agency workers, and does not change their precarious status. In fact, it allows derogations to many important aspects of employment such as the equal treatment principle which effectively maintains the precarious status of agency workers (Countouris and Horton, 2009).

In contrast with the Nordic countries, Mediterranean and East European countries have undertaken much more extensive reforms in their EPL systems that targeted both regular and temporary contracts. While these reforms have been driven by the severity of the economic crisis in the two regions, they were also vastly supported by the International Financial Institutions that provided

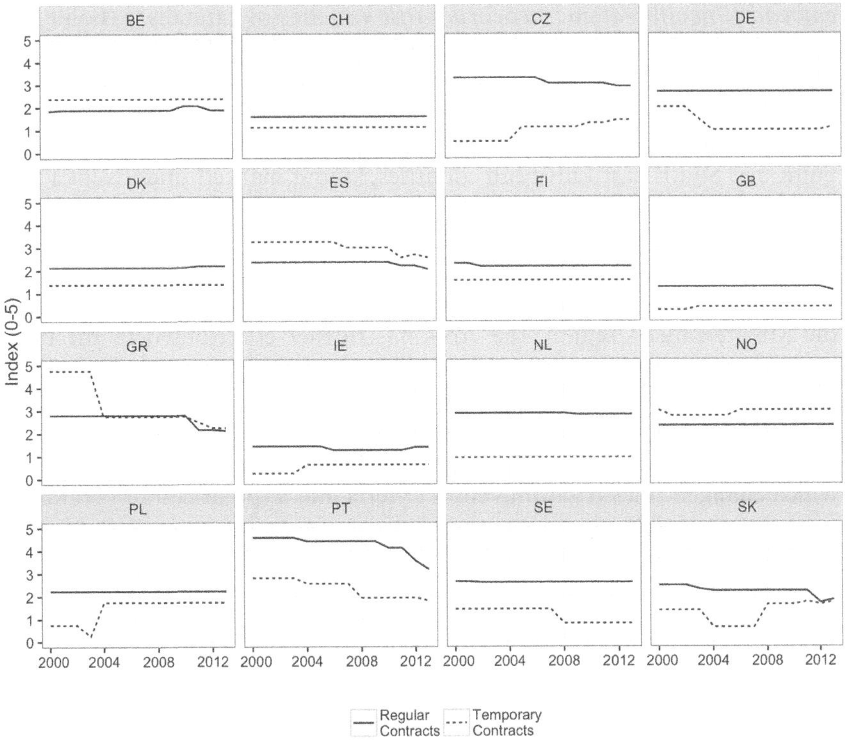

Figure 3.1 OECD employment protection legislation index for regular and temporary contracts, 2000–2013

economic assistance to countries under stress. Greece, Spain and Portugal stand out as the most active EPL reformers. In Greece, labour market deregulation went hand in hand with minimum wage and collective bargaining reforms (ILO, 2014). Reforms targeting the labour market included increasing the trial period for open-ended contracts and reducing the notice periods for firing workers but also increasing the duration of fixed-term contracts from 2 to 3 years. Similarly, in Spain, the 2012 labour market reform reduced compensation for unfair dismissals, created a new type of employment contract for small firms which allowed them to extend trial periods for up to one year and also broadened the sectors in which temporary agencies are allowed to operate (OECD, 2014; Horwitz and Myant, 2015).

Eastern European countries undertook similar reforms in the EPL systems. However, unlike in the case of Mediterranean or Nordic countries, in Eastern Europe regional heterogeneity was much higher as these countries do not easily fit in one specific employment regime. Rather, the region is characterised by different types of dependent capitalisms that combined market and state forces to different degrees, which gave rise to *neoliberal*, *embedded neoliberal* and *neocorporatist* varieties of capitalism (Bohle and Greskovits, 2007, 2012). Each of these capitalisms is characterised by different levels of EPL regulation. Whereas in the embedded neoliberal regimes that characterise Hungary, Slovakia and the Czech Republic, EPL regulation ranked from average levels to fairly strong (see Figure 3.1), in the Baltic and South East European countries, labour markets underwent a prolonged period of deregulation even before the start of the economic crisis. Moreover, as Figure 3.1 shows, EPL for temporary contracts has generally increased towards the mid-2000s as a result of reforms that adapted labour markets in these countries to EU standards. Similar to reforms passed in the Mediterranean region, the crisis has further contributed to the trend of implementing reforms to improve EPL regulation for atypical contracts while deregulating EPL for permanent contracts. For example, in Hungary the definition of temporary agency work was clarified while in Poland a large deregulation programme for around 250 professions was implemented which changed rules regarding entry criteria and apprenticeship periods.

In the case of market-driven employment regimes, many of the labour market measures passed after 2008 were part of austerity packages and sought to provide even more flexibility in the short term. In the United Kingdom, businesses with fewer than 10 employees were exempted from virtually all new domestic legislation for a period of 3 years. At the same time, in the United Kingdom, EPL reforms targeted regulation for permanent contracts by it making harder for employees to claim unfair dismissal and introducing a cap on the redundancy payments for civil servants.

The effect of EPL deregulation on national labour markets has been substantial. OECD (2015) noted that almost half of employment growth since the 1990s and up to the crisis has been in non-standard forms of work while, if the crisis is included, the number rises to almost 60 percent. Moreover, being in a non-standard contract does not increase the chances to transition into a standard job while non-standard workers are worse off in terms of job quality: generally non-standard workers receive less training, have lower levels of job security and tend to earn less. At the same time, temporary workers face higher wage penalties, experience slower wage growth and wage instability in comparison with permanent workers (OECD, 2015, p. 139). As Figure 3.2 shows, the share of temporary and part-time work in selected EU economies varies substantially between levels below 20 percent in the Czech Republic to above 50 percent in the Netherlands. Figure 3.2 also shows that in general the economic crisis has led to an increase in the share of temporary and part-time work in total employment, although the net effect of the crisis varies considerably between countries.

Interestingly, there is a large variation within employment regime clusters. Whereas in Greece the number of non-standard contracts remained fairly low in spite of a deep financial crisis, in Spain non-standard forms of work are much more common and began to rise during the crisis after an initial

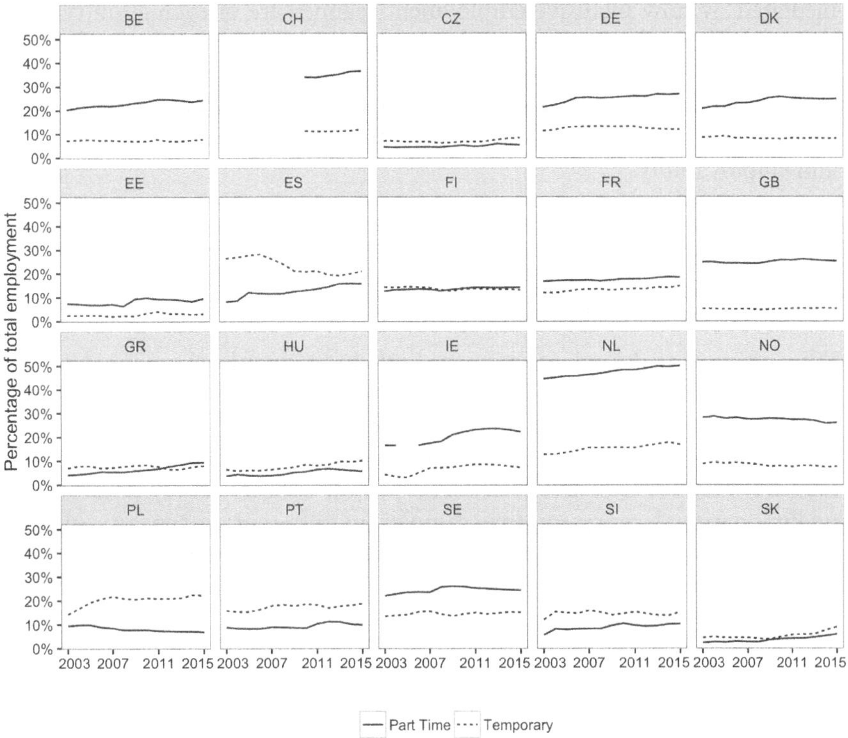

Figure 3.2 Share of part-time and temporary work in selected EU countries, 2003–2015

drop between 2003 and 2007. By comparison, in the United Kingdom, the share of non-standard employment in total employment remained fairly stable before and after the crisis. However, the economic downturn has led to a shift in the types of non-standard contracts that employers offer. In particular, in the United Kingdom a distinct employment pattern has grown substantially – the *zero-hour* contracts. Compared with other forms of atypical work, zero-hour contracts allow employers to have employees "on call" depending on availability of work. These types of contracts offer almost no protection to workers as income is unpredictable while at the same time workers have to sign exclusivity clauses which tie them to one employer even for periods when no work is available. As Hadjivassiliou, Tassinari, Speckesser and Swift (2015) note, around half a million workers in the United Kingdom were employed on zero-hour contracts in 2012–2013 and 37 percent of these workers were aged between 16 and 24 years old.

Besides the detrimental effect on labour markets, the developments described previously are also likely to impact individual perceptions about job security as well as employability. However, as the literature notes, the effect of deregulation on individual perceptions about job security is mediated by how inclusive employment regimes are in each country (Paugam and Zhou, 2007). In the following sections we carry out an empirical analysis that takes into account both the institutional framework that characterises each economy as well as the state of the economy in an attempt to check whether EPL levels impact worker' perceptions about job security and employability.

Determinants of job security

Data and variables

For our empirical analyses we use both individual-level micro data and country-level macro data. For the individual observations we rely on survey data from the European Social Survey (henceforth ESS) collected in 2004 (wave 2) and 2010 (wave 5), that is, 4 years before and 2 years after the financial meltdown of 2008. The ESS project collects survey data on high quality national representative samples in different European countries every 2 years. Next to a core questionnaire that is asked in all waves, each ESS round includes different rotating modules focusing on specific topics.[1] For this study we use waves 2 and 5 because they contain the "Family, work and well-being" module, which includes perceptions of job security together with other variables that are useful for our investigation. One of the characteristics of ESS data is that the number of countries surveyed is different from wave to wave. To maintain our sample consistency over the two time points, we select only the countries that are surveyed at both waves. Hence our initial sample consists of 20 countries: Belgium, Czech Republic, Denmark, Estonia, Finland, France, Germany, Greece, Hungary, Ireland, the Netherlands, Norway, Poland, Portugal, Slovakia, Slovenia, Spain, Sweden, Switzerland and the UK. However, due to lack of observations for some crucial variables in 2004, we need to drop four countries from this sample: Estonia, France, Hungary and Slovenia.[2] This leaves us with 16 countries, consistently observed in 2004 and 2010. From the greater group of respondents who took the ESS survey in the selected countries and waves, we keep only those individuals who provide a valid response to all our individual-level predictors. Hence, our final individual-level sample consists of 24,007 individuals.

Our first dependent variable, *perception of job security*, is measured on a 4-point Likert-type scale where respondents are asked to assess how true the statement "My job is secure" is for them. The response options range from "Not at all true" to "Very true", with smaller values indicating low perceived security and greater values indicating high perceived security. Our second dependent variable, *perceptions about employability*, is measured on a 10-point Likert-type scale where respondents are asked how difficult it would be to get a similar job if they had to leave the employer. The responses range from "Extremely difficult" to "Extremely easy", with smaller values indicating low levels of employability and higher values indicating high levels of employability.

A preliminary look at how the job security variable is distributed in our sample is provided by Figure 3.3. The figure shows the shares of respondents choosing each of the four categories in the 16 countries of our sample in 2004 and 2010. The countries are ordered from lowest to highest average perceived security.[3] In the top row of the figure are the countries in our group where citizens feel less secure about their job: Slovakia, Czech Republic, Greece and Portugal. The case of Slovakia and the Czech Republic is puzzling. Although the two countries have average levels of employment protection and relatively low shares of atypical work in total employment, they score the highest in terms of perceptions about job security. This might be related with the lack of welfare alternatives once a worker becomes unemployed (Paugam and Zhou, 2007; Chung and van Oorschot, 2012). As the literature has shown, the generosity of unemployment benefits can be linked with workers' perceptions about job security (Sjöberg, 2010). The case of Greece and Portugal, on the other hand, carries the clear mark of

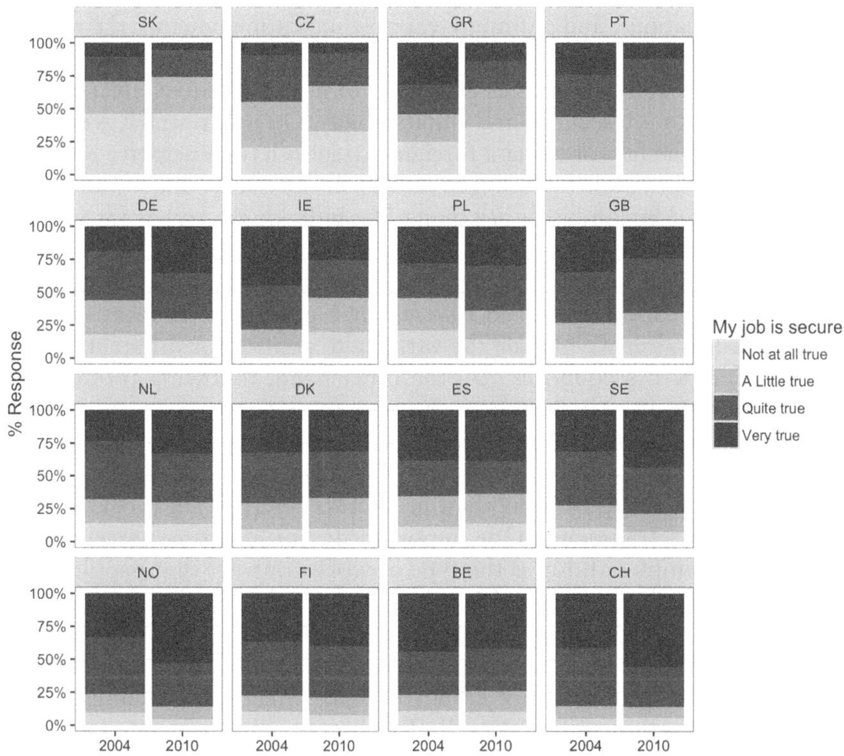

Figure 3.3 Share of respondents choosing each of the four categories on job security

the financial crisis: in both countries there has been a substantial increase between 2004 and 2010 in the tendency to respond "Not at all true" or "A little true" to the statement about job security. To give a concrete comparison, in 2004 Greek employees felt on average slightly more secure than German employees (country means of 2.61 and 2.57 respectively), while in 2010 the situation was inverted, with a far greater gap dividing the two groups (2.13 in Greece versus 2.93 in Germany). The only other country in our sample to experience a similar drop in perceived security as Greece and Portugal is Ireland, where the share of respondents choosing "Quite true" or "Very true" to the statement went to almost 80% to less than 55%, i.e. about one quarter less. However, in most of the countries the situation remained stable, with a few cases where perceptions of job security visibly increased, like Germany, Norway and to a smaller extent Poland and Sweden.

But what affects perceptions of job security and employability in the countries surveyed here? To answer this question, we look at several characteristics of the individual respondents and the countries where they live. At the individual level, we focus on sociodemographic characteristics such as age (in years), gender (a dummy variable indicating whether the respondent is female), the level of education (recoded in three categories: low, middle, and high education), and a dummy variable indicating whether the respondents are citizen of the country where they live. From previous research (Erlinghagen, 2008), we expect education to have a positive effect on perceptions of both job security and employability. On the contrary, we expect both age and the fact of being a foreign citizen to have a negative effect on our response variables. Erlinghagen (2008) shows that younger individuals are less affected by job insecurity than older individuals, and as for foreigners, we expect their working conditions to be generally more precarious, covered by limited contracts or by no work contract at all. We do not have any reason to expect gender to have either a positive or a negative effect on job security, but we include the variable to control for different sample composition across countries. On the other hand, following previous literature (Berntson et al., 2006), we expect gender to have a negative effect on employability, with women being less likely to positively perceive their labour market status.

Another key group of individual predictors refers to the working conditions of the respondents. One important factor affecting perceived job security and employability is the type of work contract that people have. To take this into account we include two dummy variables, one indicating whether respondents have a limited, fixed-term contract and one indicating whether they have no job contract at all. The type of industry by which respondents are employed may affect their feelings of job security and employability as well. To observe this effect, we include a series of dummy variables indicating the industry in which the respondents work. Following previous literature, we expect that workers in the public sector to feel the most secure about their jobs, followed by workers in manufacturing and then services (Clark and Postel-Vinay, 2009). From previous research, we also expect the size of firm for which respondents work to affect their perception of security: workers of bigger company tend in general to perceive their job as more secure than workers of smaller companies. To control for this, we include a variable recording how many employees work for the company where the respondents have their job. The indicator is coded in ordered categories, ranging from less than 10 to more than 500 employees. Finally, a crucial factor affecting job security is whether the respondent is member of a worker union. We observe this using a dummy variable. Overall, based on previous literature, we expect that trade union membership will have a positive effect on workers' perceptions about job security (Bender and Sloane, 1999; Schnabel, 2002).

The country-level data that we include come from multiple sources. We take data about gross domestic product (GDP) and unemployment rates from official national statistics. These two indictors capture two important aspects of the economic crisis that are supposed to be directly relevant for job security. GDP is a common indicator of countries' economic performance. A higher value usually indicates a growing economy, and it implies more investments and returns. A lower value, on the other hand, is an indicator of relative economic decline, and it may come together with companies cutting their workforce or going bankrupt. Hence, in contexts where GDP is higher, the average employee should have in general a safer job than in contexts where it is low.

An even more direct indicator of how much at risk a person's job is in a given context is the unemployment rate. First, it indicates that in a country at a certain point in time there are more individuals who do not have a job and arguably want one. Hence, workers should feel their position to be less secure due to higher competition. Second, unemployment is usually an important issue that receives considerable media attention. Individuals are therefore supposed to be informed about high levels of unemployment in their country, and that should affect their perceptions that jobs are, in general, less safe as more scarce. Previous studies have shown that, indeed, in countries with higher unemployment rates workers tend, on average, to feel less secure about their job (Erlinghagen, 2008). Hence, we expect a negative effect of unemployment rate on perception of job security.

We also look at the types of policies that national governments implement to protect or stimulate the labour market. An important contextual factor that may affect perceptions of job security is the employment protection legislation (EPL) operating in a given country. EPL represents the most important set of rules and instructions that regulates the hiring and firing of workers under different types of contracts. As a result, low levels of EPL means that employers can hire and fire workers easily, without many institutional barriers, while high levels of EPL indicate that employment is more secure. Furthermore, changes in EPL, have been amongst the most important labour market adjustments passed by governments that sought to address the rise in unemployment levels created by the crisis (World Bank, 2013; Adascalitei and Pignatti Morano, 2016). Finally, we use OECD data to assess the extent of active labour market policies (ALMPs) in a given country. As in the case of unemployment expenditures, ALMPs can help in buffering the consequences of job loss and help reintegrate unemployed workers in the labour market (Lübke and Erlinghagen, 2014; Van Oorschot and Chung, 2015). All the contextual-level predictors included in the models change across countries, but also between the 2 years of survey. Because the interviews are generally conducted in the middle of the year, while some yearly country indicators are averages over the whole year, we use the value of the previous year for all contextual variables. In other words, for each country, all the level-2 variables are observed in 2003 and 2009.

We use a multilevel mixed-effects regression to analyse how the individual and contextual factors described earlier affect perceptions of job security. Since our first dependent variable is measured on a 4-point ordinal scale, we specify an ordered regression model. Unlike linear models, where the intervals between values are assumed to be equally spaced, ordinal models acknowledge that values are ordered, but make no assumptions regarding the distance between any two values. For instance, in our case, the psychological leap between responding "Not at all true" and "A little true" to the statement "*My job is secure*" may be different from the one between responding "A little true" and "Quite true". In the first case, the difference is between being essentially certain that one's position is precarious and recognising some certain degree of doubt, while in the second case the difference is between two degrees of doubt – which are more abstract, and therefore separated by less clear boundaries. Ordered regression models take care of these characteristics by modelling the probability to be in a certain category against the probability to be in the previous one. Like other generalised linear models, they estimate the effect of the independent variables on a linear predictor, that is related to the outcome by the means of a link function. In this case we use a *logit* link function, therefore specifying a model that is equivalent to the more common logistic regression. The only difference is that ordinal models do not estimate an actual *intercept* (i.e. the value of the linear predictor when all independent variables take value zero), but a number of *cut-points*, which varies depending on the number of categories that the variable takes. Since in our case there are four categories, the model will estimate three cut-points: one between "Not at all true" and "A little true", one between "A little true" and "Quite true", and one between "Quite true" and "Very true". Like with intercepts, the estimated cut-points values reflect the (transformed) probability to be in the category after the cut-point against the probability to be in the category before the cut-point when all predictors have value zero. The ordinal nature of the scale is reflected by the fact that the distance between any two cut-points is not assumed to be constant, but can vary considerably across the scale.

Since our second variable is coded on a 10-point scale, we treat it as continuous and estimate a multilevel linear regression model with random effects.

Our data are structured hierarchically, with individual respondents nested within countries and years. While this would normally require modelling a cross-classified multilevel structure, we only have two year units, 2004 and 2010. Hence, to take into account time variation, we include one dummy variable taking value 1 for all the cases observed in 2010. The coefficient of this variable reflects how much more (or less) secure people perceive their job in post-crisis times compared to the pre-crisis. Of course, this effect should vary between countries: as we have seen in Figure 3.3, in some places individuals became, on average, more secure about their job, and in others less. We take into account this source of variation by nesting individuals within country-year and country units. In this way, we take into account the variation between individuals belonging to different countries, we estimate the effect of being in a post-crisis year on the whole sample, and we make sure this effect differs in different countries. Moreover, since our contextual-level predictors vary between countries but also between years, we make sure that the estimated standard errors of the contextual effects are clustered at the appropriate level.

For each of the two response variables, we specify three models. The first is the "empty" model where only the cut-points, the year 2010 dummy and the variance of the intercepts at the country-year and country-level are estimated. As we said earlier, ordinal models do not provide an estimate of an intercept, but rather of the cut-points. The unit-specific values estimated here can be interpreted as unit-specific averages: when combined with the cut-points and converted into probabilities, they tell how much the probability is to be in all four categories when all the predictors are zero. Hence, their variances reflect how much variation there is in the data among country-year averages and country averages. The second model that we estimate includes all the individual predictors discussed previously, but no contextual predictors. Finally, the third model includes all individual and contextual-level predictors. We estimate three models, improving the model specification step by step so that we can assess how much the individual and contextual predictors explain of the variance between countries, by observing the extent to which the variance of the intercepts decreases the more variables we add.

Results

Tables 3.1 and 3.2 show the results of our models. The first result worth discussing is that the "year 2010" dummy has no significant effect in the case of in job security but is significant and has a positive effect on employability. This means that, in the countries in our sample, there is no general difference between pre- and post-crisis regarding the extent to which people feel secure about their job but, counterintuitively, in the post-crisis context people feel

Table 3.1 Coefficients of the logistic multilevel analysis of job security

	Model 1		*Model 2*		*Model 3*	
	Coef.	*S.E*	*Coef.*	*S.E*	*Coef.*	*S.E*
Gender (female)			0.009	(0.024)	0.010	(0.024)
Age			0.004	(0.001)***	0.004	(0.001)***
Foreigner			-0.212	(0.056)***	-0.212	(0.056)***
Education (3 categories)			0.167	(0.018)***	0.167	(0.018)***
Union member			0.084	(0.030)**	0.083	(0.030)**
Fixed-term contract			-1.050	(0.038)***	-1.049	(0.038)***
No contract			-0.509	(0.058)***	-0.511	(0.058)***
Company size			0.025	(0.010)**	0.025	(0.010)**
Industry:[b] Public Administration			0.439	(0.048)***	0.440	(0.048)***
Industry:[b] Manufacture			-0.285	(0.033)***	-0.285	(0.033)***
Industry:[b] Agriculture & Mining			-0.012	(0.078)	-0.012	(0.078)
GDP[a]					0.320	(0.171)+
Unemployment rate[a]					-0.183	(0.091)*
Active LMP[a]					0.288	(0.132)*
EPL[a] (regular jobs)					-0.257	(0.141)+
EPL[a] (temporary jobs)					0.111	(0.117)
Year 2010	-0.051	(0.129)	-0.092	(0.134)	0.233	(0.244)
Thresholds						
1|2	-1.894	(0.180)	-2.086	(0.177)	-1.877	(0.176)
2|3	-0.639	(0.179)	-0.781	(0.176)	-0.572	(0.176)
3|4	0.916	(0.179)	0.834	(0.176)	1.043	(0.176)
Variance random intercepts						
Country: year		0.128		0.139		0.100
Country		0.379		0.340		0.159
N respondents		24007		24007		24007
N country: year		32		32		32
N countries		16		16		16
AIC		61249		59966		59960
Log likelihood		-30619		-29966		-29958

a Values refer to the previous year;
b Baseline category: services
+ = p < 0.1;
* = p < 0.05;
** = p < 0.01;
*** = p < 0.001

Table 3.2 Coefficients of the multilevel analysis of employability

	Model 1		*Model 2*		*Model 3*	
	Coef.	*S.E*	*Coef.*	*S.E*	*Coef.*	*S.E*
Gender (female)			-0.205	(0.034)*	-0.205	(0.034)*
Age			-0.039	(0.002)*	-0.039	(0.002)*
Foreigner			0.231	(0.080)*	0.228	(0.080)*
Education (3 categories)			0.264	(0.025)*	0.264	(0.025)*
Union member			-0.161	(0.042)*	-0.162	(0.042)*
Fixed-term contract			-0.178	(0.052)*	-0.177	(0.052)*
No contract			-0.003	(0.080)	-0.003	(0.080)
Company size			-0.053	(0.014)*	-0.053	(0.014)*
Industry:[b] Public Administration			-0.697	(0.065)*	-0.696	(0.065)*
Industry:[b] Manufacture			-0.448	(0.047)*	-0.448	(0.047)*
Industry:[b] Agriculture & Mining			-0.226	(0.110)*	-0.225	(0.110)*
GDP[a]					0.587	(0.198)*
Unemployment Rate[a]					-0.492	(0.113)*
Active LMP[a]					0.243	(0.196)
EPL[a] (regular jobs)					-0.195	(0.217)
EPL[a] (temporary jobs)					-0.203	(0.155)
Year 2010	0.2376	(0.212)	0.245	(0.220)	0.926	(0.283)*
Intercept	4.420	(0.217)*	4.547	(0.233)*	4.120	(0.241)*
S.D. random intercepts						
Country: year		0.592		0.139		0.100
Country		0.626				
Residual		2.648		0.340		0.159
N respondents		23852		23852		23852
N country: year		32		32		32
N countries		16		16		16
AIC (REML)		114284		113164		113148
Log likelihood		-57142		-56582		-56574

a Values refer to the previous year;
b Baseline category: services
* = $p < 0.05$

that their chances of obtaining a similar job are higher. Of course, failing to see an effect of the crisis on job security does not necessarily mean that the effect is not there. First, our post-crisis survey was conducted in 2010, only 2 years after the beginning of the financial crisis. Hence, it might just need more time for the psychological implications of changing economic conditions to reveal themselves. Second, while the model provides evidence for an *average* effect, the crisis might have affected some groups of citizens more than others. Third, the positive effect of the crisis on employability might be driven by that fact that workers who remained employed 2 years after the downturn perceived themselves as sufficiently competitive in the labour market.

Looking at the individual characteristics, we note that all variables have a significant on self-perceived job security effect except for gender. Older people are more likely to feel secure about their job, a finding that contradicts the findings discussed by Erlinghagen (2008), but is perfectly plausible when we consider that older people are more likely to have longer tenures. Other effects go in the expected direction. Being a foreigner implies feeling on average less secure about one's job, as well as having a fixed-term contract or having no contract at all. Moreover, education has a positive effect on perceived job security, as well as being a member of a trade union, and working for a larger company. Finally, the industry for which an individual works matters as well. Unsurprisingly, people employed in the public administration feel on average more secure about their job than those employed in the service sector. However, less intuitively, being employed in manufacturing comes with significantly lower perceived security than working in services. This might be driven by the fact that workers in manufactoring might have been faced with important restructurings, which might drive down their perceptions about job security.

By comparison, as expected, gender has a negative effect on employability, with women feeling less secure about finding a similar job. At the same time age and being in a fixed-term contract have a negative effect on employability. Moreover, in comparison with the services workers in the public administration, manufacturing and agriculture feel less competitive on the labour market. This effect might be driven by the higher mobility that workers in the services enjoy in comparison with the other sectors of the economy. At the same time, workers in manufacturing might find it difficult to find a new job once unemployed, thus feeling less secure about their future. Surprisingly, being a foreigner has a positive impact on self-perceived employability.

Among the contextual variables, the unemployment rate has a significant effect on both job security and employability, which goes in the expected direction: the higher the level of unemployment in a given country at a certain point in time, the less secure and competitive people feel about their job, on average. To fully appreciate this effect, Figure 3.4 shows the predicted probabilities to be in each of the four categories of our job security variable over the range of unemployment rates observed in our data. When unemployment is at its lowest, as in countries such as Norway, Switzerland or Ireland before the crisis, almost three quarters of the citizens find the

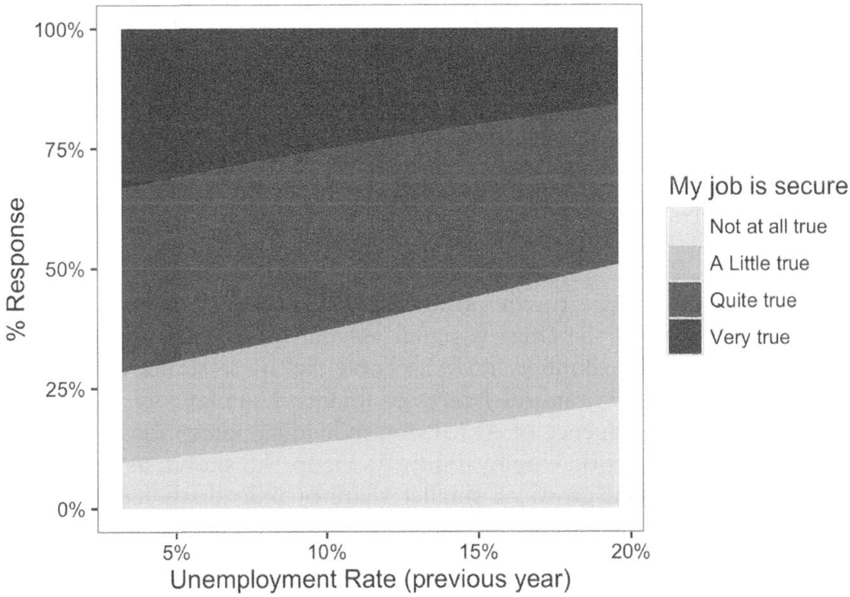

Figure 3.4 Predicted probability of job security at different levels of unemployment

statement "*My job is secure*" to be either quite true or very true. Conversely, when the unemployment is at its highest, like in Greece or Spain after the crisis, the figure drops to a half: not a small share, but substantially reduced. This finding underlines that when thinking about job security, usually workers consider the state of the economy as the main proxy for assessing their own position. It is thus not surprising that the issue of unemployment surfaced very often in the political discourse surrounding the policy measures designed to counteract the effects of the economic crisis. However, the treatment, which as discussed earlier, involved a range of measures targeted to deregulate labour markets, was not effective in terms of addressing the unemployment issue.

An interesting result is the negative effect on job security, albeit only significant at $p < 0.1$, of EPL for regular jobs. Substantively, this result suggests that in countries with more protected regular jobs, the more insecure workers are about their jobs. While this finding is all but robust, it suggests that employment protection legislation may not translate into jobs that are more secure. Therefore, the effect might be the result of the discrepancies that exist in many countries between the regulation and enforcement. Since EPL captures only the regulatory dimension of the labour market, while ignoring how the rules are enforced in different economies, it is possible that even though strict regulation does exist, government agencies do not necessarily enforce it. This is the case in many East European and Mediterranean countries where labour related conflicts are costly for workers and implementation issues abound. Furthermore, as Clark and Postel-Vinay (2009) note, stricter EPL can lead to longer unemployment durations and make it more difficult for workers in atypical contracts to maintain or upgrade their labour market status. At the same time, stricter EPL might lead to more temporary jobs, and thus inflate the share of those who feel insecure about their jobs (Clark and Postel-Vinay, 2009).

Furthermore, GDP growth positively impacts both job security and employability, albeit the effect is significant only at $p < 0.1$ in the case of job security. As the economy grows, people feel more secure about their job and that they have more chances of finding a similar job. Finally, we find a significant influence of ALMPs on individual perceptions about job security but no effect on employability. As Figure 3.5 shows, as the expenditure per individual grows, a smaller share of individuals feels insecure about their jobs. The finding suggests that although more generous ALMPs might make workers feel more secure about their labour market status, once unemployed, ALMPs might not necessarily contribute to improving their chances of securing a similar job.

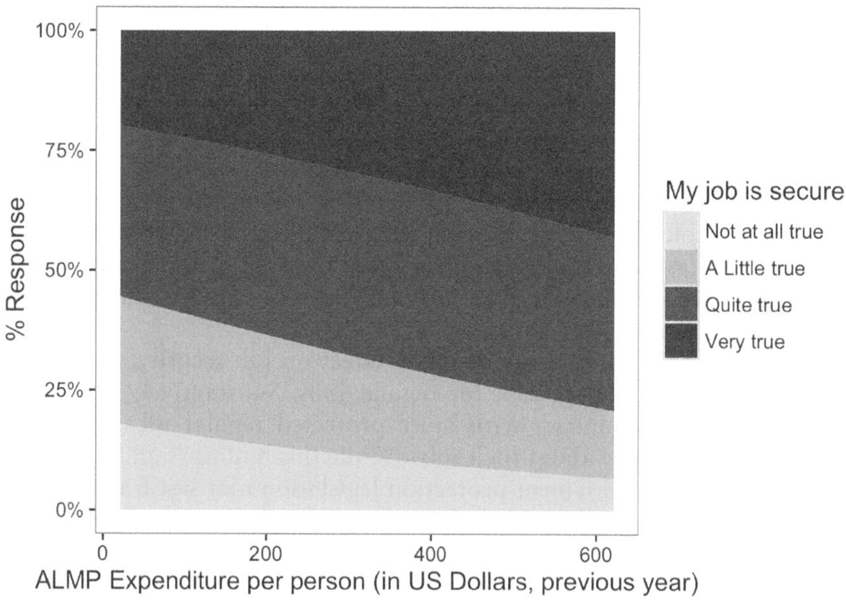

Figure 3.5 Predicted probability of job security at different levels of ALMP expenditure

Conclusion

This chapter has analysed the impact of economic and institutional factors on workers' self- perceptions about job security and employability. It has discussed the implications of the crisis-driven reforms in EPL systems and has shown that in most European countries these were associated with an increase in the number of atypical contracts. It has shown that individual perceptions about job security are negatively impacted both by stricter EPL regulations and a higher unemployment level. Furthermore, the paper showed that ALMPs and GDP growth have a positive impact on perceived job security. Employability was positively impacted by GDP growth and negatively impacted by unemployment levels. At the same time, the paper found that a host of individual-level predictors impacted perceptions about job security: whereas union membership, education, the size of the company as well as working in the public sector lead to higher levels of self-perceived job security, being a foreigner, being on a fixed-term contract and working in industry are associated with lower rankings of self-perceived job security. In comparison, self-perceived employability was negatively associated with gender, age and being on an atypical contract.

In light of these findings, a number of questions remain open about the links between institutions and individual perceptions about job security and employability. First, it seems that workers do not trust that ALMPs are an effective tool for ensuring their re-employment. Second, the links between EPL and individual perceptions about job security require more examination. Although are findings remain rather speculative in this aspect, it might be that what we are capturing in our analysis is a labour market dualisation effect in which outsiders do not benefit from increases in EPL for regular workers which negatively impacts workers on atypical contracts. Third, rather than reacting to institutional changes, workers' self-perceptions about job security and employability are more sensitive to macroeconomic changes, particularly in GDP levels and unemployment.

Notes

1 See www.europeansocialsurvey.org/data/module-index.html for more information on ESS data and its modules.
2 In Hungary and France, we miss individual-level data from ESS; specifically, the variable on the industry sector of the company where the respondents work is missing in Hungary, and the variable on the type of employment contract that the respondents have is missing in France. In Estonia and Slovenia, we miss country-level data from OECD about employment protection legislation.
3 To overcome the imbalance in number of observations between the 2004 and 2010 samples, we first calculated the country averages for every year, and then calculated the average between the 2 years.

References

Adascalitei, D. and Pignatti Morano, C. (2016). Drivers and effects of labour market reforms: Evidence from a novel policy compendium. *IZA Journal of Labor Policy*, 5(15), pp. 1–32.

Bender, K. and Sloane, P. (1999). Trade union membership, tenure and the level of job insecurity. *Applied Economics*, 31(1), pp. 123–135.

Blanchard, O. (2006). European unemployment: The evolution of facts and ideas. *Economic Policy*, 21(45), pp. 7–59.

Bohle, D. and Greskovits, B. (2007). Neoliberalism, embedded neoliberalism and neocorporatism: Towards transnational capitalism in central-eastern Europe. *West European Politics*, 30(3), pp. 443–466.

Bohle, D. and Greskovits, B. (2012). *Capitalist Diversity on Europe's Periphery*. Cornell Studies in Political Economy. Ithaca, NY: Cornell University Press.

Chung, H. and van Oorschot, W. (2012). The impact of perceived and actual unemployment benefit generosity and unemployment rates on the employment security of workers. In Ervasti, H., Goul Andersen, J., Fridberg, T. and Ringdal, K. (Eds.) *The Future of the Welfare State*. Cheltenham and Northampton, MA: Edward Elgar Publishing, pp. 46–67.

Clark, A. and Postel-Vinay, F. (2009). Job security and job protection. *Oxford Economic Papers*, 61(2), pp. 207–239.

Countouris, N. and Horton, R. (2009). The temporary agency work directive: Another broken promise? *Industrial Law Journal*, 38(3), pp. 329–338.

Cutuli, G. and Guetto, R. (2013). Fixed-term contracts, economic conjuncture, and training opportunities: A comparative analysis across European labour markets. *European Sociological Review*, 29(3), pp. 616–629.

Erlinghagen, M. (2008). Self-perceived job insecurity and social context: A multilevel analysis of 17 European countries. *European Sociological Review*, 24(2), pp. 183–197.

European Commission. (2010). *Communication From the European Commission to the European Parliament, the Council, the European Economic and Social Committee and the Committee of Regions: An Agenda for New Skills and Jobs: A European Contribution Towards Full Employment*. Brussels: European Commission.

Gallie, D. (2013). *Economic Crisis, Quality of Work, and Social Integration: The European Experience*. Oxford: Oxford University Press.

Hadjivassiliou, K., Tassinari, A., Speckesser, A. and Swift, S. (2015). *Country Report: United Kingdom*. STYLE Working Papers. Available at: www.style-research.eu/wordpress/wp-content/uploads/2015/03/UK_WP3-Task-3-National-Report-IES-17.6.2015.pdf.

Horwitz, L. and Myant, M. (2015). *Spain's Labour Market Reforms: The Road to Employment – or to Unemployment*? Working Paper 2015.03. Brussels: European Trade Union Institute.

ILO. (2014). *Greece Productive Jobs for Greece*. Studies on Growth with Equity. Geneva: International Labour Office.

Lübke, C. and Erlinghagen, M. (2014). Self-perceived job insecurity across Europe over time: Does changing context matter? *Journal of European Social Policy*, 24(4), pp. 319–336.

OECD. (2014). *The 2012 Labour Market Reform in Spain: A Preliminary Assessment*. Paris: OECD Publishing.

OECD. (2015). *In It Together: Why Less Inequality Benefits All*. Paris: OECD Publishing.

Paugam, S. and Zhou, Y. (2007). Job insecurity. In Gallie, D. (Ed.) *Employment Regimes and the Quality of Work*. Oxford: Oxford University Press, pp. 179–204.

Schnabel, C. (2002). *Determinants of Trade Union Membership*. Discussion Paper No. 15. Friedrich-Alexander-Universität Erlangen-Nürnberg, Lehrstuhl für Arbeitsmarkt und Regionalpolitik. Available at: www.econstor.eu/bitstream/10419/28298/1/361174594.PDF [Accessed 27 November 2017].

Sjöberg, O. (2010). Social insurance as a collective resource: Unemployment benefits, job insecurity and subjective well-being in a comparative perspective. *Social Forces*, 88(3), pp. 1281–1304.

Sverke, B. and Marklund, S. (2006). Predicting perceived employability: Human capital or labour market opportunities? *Economic and Industrial Democracy*, 27(2), pp. 223–244.

van Oorschot, W. and Chung, H. (2015). Feelings of dual-insecurity among European workers: A multi-level analysis. *European Journal of Industrial Relations*, 21(1), pp. 23–37.

World Bank. (2013). *The World Development Report 2013: Jobs*. Washington, DC: World Bank. Available at: https://openknowledge.worldbank.org/handle/10986/11843 [Accessed 27 November 2017].

4 Quality of working time in the police

The experience of shift extensification for officers and staff

Dora Scholarios, Hannah Hesselgreaves and Raymond Pratt

Introduction

For employers, work scheduling which allows labour flexibility is essential given wider trends in employment, such as more globalised production and business services. This means that employers are able to increase, reduce or vary the distribution of working hours according to demand (Lambert, 2008; Rubery, Ward, Grimshaw and Beynon, 2005). As highlighted in Chapter 1, employer-led flexibility suggests flexibility which is good for employers without particular concern for employee influence or interests. In his typology of flexibility and stability, Jonsson (2007) also differentiates between the contrasting positions of employers and employees in the desirability of flexibility. With regard to working time, employer-desired variability imposed on employees may include requiring employees to work overtime or unsocial hours, such as night or weekend working, and other non-standard working arrangements which have increased in prominence over the last decade; e.g. reduced or zero hours contracts, flexitime, shift-working or compressed hours (Bewley, Rincon-Aznar and Wilkinson, 2014).

This chapter focuses on the unpredictable or unstable aspects of working time which are driven by employers' operational needs (see also Jonsson's, 2007, p. 36, discussion of flexibility in terms of situations where employees are flexible for the employer). It has been argued that this form of unpredictable working time has not been sufficiently recognised relative to other working time arrangements (Henly and Lambert, 2014). Extended working hours which result from variable (Nabe-Nielsen et al., 2012) or unpredictable (Henly and Lambert, 2014) work demands direct attention to employees' daily experience of shifts. Arguably, unplanned variations in employee working time are a much more common occurrence than has been acknowledged in literature on work scheduling or shiftwork more generally. Lambert (2008) warns that some data capture of fluctuating working hours will inevitably underestimate its prevalence. Unlike paid overtime, for example, how work is distributed in a typical working shift (e.g., taking important customer calls at the end of one's shift) or dealing with uncertain capacity (e.g., covering for staff sickness absence) is seldom formally logged (Van den Bergh, Beliën, De Bruecker, Demeulemeester and De Boeck, 2013).

Such discrepancies between hours rostered and actual hours caused by unplanned variation means that employees often face having little control over their work schedules and hence experience instability, regardless of formal shift rosters. This is likely to impact job quality in a number of ways. It has been well established that control over working time allows employees to more effectively manage the boundaries between work and life (Grosswald, 2004). Work time control also aids sleep and recovery from work, reduces exhaustion and the risk of health problems (Kattenbach et al., 2010; Nijp, Beckers, Geurts, Tucker and Kompier, 2012) and generally increases satisfaction with one's work schedule (Swanberg, McKechnie, Ojha and James, 2011). Lack of control within a single shift may have few knock-on effects; however, persistent absence of control over shift start, duration or finish may lead to a longer term degradation of the quality of both work and non-work life.

We refer to this instability in daily working hours as shift extensification. The chapter aims (1) to establish the degree to which shift extensification impacts one particular public service context – the police – and (2) to conceptualise the processes through which it may create cumulative intensity in working time over a shift pattern, with consequences for employees' personal lives. We present primarily qualitative data from a survey of four UK police services which spanned a number of occupations, including officers and staff, thus allowing us to explore two policing environments. While officers may face greater risks in their daily duties, civilian working environments in the police are also facing greater demands given increasingly squeezed resources. In this public sector context, the recent climate of austerity has had a significant impact on staffing levels (HMIC, 2014; Loveday, 2015). Arguably, this also creates a climate of potentially greater demand from management for working time flexibility from employees for whom shifts may be becoming more unstable. There have been relatively few research studies focusing on the civilian police workforce, despite indications that policing will increasingly depend on civilian roles given the resourcing challenges in meeting rising public demand (Flanagan, 2008). Our analysis of the police context also has relevance for any front-line emergency, health and service settings, where the compatibility of service demands and labour supply may make the occurrence of shift extensification a frequent reality for many employees.

The chapter first reviews our conceptualisation of shift extensification as a dimension of work time quality before detailing further issues of working time and shifts in the police context. We then present our qualitative analysis of open text comments from a large-scale survey of four UK police services. Our data presents descriptive analysis of the extent to which shift extensification is evident for these police respondents and exploratory analysis of how they represent this extensification and its impact on their lives.

Understanding quality of working time through shift extensification

Extensification, or 'overflowing work', refers generally to the spillover of work from one domain to another, most commonly from work to non-work life. The best known applications of this concept have explored the effects on individuals and households in terms of work-life balance. We apply the concept of overflowing work to the formally defined shift, focusing on the degree to which shifts extend in terms of duration. Extended hours may apply to a single shift, as in work overflowing beyond the formal boundaries of the shift's completion, or the need to work overtime.

The importance of extended shifts for how employees experience working time is indicated in one recent study, where short notice was identified as the most problematic aspect of working hours controlling for a range of demographic factors (Åkerstedt and Kecklund, 2017). Implicit in such findings is the suggestion that employees dislike the instability and the lack of control in determining their working hours, and how they manage the boundary between work and their non-work lives. When such unplanned shift extensification occurs often, there is likely to be cumulative knock-on effects resulting from reduced control over the work-life interface (Grosswald, 2004).

Generally, employee control over working time is recognised as an important indicator of job quality (Green et al., 2013; Muñoz de Bustillo, Fernández-Macías, Antón and Esteve, 2011). This includes employee time and schedule control, for example, over daily hours or time off (Albrecht, Kecklund, Tucker and Leineweber, 2016), and the notice given by employers when arrangements are changed (Green et al., 2013).

Work time control has also been associated with a range of employee attitudinal and health outcomes (see Theorell, 2010 and Harma and Kecklund, 2010 for an overview). Findings suggest proximal effects on work-life boundary management (affecting work-family conflict or the experience of rest/leisure time) and attitudes regarding working hours (Golden, Henly and Lambert, 2013; Swanberg et al., 2011), as well as more distal and longer term effects on sleep, recovery from shifts and subjective and actual health complaints. To illustrate, it is generally well accepted that work time control reduces work-non-work life conflict and exhaustion (Nijp et al., 2012; Kattenbach et al., 2010); leads to more satisfaction with leisure time (Costa, Sartori and Åkerstedt, 2006); aids sleep and recovery from work (Åkerstedt et al., 2002); and reduces the risk of sickness absence and health problems (Ala-Mursula, Vahtera, Pentti and Kivimäki, 2004; Takahashi et al., 2012). The ability to effectively manage one's work-life boundary relates directly to the need for recovery time; for example, at least 12 hours of rest between shifts is recommended (Pallesen et al., 2010) as well as working forward-rotating shifts and fewer night and weekend shifts (Bambra, Petticrew, Whitehead, Sowden and Akers, 2007).

Unpredictable or short notice changes to hours have been associated with worrying effects on health. These indicate a link between short notice changes to hours and higher prevalence of subjective health complaints, such as anxiety and heart disease (Costa et al., 2004), sleepiness and fatigue (Janssen and Nachreiner, 2004), and adverse mental health, especially in low reward situations (Van Der Hulst and Geurts, 2001). Work-time influence also buffers the adverse effects of shiftwork by increasing predictability (Nabe-Nielsen, Garde, Albertsen and Diderichsen, 2011). Assuming the benefits from recovery time and maintaining good health, organisations are also thought to benefit by allowing their employees greater control over their working time, with lower absence or turnover rates in the longer term (Baltes, Briggs, Huff, Wright and Neuman, 1999).

Flexible working arrangements which offer employees some choice over core hours and start/finish times have become more prevalent, most commonly through reduced hours and flexitime (Åkerstedt and Kecklund, 2017; Kerkhofs, Román and Ester, 2010; van Wanrooy et al., 2013). In principle, the offer of flexible working should allow employees to negotiate a balance between work and non-work activities to meet their lifestyle preferences (Janssen and Nachreiner, 2004). Many jobs, however, are not conducive to employee-led flexibility as they require continuous and overlapping shifts, or depend on rigid formalised shift structures. The primary constraint to flexible working provision, as cited by 53 per cent of managers in a national UK survey, is the nature of work or operating hours (van Wanrooy et al., 2013). Such constraints also may particularly affect lower-wage, front-line positions (Lambert, 2008; Swanberg et al., 2011).

Moreover, we argue that shift extensification applies just as much to understanding working time quality for those on flexible working arrangements. Although these employees have greater putative control, the working environment often means such control is not attainable. Using Jonsson's (2007) typology, employees may derive some stability from knowing their working hours on a flexible working arrangement but still may experience instability as a result of a different element of their working time – in the present case, extended shifts. In some contexts, such as policing (Dick, 2009), the culture may mean that managers are reluctant to meet employee requests for flexibility (e.g., reduced hours) and employee control over work schedules is sacrificed for organisational goals. Similarly, employee-negotiated work scheduling, referred to as self-rostering, often fails or is unpopular due to the need to accommodate other employees' demands (Ingre et al., 2012). Again, therefore, apparent employee influence over work scheduling is constrained by employer needs or the schedules of co-workers.

Working time in the British police service

Policing has been found to be amongst the most stressful occupations. Police officers face significant operational stressors, such as risk of violence or injury (Houdmont, Kerr and Randall, 2012; Hall, Dollard,

Tuckey, Winefield and Thompson, 2010), while police staff are experiencing growing work demands as a result of resourcing issues (see for example, the case of police call handlers, Lumsden and Black, 2017). Adding to this, the current context of austerity in the UK has led to reforms in police management which are driven by doing 'more with less' (HMIC, 2014; Loveday, 2015; Winsor, 2012). This often means an implicit requirement for willingness to work longer hours or beyond the rostered shift. For both officers and staff, therefore, the climate of 'austerity policing' (Brogden and Ellison, 2012) means that shift extensification may be a defining feature of work.

Long working hours are not unexpected in police work. Hewlett and Luce's (2006) account of 'extreme work' includes a minimum of 60 hours per week at work and time-based demands, including 'unpredictable flows of work'. They argue that for some professions long hours are a 'badge of honour'. In the police, Turnbull and Wass's (2015) examination of extreme work highlights long hours as a vehicle for meeting operational demands. Although dealing with challenging people, situations and environments is mainly accepted as part of policing, participants in Turnbull and Wass's study also described the extensification of working time as unacceptable, thereby suggesting some resistance to the normalisation of such work scheduling practices.

Within the UK, police shift patterns are informed by the European Working Time Directive (2003/88/EC) (see for example the guidance of the Police Federation, 2016). With respect to hours of work, the Directive recommends a limit of weekly working hours to an average of 48; a minimum daily rest period of 11 consecutive hours in every 24 hours; and a minimum weekly uninterrupted rest period of 24 hours. It also provides extra protection for night workers (i.e., average working hours must not exceed 8 hours per 24-hour period and night workers must not perform heavy or dangerous work for longer than 8 hours in any 24-hour period). In addition, there is clear guidance on best practice provided by the Police Regulations 2003 on adequate notice for bringing forward a rostered shift (notice should be provided at least 8 hours before) or providing compensation for duty on a rostered rest day. All of these regulations, however, are subject to 'exigencies of duty' (i.e., when a pressing demand necessitates a change of duty roster) and there has been an acknowledged excessive use of night shifts and limited availability of 11 hours of rest between shifts within the police service. The need for recovery between shifts through leisure activity is especially important for police (Iwasaki, Mannell, Smale and Butcher, 2005). Kinman, McDowall and Cropley (2012), in a study of one UK police force, found that unpredictable demands interfere with recovery which could take a number of forms; for example, spending time with family and friends or taking exercise. These authors interpreted their findings as showing that in the absence of time for recovery between shifts, strain-based work-life conflict was more likely, with implications for well-being and health, and recommended interventions to provide advice on implementing recovery strategies.

The recommended shift pattern within the UK police is the Variable Shift Arrangement (VSA). In a review of rostering and deployment, the UK Home Office (2004) concluded that a VSA was the preferable pattern on the grounds of demand-supply concerns during periods of intense activity. This was in contrast to the 8-hours fixed shift (called the Regulation Shift Pattern) which was considered insufficient for meeting increasing demands for flexibility. VSAs were to be viewed as planning principles for three-month duty rosters using shifts of greater than 8 hours. They offered managers an opportunity to match service demand and supply and at the same time, address police officer concerns regarding working a regulated shift pattern with no flexibility. In principle, therefore, the VSA represented demand-led flexibility while still providing employees with a balance between flexibility and predictability or stability (due to the three-month duty roster). In a sign of increasing stringency, though, the recent Winsor (2012) review has allowed Chief Constables greater control in implementing shift arrangements, thus yielding further towards an employer-led flexibility model.

It is also true that most forces also operate a mixture of part-time, flexible and compressed hours. Flexible working, including job-sharing, term-time contracts, annualised hours and more flexible start and finish times, is regarded as 'best practice', and has been shown as effective in reducing sickness absence in British police services (Hayday, Broughton and Tyers, 2007). Nevertheless, this is negotiated individually between the officer and their supervisor, with some forces requiring a percentage of the flexible hours during unsocial hours (evenings/weekends and nights) (Home Office, 2007). In addition, as noted previously, the culture of policing has meant that such requests are often sacrificed in order to meet operational goals (Dick, 2009).

Research questions

For many front-line occupations, non-standard working times, such as night work or weekend working, are accepted working norms. However, unexpected extensions to shifts are seldom formally acknowledged, or studied, even though the consequences of unpredictability and low employee control over work schedules can be significant. The aim in this chapter was to explore specifically the concept of unplanned shift extensification. Our first research question examines a number of indicators of shift extensification based on the recommendations of the European Working Time Directive to determine the extent to which this is an issue for different police occupations. Shift extensification defined in this way implies that the extended hours worked are unexpected. Paid overtime, in contrast, would be considered planned shift extensification and is not the primary concern of this chapter. Our first question is:

1 To what extent does shift extensification exist for police officers and staff?

A second research aim is to elaborate on how individuals experience shift extensification and particularly how they report that it affects working and private life. Our earlier arguments propose that persistent experiences of unpredictable extended hours have cumulative effects, for example, on time for recovery between shifts. Creeping extensification at the fringes of shifts (i.e., both at the end and rolling over into the recovery time before the beginning of the next) means that even employees on a fixed or rostered shift pattern may experience low work-time control and hence poor working time quality. A second research question, therefore, is as follows.

2 In what ways does shift extensification impact experiences of time quality in both work and non-work lives?

Methodology

Data and sample

Data are drawn from a survey of police officers and staff in four UK police forces, one large urban/suburban force and three smaller rural/suburban forces. An electronic survey, with two email reminders, was administered in 2011 via Force email systems and returned on a secure web server. Paper versions were also available. Response rates for police officers varied from 45 per cent for one of the smaller forces to a mean of 27 per cent for the other three; for police staff, there was a much lower response rate of 15 per cent.

As a percentage of the target population of all officers in the four police forces, the officers' response rate is typical for online surveys (Sheehan, 2001), and is likely affected by the length of the survey and the researchers not having direct access to the internal email systems to conduct further, personalised follow-ups with individuals. The low response rate for police staff may be due to the greater fragmentation of occupations which these represent, the lower salience of a survey on shiftwork and safety (as the larger project was advertised) for this group, and again, the reliance on organisational gatekeepers to distribute the survey.

For police staff, respondents were asked to indicate their job title from which we formed four occupational groups – Police Community Service Officers, control room staff, operational policing and support roles. Police

Community Service Officers are uniformed civilian members of police support staff who may patrol with constables but who have limited powers. They are also contracted to work a greater number of hours than constables. Control room staff (which includes call handlers, controllers and dispatchers) deal with judging priority level of calls, vulnerable callers and safeguarding of evidence, and are considered the first line in the investigation process (HMIC, 2017). Increasing call numbers and fewer resources (HMIC, 2014) have meant this workforce are facing particular pressures meeting their local call handling targets. Police officers may also be brought in to manage calls where there are staff shortages to meet demand. Therefore, the control room is an intensified work environment with pressures on staffing (Lumsden and Black, 2017). Operational policing represents a range of roles, including police custodian, crime scene investigator and research/intelligence officers. Support roles represent administrative, business or strategic development roles.

The respondent profiles did not indicate any obvious bias suggesting representativeness for these forces. For example, women comprise 23 per cent of officers in England and Wales and a lower proportion are PCSOs than other police staff roles (Flanagan, 2008). Both of these are broadly in line with our proportions (see Table 4.1).

We focus only on respondents on two formal shift arrangements – Variable Shift Arrangements (VSAs) and Regulation Shift Pattern (RSP; 8-hours fixed shift). VSAs allow greater management-driven flexibility than fixed shifts to accommodate demand while still in principle allowing some predictability for employees since they are based on three-month duty rosters.

The final sample size was 3257, with the majority (57 per cent) police constables (N = 1843), 19 per cent police sergeants and inspectors (N = 601) and 25 per cent police staff (N = 813) (Table 4.1).

Survey measures

Working pattern variables

Shift pattern was represented by either the VSA or RSP. The predominant shift pattern was the VSA for both officers and staff, although staff support roles had a small majority working RSPs (Table 4.2). *Unsocial hours* were measured by two variables: (a) night worker (0/1), defined as being rostered for at least three hours between 24:00 and 03:00 and (b) the number of weekend days usually worked each month (0–8). In addition, respondents were asked if they worked *overtime* and how many hours/week on average (0 'none', 1 '< 4 hours/week', 2 '4 or more hours per week'). We also asked if they worked on a *Flexible Working Arrangement* (0/1, 1 = yes). For officers, flexible working referred to particular types of requests for a reasonable adjustment to hours (e.g., Time Off In Lieu, shift adjustments such as

Table 4.1 Sample description

	Police officers				*Police staff*									
	Constables N = 1843		*Sergeants/ Inspectors* N = 601		*All police staff* N = 813		*PCSO* N = 147		*Control room* N = 298		*Operational policing* N = 162		*Support roles* N = 206	
	Mean/N	*SD/%*	*Mean/N*	*SD/%*	*Mean/N*	*SD/%*	*Mean/N*	*SD/%*	*Mean/N*	*SD/%*	*Mean/N*	*SD/%*	*Mean/N*	*SD/%*
Months on shift pattern	28	36.40	39	43.74	44	41.62	31	20.33	42	40.40	46	46.28	54	47.84
Tenure (1–4)	2.42	1.17	3.49	.73	2.20	1.20	1.63	.95	2.17	1.16	2.24	1.22	2.61	1.25
Age (years)	38	8.28	43	6.19	42	11.85	39	11.73	41	11.71	42	11.29	45	11.88
Female	516	28%	92	15%	455	56%	66	45%	195	65%	92	57%	102	50%
Dependents	750	41%	133	22%	354	44%	91	62%	176	59%	85	53%	106	52%
Married/ cohabiting	1093	59%	467	78%	557	69%	56	38%	121	41%	77	48%	100	49%

Note. Total N = 3257 PCSO 'Police Community Support Officer'; Control room – includes Call handlers/Controllers/Dispatchers; Operational policing – includes police custodian/CSI/response/intelligence officers; Support roles – includes Admin, Researchers, Strategic/business roles

Tenure: 1 'less than 5 years', 2 '5–9 years', 3 '10–14 years', 4 '15 years or more'

Table 4.2 Working time patterns

	Police officers				*Police staff*[a]									
	Constable		*Sergeant/ Inspector*		*All police staff*		*PCSO*		*Control room*		*Operational policing*		*Support roles*	
	N	%	N	%	N	%	N	%	N	%	N	%	N	%
Shift pattern														
Variable shift arrangement	1282	69.6	444	73.9	536	65.9	64	43.5	277	93.0	109	67.3	86	41.7
Regulated shift pattern	561	30.4	157	26.1	277	34.1	83	56.5	21	7.0	53	32.7	120	58.3
Night worker	1357	74.2	452	75.7	427	53.2	8	5.5	248	84.6	100	62.1	71	35
Weekend work (3 days or more/month)	1370	75.7	433	73.4	478	60.9	75	52.8	215	75.4	108	67.5	80	40.4
Work FWA	418	22.7	149	24.8	252	31.1	44	30.1	87	29.2	35	21.6	86	42.4
Overtime														
None	373	20.2	123	20.5	372	45.8	71	48.3	102	34.2	80	49.4	119	57.8
1–3 hours/week	936	50.8	259	43.1	267	32.8	67	45.6	100	33.6	46	28.4	54	26.2
> 3 hours/week	533	28.9	219	36.4	174	21.4	9	6.1	96	32.2	36	22.2	33	16.0
Shift extensification[b]														
4 nights in row	1123	61.7	327	55.1	355	46.8	13	10.0	191	65.6	84	54.5	67	36.6
< 11 hrs rest betw shifts	556	31.0	151	25.7	100	13.3	25	18.4	28	9.9	22	14.6	25	13.7
Shifts of > 10 hours	921	51.0	299	50.9	129	17.0	12	9.0	68	23.9	27	17.1	22	12.0
Seldom 1 day off betw work periods	1078	59.5	258	60.1	528	69.2	91	65.9	211	73.5	104	68	122	65.6

(*Continued*)

Table 4.2 (Continued)

	Police officers				*Police staff*[a]									
	Constable		*Sergeant/ Inspector*		*All police staff*		*PCSO*		*Control room*		*Operational policing*		*Support roles*	
	N	%	N	%	N	%	N	%	N	%	N	%	N	%
Mins detained at end of shift														
none	425	23.1	124	20.6	594	73.1	101	68.7	248	83.2	100	61.7	145	70.4
up to 30 mins	389	21.1	180	30.0	133	16.4	30	20.4	34	11.4	32	19.8	37	18.0
betw 30 and 60 mins	588	31.9	190	31.6	62	7.6	16	10.9	10	3.4	19	11.7	17	8.3
betw 60 and 90 mins	88	4.8	31	5.2	3	0.4	0	0.0	2	0.7	1	0.6	0	0.0
betw 90 and 120 mins	252	13.7	55	9.2	15	1.8	0	0.0	3	1.0	6	3.7	6	2.9
over 120 mins	101	5.5	21	3.5	6	0.7	0	0.0	1	0.3	4	2.5	1	0.5
	Mean	*SD*	*Mean*	*SD*	*Mean*	*SD*	*Mean*	*SD*	*Mean*	*SD*	*Mean*	*SD*	*Mean*	*SD*
No. days detained at end of shift in average week (0–7)	1.41	1.12	1.78	1.41	.47	.94	.43	.83	.33	.88	.68	1.08	.55	.94

Notes:

a PCSO 'Police Community Support Officer'; Control room – includes Call handlers/Controllers/Dispatchers; Operational policing – includes police custodian/CSI/response/intelligence officers; Support roles – includes Admin, Researchers, Strategic/business roles

b The first four indicators reflect deviation from the European Working Time Directive. Percentages represent those reporting either 'sometimes' or 'often' unless indicated otherwise early start to accommodate family demands or late shifts to accommodate a disability; e.g., arthritis which may be worse in the morning).

Shift extensification variables

Four questions asked about the extent to which the shift pattern deviated from EU Working Time Regulations (e.g., Åkerstedt and Kecklund, 2005). These measured frequency of experiencing (1) at least four night shifts in a row; (2) < 11 hours rest between tours of duty; (3) working shifts of > 10 hours; and (4) not having one day off between work periods (all measured on a scale of 1 'almost never', 2 'a few times per year', 3 'a few times per month', 4 'several times per month'). An additional two questions asked about being detained at the end of the rostered shift: times per week on average detained at end of shift (0 'never', 1 '1/week', 2 '2/week', 3 '3–7/week'); and minutes detained on average at end of shift (0 'none', 1 'up to 30 mins', 2 '30–60 minutes', 3 '60–90 minutes', 4 '90–120 minutes', 5 'over 120 minutes').

Biographical and job variables

The survey also provided measures of: the number of months on the shift pattern; tenure with police (measured on a 4-point ordinal scale (1 'less than 5 years', 2 '5–9 years', 3 '10–14 years', 4 '15 years or more')); age (in years); gender (0/1, 1 = female); one or more dependent relatives (0/1); and whether respondents were married/cohabiting (0/1). Each of these variables has been shown to impact responses to shiftwork and working unsocial hours (see review by Tucker and Folkard, 2012). We include these only to gain a clearer picture of the respondent profile.

Qualitative data

Each survey offered the opportunity for open-ended comments about each individual's experiences of shiftwork. This option was taken up by a total of 2198 respondents – 1669 officers (68 per cent of all officer respondents) and 529 police staff (65 per cent of all staff respondents). This data was used to address Research Question 2 on how shift extensification shapes the quality of working time. We included all available respondents in our analysis.

Analysis

The analysis of 2198 open text comments (1669 from officers and 529 from police staff) used an open coding system, although explicitly sought to identify references to two themes particularly: (1) different forms of unplanned extensions to shifts and their effects on individuals' work-life boundary and (2) the role played by management in shift extensification. Table 4.3 provides a breakdown of terms referenced and frequencies.

Table 4.3 Thematic area frequencies

Theme	*Terms*	*Officers (n = 1669)*	*Staff (n = 529)*
Extensification and its effects on the work-life boundary	References to: travel or commute, increased hours, finishing times later, working a shift pattern that compounds the effects of the shift itself – quick change overs, quick turn arounds, few days off in a pattern, being on call, attending court, short notice periods, reduced rest days, working on, or cancelling of, rest days, or a shift ending on a rest day, changes to shift patterns, training days, on call, overtime	603 cases, 804 references	71 cases, 90 references
Management	Management or manager, seniors or supervisor, employer, policy, power	136 cases, 175 references	18 cases

Findings

Research question 1: evidence of shift extensification

Table 4.2 shows the profile of the sample with respect to working patterns and shift extensification. Deviation from the recommendations of the European Working Time Directive was most common amongst constables and sergeants/inspectors, although control room staff also show high proportions of 'sometimes' or 'often' working four nights in a row. A majority of officers 'sometimes' or 'often' work shifts of more than 10 hours. Across both officers and police staff, 60 per cent or more seldom have one day off between work periods. This figure was highest amongst control room staff (74 per cent) and operational policing staff (68 per cent).

Generally, officers are more likely to be detained at the end of their shifts – only 23 and 21 per cent of constables and sergeants/inspectors, respectively, say they are never detained while over 70 per cent of police staff overall indicate this. Most likely staff to be detained are those in operational policing. When asked the number of times in one week they are typically detained, officers report more days per week than staff with an average of 1.4 and 1.8 days for constables and sergeants/inspectors, respectively. When this is examined in more detail, 40 and 30 per cent of constables and sergeants/inspectors, respectively, indicated about once per week and 25 and 42 per cent, respectively 2–3 times per week, suggesting that it is likely to be part of an average working week for at least 70 per cent of officers. Senior officers also seem to be detained more often than constables. The majority of officers indicate being detained on average between 30 and 60 minutes after their formal shift end, although 20 per cent of constables indicated over 90 minutes on average.

Unsocial hours are common for officers, control room staff and those in operational policing, who are more likely to work nights. Weekend working is common across all occupations. FWAs are used in approximately one-third of all roles and more (42 per cent) for those in support roles. Overtime is more common amongst officers and control room staff.

Research question 2: shift extensification and time quality

The nature of shift extensification

The open text comments asking respondents to reflect on their experience of shiftwork, whether this spanned unsocial hours or not, provided an insight into how shift extensification is experienced. As suggested by the survey data, police officers were more affected by these examples of unplanned extended hours, but some police staff were also affected, notably, in the front-line roles of the control room and operational policing, where presumably work demands can be unpredictable.

In respondents' comments, extensification was shown to be either integral to the shift pattern itself or an unintended consequence of the need to meet operational demands. In the former case of actual shift patterns creating extensification, common examples were flexible start and finish times which stretch the shift into rest days, and frequent but shorter working days resulting in fewer rest days ('quick change overs'). This includes increased travel time, thus further limiting non-work time. From the open text comments, a total of 603 officers (36 per cent) and 71 staff (13 per cent) described these various types of extensification, although there were nearly 300 more individual references to them (where one respondent perhaps described multiple examples). Our evidence that shift extensification was more of an issue for officers than most police staff (Table 4.2) is consistent with there being relatively fewer comments from staff than officers. A significant contributor to these frequencies was the reduction of rest days because of changes to shifts, substitution with training days or, more commonly, working a night shift into the beginning of the rest day (hence quick change overs – when one of the rest days is not a complete one).

The following quotation illustrates in a concrete way how changes to shifts are implemented despite the specified Variable Shift Arrangements (VSAs) which set out shift patterns weeks in advance. VSAs may only be changed in accordance with the workforce agreement (Police Federation, 2016), although senior officers can make demand-led changes due to 'exigency of duty'. This instability in hours has a knock-on effect across a shift pattern and rostered rest days.

> My shift pattern is basically a rest day pattern; over 50% of my shifts are regularly changed and these changes often do not comply with VSA protocol e.g. from a 0800–1600 shift to 1600–0000 shift; this is done with little notice and with utter disregard for family responsibilities.
>
> (Sergeant, Roads Policing, VSA, works nights, Ref 2345)

The survey findings showed police officer shifts were more likely to deviate from the recommendations of the European Working Time Directive. The following officers illustrate the range of issues raised with the formal shift patterns, even when their formal shift pattern was the fixed 8-hour Regulated Shift Pattern (RSP) rather than the VSA, and officers were not formally rostered as night workers (defined as being rostered for at least three hours between 24:00 and 03:00).

> A new shift pattern has been implemented and this has led to a whole rest day being removed for a training day and given back the hours spread over the 5 week pattern. This has led to almost never getting away on time and one rest day in between shifts every 5 weeks.
>
> (Officer, VSA does not work nights Ref 1311)

> Quick change overs and single days off are truly soul destroying! Whereas a 2 or 3 day rest period gives you time to decompress and spend quality time with your family.
>
> (Officer, VSA does not work nights, Ref 1224)

> The current shift pattern that we work which has night shifts into rest days and morning shifts after rest days affects the quality of time off. The shift pattern also provides only one weekend in five off which is not frequent enough and generally brings the feeling of constantly being in work.
>
> (Officer, RSP works nights, 3025)

These quick change overs and additional training days are, in some cases, examples of actual increases in working time. In other cases, they reflect a problem of working time distribution or spacing, such that hours are bundled together. This impedes the availability and quality of personal time. These effects intensify the experience of working time arrangements, either through extended single periods of working time in a shift pattern, or through the pervading effects of related time costs (i.e., the increased need for travel time and recovery time).

The second set of scheduling characteristics is not structural to the design of the shift patterns, but is the consequence of operational demands. Here, working time is extended by unpaid overtime, variations or deviations to the published shift pattern, being called into court and being on call. In this one illustration, the unpredictable demands of the job take over personal lives.

> As the father of two young children under the age of three and a partner that is also in the police force we get 1 day off together in 8 weeks, the last day we were due to have there was a murder and I worked it and my rest days so we have had one day off together in 16 weeks; how can that be good for family life; we run our lives by text message never knowing what this effect may have on our children, shifts wreck everybody's life.
>
> (Officer, VSA does not work nights, Ref 1282)

Unpredictability which restricts the ability to plan was noted particularly, although not exclusively, by those who have children and illustrates further consequences in one's private life. Both police staff and officers reported feeling pressure to overcompensate, at personal cost. For example, they talked about making 'spare time go further', juggling social life with family time and getting less sleep. Child care arrangements and rest days would suffer as a result of changing shifts at short notice, especially for particular roles (e.g., proactive intelligence). The following two examples indicate how decision making and planning are directly affected adversely by shift instability, leading to a lack of flexibility for the employee.

> Particularly where you don't have a regular weekday off. If your only childcare option is a childminder or nursery you will have to pay full-time (5 days per week) regardless of whether you need that or not because their business model doesn't allow for the flexibility you need as a shift worker and the changes in weekday rest days. They want to be able to 'sell' that one day a week to someone else and this is obviously much easier to do if they can guarantee a particular day of the week.
>
> (Staff, RSP does not work nights, Ref 852)

> It is not the shift work, we only know now 90 days in advance what shift we are likely to be working and that can be narrowed down to a shift change up to 30 days prior to working it so childcare, and leisure activities and making doctors' appointments etc. are getting harder to do.
>
> (Staff, VSA nights, Ref 519)

It seems that one effect of unpredictable working hours is to over-allocate time to work in the planning of family activities and childcare. We interpret this as a form of extensification as it has the effect of suspending non-work life or not allowing what is formally allocated as recovery time. The preceding illustrations indicate that this occurs for both officers and staff, and regardless of whether shifts span unsocial hours or not. This extensification into non-work life is examined now in more detail.

Personal life and recovery

Beyond the family structure, many comments described how unpredictable shift extensification made any activity which requires time coordination with others precarious. For example, involvement in family occasions becomes challenging, and individuals are often deemed unreliable by their families, or even left out; one respondent said that their family 'no longer extended invitations' to them for family functions. These adjustments to personal activities as a result of unpredictable working hours created a form of paralysis in private life, especially during the life of a shift rotation, as illustrated by the following call handler:

> Family and friends have eventually got used to my shift pattern, initially not knowing when I was working one day from the next, phone calls at 1100 am on a Saturday morning 'are you coming to the rugby today', 'no I've been on nights I'm in bed', used to be the reply. But it appears over time that everyone has got used to them. The shifts did take time to adjust to, coming from working a 9–5 Monday to Friday job to the shifts I'm on now. Sometimes it feels there's no time left in the day to do anything particularly on late shifts (1100hrs–2100hrs), can't get anything done in the morning, and by the time you finish at 2100hrs you're normally too knackered to do anything, even eating your tea's a task. Then we get two days off after a set of four late's, the first one normally used for recovery from the shifts, the second one seems wasted as most people will be in bed ready for the 7 o clock start the following day.
>
> (Staff, Command and Control Radio Operator, VSA nights, Ref 1128)

There were many examples of shift extensification rendering personal time useless because of the effects of tiredness. Fatigue and recovery time penetrated personal time, and this time was therefore seen as unavailable to self or family. In addition to 382 respondents commenting about rest days, 438 officers (26 per cent of comments) and 103 staff (20 per cent of comments) mentioned tiredness affecting their non-work life, or what might be classified as work-related fatigue. 'Joke' rest days were frequently mentioned, perhaps where a sequence of night shifts which would mean less sleeping hours would lead to spending most of one's rest day asleep. The cumulative effect of shifts on rest days is captured the following two examples:

> I tend to find that it takes me the day off to recover from the early shifts then I am straight back on the lates and again recovering on the following two days. I am also feeling that tired under the 9 week shift pattern that I have been taking leave to recover and spend time with family – this then has a knock on effect when planning a family holiday.
>
> (Constable, VSA does not work nights, Ref 847)

> Working nights into rest days is difficult, especially when family and friends think that you're on 'days off'. This means trying to go to bed on the first 'rest' day at say 11pm, which is 9 hours earlier than the previous (or same as it is) day. . . . As most of the rest days include working into them the actual rest hours are reduced. . . . I've spoken with the occupational health unit who tell me that there are 'worse shift patterns'. . . . I've expressed my concerns with senior management (Supt) and told him directly that I feel that the current shift pattern is 'a joke'.
>
> (Constable, Firearms, VSA works nights, Ref 3647)

The value of high-quality personal time was increased because it was perceived to be elusive, thus compelling respondents to 'make the most' of it by squeezing in non-work activities and so intensifying home life. This, in turn, resulted in less rest time.

> Fatigue plays a big part in this, which is the direct result of shift work. Or, as the case is with me, you then find that you try to do too much so that you can meet as many commitments as possible. This results in actually getting less sleep and being busier during your rest days than you are during a shift cycle!
>
> (Constable, VSA works nights, Ref 388/94)

This data suggests that the lack of control over scheduling goes beyond the effects of shiftwork or unsocial hours in the consequences for non-work life. Shift extensification is indeed a feature of many police officers' and staff's working life. This not only increases time worked, but impacts the efficiency and quality of personal time and recovery.

Employer-led 'regular uncertainty'

Many attributed the work-life conflict resulting from shift extensification to management. Some respondents considered working time arrangements as an expression of lack of care from management – essentially flexibility for management at the expense of instability for employees (175 references (11 per cent of comments) from officers and 18 (3 per cent of comments) from staff). In these descriptions, respondents appraised how much employers are caring and considerate towards employees (four individuals referred to them as 'the powers that be'), and the extent to which these 'powers' prioritise service delivery and performance metrics over employees and their well-being. Some respondents interpreted the offering of work-life balance as policy rhetoric to uphold the image of the service rather than genuine empathy for employees' needs.

> The policy would like you to believe there is a work/life balance – this is not the case – my family life has suffered and I have missed many important events due to the lack of understanding from my superiors and no work/life balance.
>
> (Staff, Control Room, Communications Officer, VSA works nights, Ref 440/3561)

> The Police Service makes considerable effort to portray a caring attitude towards their officers and quotes the mantra of work life balance. In reality the job needs doing. Officers on section are able to hand over the jobs but within CID there is no one to hand it to so we can go home at a reasonable time. As a result we stay on until the job is dealt with. . . . The public are not allowed to see how cost cutting will effect the service provided. The service is sinking and no one wants to say anything.
>
> (Officer, Roads Policing, VSA does not work nights, Ref 1317/1706)

Some described the general unrest and negative reactions to management's apparent prioritisation of service over employee welfare, often extending working time into rest days.

> Whilst working in a core policing unit on standard 8–4 day shifts the demands of supervision mean the regular short notice change of duties. Scant regard is paid to personal requirements and contractual boundaries. There is an 'if you don't like it then leave' attitude from senior supervisors. Whilst it is appreciated that operational matters have priority the regular uncertainty is at times depressing.
>
> (Staff, Investigation Support Officer, Serious and Organised Crime Group, RSP does not work nights, Ref 811/1287)

> The problem is when management dictate change of shifts. It impacts not just on me but reverberates around partner, children, brother, mother and friends. I have had one very embarrassing experience where I had to let people down due to deviation of shifts. This has left a bitter taste – it impacted badly and I was shamed. As management have the upper hand due to cuts at this time a 'management by fear' culture is starting to take hold.
>
> (Staff, Call Handler, VSA works nights, Ref 379/2324)

Acceptance

Finally, it should be acknowledged that a significant number of comments accepted that shiftworking is an expectation of policing which employees, and even family members, are willing to meet at personal cost. The following quotation illustrates these sentiments:

> I have been a police officer for 22 years and shift work has been an important part of my working life whilst doing this job. I have found that supervision have been flexible in their dealings with staff when it comes to family issues over shifts, so in that respect the balance has always been good. It is important to remember we have joined a profession where the demands and expectations are high and the requirements for ALL officers to be able to work 24/7 providing good and adequate service to the public. I've never forgotten that and my family except [accept] that the demands the service expect from me.
>
> (Constable, Roads Policing, VSA does not work nights, Ref 1225/1618)

There were also many respondents who went further and, despite potential negative effects on personal life, protected the professional identity of the police service as hard working and stoic. These perceptions support the notion of policing as extreme work (Hewlett and Luce, 2006), where long and flexible hours to meet service demands, regardless of the inevitable instability for employees, are a normative expectation. These attitudes are reflected in the following two examples:

> Depending on which week of the fixed pattern, sometimes there is enough time to balance work and home but mainly it is difficult. But that's the job. With the restrictions on budget and overtime, on occasion now you are expected to work without getting paid the extra time it takes to complete jobs. . . . You just have to do what it takes and it is expected when you join this type of work.
>
> (Constable, CID, VSA does not work nights, Ref 1344)

> Shiftwork isn't great, but I knew what it was going to be like before I joined the Police. We are a 24 hour service and we get a good pension because we know we are going to die 5 yrs earlier on average because of shift work. . . . It affects my life in as much as I can't always plan things because I know, being a Detective in CID, if an incident happens then I will be late home because the nature of the job is that you stay with an investigation or a prisoner until you have finished. That's the job and that's the way it will always be. Being in the police is a vocation and a way of life, too many people join expecting it to be a 9–5 job and whinging and moaning if they have to stay half an hour over their shift.
>
> (Constable, CID, VSA does not work nights, Ref 2035)

Discussion

As indicated in the preceding final quotation, it could be argued that the experience of shift extensification is a personal one and as such cannot be assumed to be a new type of job stressor, with implications for job quality, impacting front-line work like policing. In this chapter, we have argued that shift extensification represents instability for the employee which often goes unrecognised and unmeasured, and have tried to conceptualise how this takes form and impacts employee lives. Our chosen empirical context is police work where a long hours culture is often accepted as the norm (Turnball and Wass, 2015). In the UK, as in other countries, policing also has been exposed to significant external pressures, most notably the effects of budget cuts following the 2008–2009 economic and financial crisis, which have led some to describe current management systems as 'austerity policing' (Brogden and Ellison, 2012). These pressures, as in other similar contexts, make employer-led demands for flexibility which require adjustments to employee work schedules more likely, regardless of the consequences for non-work life.

The chapter reports on evidence from police officers and staff in four UK police services. The findings suggest that unplanned extensions to formal shifts are a feature of work for most police officers and some staff, such as call handlers and those in operational policing roles. Elsewhere, we reported evidence for the effects of such unpredictability in working time on police officers' work-life conflict and perceived stress and, in turn, sleep and self-reported health (Scholarios, Hesselgreaves and Pratt, 2017). The effects in the latter study were shown to go beyond the effects of working unsocial hours. The qualitative data which we present in this chapter demonstrates a number of forms of shift extensification and shows complex effects on employees' lives generated by employer-led flexibility and the experience of instability for the employee. It allows us to understand the nature of shift extensification better. Most notably, the comments made by respondents themselves demonstrate the mechanisms through which extended hours and unpredictable shift patterns intensify non-work life and contribute to negative well-being and health outcomes as demonstrated in Scholarios et al. (2017).

By conceptualising shift extensification in this way, we further understanding in several ways. Firstly, it allows us to consider working time quality beyond the definitions of unsociable hours (night working and weekend working). The comments from officers and staff spanned night workers and those not rostered to work at night, and different roles and shifts. Our approach adds two additional elements to the problems usually associated with working unsocial hours. The first is that we should be aware of extended working time as an integral part of daily work scheduling and each shift, in addition to other types employer-driven flexibility such as the effects of overtime, being on-call or unpaid hours. The second element refers to those areas of life that are controlled by working time, but are not directly measured as time *at* work (for example, journey time and recovery time). By aiming to conceptualise the 'fringes' of shifts – the beginning or end of a rostered shift, and the overlap with non-working time across a shift pattern – we extend the notion of how working time quality is experienced. Capturing a similar notion, Kecklund, Sallinen and Axelsson (2016) have discussed some of the factors that limit sleep during off-duty time, and include commuting, eating, domestic and social responsibilities. They emphasise the importance of timing of non-work duties among shiftworkers to maintaining sufficient sleep. In our study, the examination of some of these non-work aspects and their timing highlights how working time, and time committed to activities like commuting and sleeping *because* of shiftwork, can dictate many other areas of life. They restrict engagement with life activities outside of work but could still be considered elements of extended work time (what we have labelled shift extensification) because they are connected to working time and do not contribute to non-work time; indeed they limit it.

Secondly, the findings develop our understanding of shiftworkers' experiences of working time by offering qualitative descriptions of features which are disruptive. Many of these features are evident in working time research; 'quick returns' (defined as < 11 hours; the minimum inter-shift interval by the European Working Time Directive), lacking influence over working hours, long working hours, being frequently on-call and lacking employee-led flexibility (Tucker, Bejerot, Kecklund, Aronsson and Åkerstedt, 2013). Our study examines how these disruptive features serve to extend and intensify working hours, and reduce recovery opportunities. Thus, the findings indicate the undermining of recovery time through shift design, consistent with other authors (e.g., Beckers, Kompier, Kecklund and Härmä, 2012; Kecklund et al., 2016). Sallinen and Kecklund (2010) also noted this effect, irrespective of shift pattern and Eriksen and Kecklund (2007) found that flexible shifts offered police officers more sleep, because of the longer rest time between shifts. Flexible working arrangements in general, where work-time control and hence some stability is returned to employees, may help mitigate the effects of extended working hours, for example, in aiding recovery or helping to manage work-family conflict (see, for example, Kattenbach, Demerouti and Nachreiner, 2010).

Domestic roles and gender clearly may be an important factor. The male-orientated environment of policing, and the culture which therefore dictates the pattern of working time, may have a different effect for men and women, although in the present analysis we did not distinguish by gender. In their study of doctors, Tucker et al. (2013) found that attitudes towards disruptive working time were partly related to gender. This may reflect women working in male-orientated (medical) professions, where it could be argued that work schedules do not accommodate domestic roles and responsibilities and may appear to favour men. Related to domestic roles and conflicts with professional working time is our respondents' focus on the non-work domain in their descriptions. Ingre, Akerstedt, Ekstedt and Kecklund (2012) reported that a lack of predictability of time for family and leisure was associated with preferences for fixed shifts. These preferences, termed 'personal' fit, are described in considerable detail in our data, as respondents compare their domestic needs with the time available within their shift pattern. Such comments were just as likely from men as from women.

Our third contribution is to wider workforce issues facing public sector contexts where there are growing work demands and restricted resources to dedicate to staffing (Bach, 2016). This study allows us to reflect on the wider implications of how the quality of working time is being affected by the erosion of employee control over shift length and rest periods between shifts to meet strategic requirements for flexible scheduling; this is an issue across public sector services as well as other front-line occupations. Some of our respondents also pointed to a 'management by fear' culture driving and sustaining this imposition of time pressures.

Conclusion

In conclusion, better understanding of how employees experience time and control over time is fruitful. Eriksen and Kecklund (2007) in their study of police officers in Sweden found that sleep and wakefulness problems were more associated with attitudes towards working hours than associated with actual working hours themselves. In other words, it is not the long hours in themselves which are viewed negatively; it is when working time encroaches on what years of research has shown is essential for the positive well-being and health of those who work on shifts – recovery time, either through family/leisure activity or sleep, and opportunity to effectively balance the work-life boundary. Our focus on shift extensification in the police provides one illustration of the potential silent erosion of control at the fringes of working time which may be having a growing impact on job quality.

References

Åkerstedt, T. and Kecklund, G. (2005). The future of work hours – the European view. *Industrial Health*, 43(1), pp. 80–84.

Åkerstedt, T. and Kecklund, G. (2017). What work schedule characteristics constitute a problem to the individual? A representative study of Swedish shift workers. *Applied Ergonomics*, 59, pp. 320–325.

Åkerstedt, T., Knutsson, A., Westerholm, P., Theorell, T., Alfredsson, L. and Kecklund, G. (2002). Sleep disturbances, work stress and work hours: A cross-sectional study. *Journal of Psychosomatic Research*, 53(3), pp. 741–748.

Ala-Mursula, L., Vahtera, J., Pentti, J. and Kivimäki, M. (2004). Effect of employee worktime control on health: A prospective cohort study. *Occupational and Environmental Medicine*, 61, pp. 254–261.

Albrecht, S. C., Kecklund, G., Tucker, P. and Leineweber, C. (2016). Investigating the factorial structure and availability of work time control in a representative sample of the Swedish working population. *Scandinavian Journal of Public Health*, 44(3), pp. 320–328.

Bach, S. (2016). Deprivileging the public sector workforce: Austerity, fragmentation and service withdrawal in Britain. *The Economic and Labour Relations Review*, 27(1), pp. 11–28.

Baltes, B. B., Briggs, T. E., Huff, J. W., Wright, J. A. and Neuman, G. A. (1999). Flexible and compressed workweek schedules: A meta-analysis of their effects on work-related criteria. *Journal of Applied Psychology*, 84(4), pp. 496–513.

Bambra, C., Petticrew, M., Whitehead, M., Sowden, A. and Akers, J. (2007). *Project Final Report: The Health and Wellbeing Effects of Changing the Organisation of Shift Work: A Systematic Review*. Public Health Research Consortium.

Beckers, D., Kompier, M., Kecklund, G. and Härmä, M. (2012). Worktime control: Theoretical conceptualization, current empirical knowledge, and research agenda. *Scandinavian Journal of Work, Environment & Health*, 38(4), pp. 291–297.

Bewley, H., Rincon-Aznar, A. and Wilkinson, D. (2014). *An Assessment of the Changing Use of Flexible Employment and Implications for the National Minimum Wage, Including Compliance (No. 11815)*. Chicago: National Institute of Economic and Social Research.

Brogden, M. and Ellison, G. (2012). *Policing in an Age of Austerity*. Routledge.

Costa, G., Åkerstedt, T., Nachreiner, F., Baltieri, F., Carvalhais, J., Folkard, S. et al. (2004). Flexible working hours, health, and well-being in Europe: Some considerations from a SALTSA project. *Chronobiology International*, 21, pp. 831–844.

Costa, G., Sartori, S. and Åkerstedt, T. (2006). Influence of flexibility and variability of working hours on health and well-being. *Chronobiology International*, 23(6), pp. 1125–1137.

Dick, P. (2009). Bending over backwards? Using a pluralistic framework to explore the management of flexible working in the UK police service. *British Journal of Management*, 20(s1), pp. S182–S193.

Eriksen, C. A. and Kecklund, E. (2007). Sleep, sleepiness and health complaints in police officers: The effects of a flexible shift system. *Industrial Health*, 45, pp. 279–288.

Flanagan, R. (2008). *The Review of Policing*. Final Report. London: Home Office.

Golden, L., Henly, J. R. and Lambert, S. (2013). Work schedule flexibility: A contributor to happiness? *Journal of Social Research and Policy*, 4(2), p. 107.

Green, F., Mostafa, T., Parent-Thirion, A., Vermeylen, G., Van Houten, G., Biletta, I. and Lyly-Yrjanainen, M. (2013). Is job quality becoming more unequal? *Industrial and Labor Relations Review*, 66(4), pp. 753–784.

Grosswald, B. (2004). The effects of shift work on family satisfaction. *Families in Society: The Journal of Contemporary Social Services*, 85(3), pp. 413–423.

Hall, G. B., Dollard, M. F., Tuckey, M. R., Winefield, A. H. and Thompson, B. M. (2010). Job demands, work-family conflict, and emotional exhaustion in police officers: A longitudinal test of competing theories. *Journal of Occupational and Organizational Psychology*, 83(1), pp. 237–250.

Harma, M. and Kecklund, G. (2010). Shift work and health: How to proceed? Editorial. *Scandinavian Journal of Work, Environment & Health*, 36(2), pp. 81–84.

Hayday, S., Broughton, A. and Tyers, C. (2007). *Managing Sickness Absence in the Police Service: A Review of Current Practices*. London: HSE.

Henly, J. R. and Lambert, S. J. (2014). Unpredictable work timing in retail jobs. Implications for employee work–life conflict. *Industrial and Labor Relations Review*, 67(3), pp. 986–1016.

Her Majesty's Inspectorate of Constabulary (HMIC). (2014). *State of Policing*. HMIC.

Her Majesty's Inspectorate of Constabulary (HMIC). (2017). *PEEL: Police Effectiveness*. HMIC.

Hewlett, S. A. and Luce, C. B. (2006). Extreme jobs: The dangerous allure of the 70-hour workweek. *Harvard Business Review*, 84(12), pp. 49–59.

Home Office. (2004). *Study of Police Resource Management and Rostering Arrangements*. London: Home Office.

Home Office. (2007). *Flexible Working in the Police Service*. London: Home Office.

Houdmont, J., Kerr, R. and Randall, R. (2012). Organisational psychosocial hazard exposures in UK policing: Management Standards Indicator Tool reference values. *Policing: An International Journal of Police Strategies and Management*, 35(1), pp. 182–197.

Ingre, M., Akerstedt, T., Ekstedt, M. and Kecklund, G. (2012). Periodic self-rostering in shift work: Correspondence between objective work hours, work hour preferences (personal fit), and work schedule satisfaction. *Scandinavian Journal of Work, Environment & Health*, 38(4), pp. 327–336.

Iwasaki, Y., Mannell, R. C., Smale, B. J. and Butcher, J. (2005). Contributions of leisure participation in predicting stress coping and health among police and emergency response services workers. *Journal of Health Psychology*, 10(1), pp. 79–99.

Janssen, D. and Nachreiner, F. (2004). Health and psychosocial effects of flexible working hours. *Revista de saude publica*, 38, pp. 11–18.

Jonsson, D. (2007). Flexibility, stability and related concepts. In Furåker, B., Håkansson, K. and Karlsson, J. Ch. (Eds.), *Flexibility and Stability in Working Life*. New York, NY: Palgrave Macmillan, pp. 30–41.

Kattenbach, R., Demerouti, E. and Nachreiner, F. (2010). Flexible working times: Effects on employees' exhaustion, work-nonwork conflict and job performance. *Career Development International*, 15(3), pp. 279–295.

Kecklund, G., Sallinen, M. and Axelsson, J. (2016). Optimizing shift scheduling. In Kryger, M., Roth, T. and Dement, W. (Eds.) *Principles and Practice of Sleep Medicine* (6th ed.). Elsevier.

Kerkhofs, M., Román, A. and Ester, P. (2010). *Flexibility Profiles of European Companies: European Company Survey 2009*. Luxembourg: Publications Office of the European Union.

Kinman, G., McDowall, A. and Cropley, M. (2012). *Work–Family Conflict and Job-Related Wellbeing in UK Police Officers: The Role of Recovery Strategies*. Available at: http://epubs.surrey.ac.uk/787223/ [Accessed 16 September 2017].

Lambert, S. (2008). Passing the buck: Labor flexibility practices that transfer risk onto hourly workers. *Human Relations*, 61(9), pp. 1203–1277.

Loveday, B. (2015). Police management and workforce reform in a period of austerity. In *Police Services*. Springer International Publishing, pp. 115–127.

Lumsden, K. and Black, A. (2017). Austerity policing, emotional labour and the boundaries of police work: An ethnography of a police force control room in England. *British Journal of Criminology*, 58(3), pp. 606–623.

Muñoz de Bustillo, R., Fernández-Macías, E., Antón, J. I. and Esteve, F. (2011). E pluribus unum? A critical survey of job quality indicators. *Socio-Economic Review*, 9(3), pp. 447–475.

Nabe-Nielsen, K., Garde, A. H., Albertsen, K. and Diderichsen, F. (2011). The moderating effect of work-time influence on the effect of shift work: A prospective cohort study. *International Archives of Occupational and Environmental Health*, 84(5), pp. 551–559.

Nabe-Nielsen, K., Garde, A. H., Aust, B. and Diderichsen, F. (2012). Increasing work-time influence: Consequences for flexibility, variability, regularity and predictability. *Ergonomics*, 55(4), pp. 440–449.

Nijp, H. H., Beckers, D. G., Geurts, S. A., Tucker, P. and Kompier, M. A. (2012). Systematic review on the association between employee worktime control and work-non-work balance, health and well-being, and job-related outcomes. *Scandinavian Journal of Work, Environment & Health*, pp. 299–313.

Pallesen, S., Bjorvatn, B., Magerøy, N., Saksvik, I. B., Waage, S. and Moen, B. E. (2010). Measures to counteract the negative effects of night work. *Scandinavian Journal of Work, Environment & Health*, pp. 109–120.

Police Federation. (2016). *Quick Reference Guide*. Research and Policy Support, Police Federation of England and Wales HQ. Available at: http://www.polfed.org/documents/QRG_-_Version_2.pdf [Accessed September 2017].

Rubery, J., Ward, J., Grimshaw, D. and Beynon, H. (2005). Working time, industrial relations and the employment relationship. *Time and Society*, 14, pp. 89–111.

Sallinen, M. and Kecklund, G. (2010). Shift work, sleep, and sleepiness: Differences between shift schedules and systems. *Scandinavian Journal of Work, Environmental & Health*, 36(2), pp. 121–133.

Scholarios, D., Hesselgreaves, H. and Pratt, R. (2017). Unpredictable working time, well-being and health in the police service. *The International Journal of Human Resource Management*, pp. 2275–2298.

Sheehan, K. B. (2001). E-mail survey response rates: A review. *Journal of Computer-Mediated Communication*, 6(2).

Swanberg, J. E., McKechnie, S. P., Ojha, M. U. and James, J. B. (2011). Schedule control, supervisor support and work engagement: A winning combination for workers in hourly jobs?. *Journal of Vocational Behavior*, 79(3), pp. 613–624.

Takahashi, M., Iwasaki, K., Sasaki, T., Kubo, T., Mori, I. and Otsuka, Y. (2012). Sleep, fatigue, recovery, and depression after change in work time control: A one-year follow-up study. *Journal of Occupational and Environmental Medicine*, 54(9), pp. 1078–1085.

Theorell, T. (2010). Flexibility at work in relation to employee health. In Cooper, L. C., Campbell Quick, J. and Schabracq, J. M. (Eds.) *International Handbook of Work and Health Psychology* (3rd ed.), pp. 251–267. Chichester: John Wiley & Sons.

Tucker, P., Bejerot, E., Kecklund, G., Aronsson, G. and Åkerstedt, T. (2013). *Doctors' Work Hours in Sweden: Their Impact on Sleep, Health, Work-family Balance, Patient Care and Thoughts about Work*. Stress Research Report. Stockholm: Stress Research Institute. Available at: www.stressforskning.su.se/english/publications/reports [Accessed 15 September 2017].

Tucker, P. and Folkard, S. (2012). *Working Time, Health and Safety: A Research Synthesis Paper*. Geneva: International Labour Office.

Turnbull, P. J. and Wass, V. (2015). Normalizing extreme work in the police service? Austerity and the inspecting ranks. *Organization*, 22(4), pp. 512–529.

Van den Bergh, J., Beliën, J., De Bruecker, P., Demeulemeester, E. and De Boeck, L. (2013). Personnel scheduling: A literature review. *European Journal of Operational Research*, 226(3), E-mail survey response rates: A review. *Journal of Computer-Mediated Communication*, 6, pp. 2367–2385.

Van Der Hulst, K. and Geurts, S. (2001). Associations between overtime and psychological health in high and low reward jobs, *Work and Stress: An International Journal of Work, Health and Organisations*, 15(3), E-mail survey response rates: A review. *Journal of Computer-Mediated Communication*, 6, pp. 2227–2240.

Van Wanrooy, B., Bewley, H., Bryson, A., Forth, J., Freeth, S., Stokes, L. and Wood, S. (2013). *Employment Relations in the Shadow of Recession: Findings From the 2011 Workplace Employment Relations Study*. Basingstoke: Palgrave Macmillan.

Winsor, T. P. (2012). *Independent Review of Police Officer and Staff Remuneration and Conditions: Final Report* (vol. 8325). The Stationery Office.

5 'Supply chain capitalism'

Exploring job quality for delivery workers in the UK

Kirsty Newsome, Sian Moore and Cilla Ross

Introduction

The focus of this chapter is to explore the dynamics and impact of supply chain capitalism upon the job quality and work quality (Muñoz de Bustillo, Fernández-Macías and Antón, 2009) of parcel delivery workers in the UK. While Muñoz de Bustillo's focus is upon work quality and *employment quality*, the chapter focuses not just on directly employed workers, but also on dependent self-employment and the apparent extraction of parcel delivery workers from an employment relationship – we thus formally refer to 'job' rather than 'employment quality'. However, the data presented in the chapter exposes the fiction of 'self-employment' in parcel delivery, promoting further consideration of contractual arrangements as a measure of job quality. It necessarily invokes the UK's institutional support for dependent self-employment, although this has been the subject of legal contestation over worker rights (Behring and Harvey, 2015).

The purpose of the chapter is not to provide an extensive discussion of the debates on job quality. These debates have been rehearsed elsewhere and subject to concentrated academic debate over recent times (see Chapter 1, Findlay, Kalleberg and Warhust, 2013; Kalleberg, 2011; Osterman, 2013) Now seemingly widely accepted, job quality is regarded as a multi-dimensional phenomenon influenced by a variety of factors and contexts. Subject to interrogation by multiple social science disciplines, attempts to 'measure' job quality is understandably regarded as problematic. For economists, debates on job quality seem to be grounded upon pay as a proxy for good quality jobs. Psychologists appear to be preoccupied with individual notions of job satisfaction and well-being as a measure for job quality. Writers from a sociological tradition understand job quality as predicated upon the dynamics of the employment relationship. For writers in this tradition the dimensions of job quality can best be understood as an outcome of the employment relationship influenced by a variety of contextual factors and institutional and regulatory regimes (Gallie, 2007). Indeed, more recent debates have come to recognise the importance of agency (individual and/or collective) in shaping the dynamics of job quality (Hoque, Earls, Conway and Bacon, 2017; Simms, 2015). Moreover, these interventions have highlighted the fluid nature of job quality, reflecting an outcome of the power dynamics of interests within the workplace. Notwithstanding the machinations of the debates on job quality regarding appropriate territories and level of analysis, there does appear to be some level of agreement as to what can be considered the 'dimensions of job quality'. Broadly speaking, these dimensions of job quality appear to coalesce around key themes notably: job security; autonomy and discretion; skill and skill formation systems; and work pressures (Gallie, 2007; Muñoz de Bustillo et al., 2009; Holman, 2013). Yet, while these dimensions of job quality might include contractual status as an indicator of security, there has been little focus upon so-called 'self-employment'. It is not mentioned in Muñoz de Bustillo, Fernández-Macías, Antón and Esteve (2011), although their previous report for the EU (2009), written prior to the substantial rise in self-employment in the UK, excludes this group of workers whilst acknowledging the existence of false self-employment and concluding that *quality of work* indicators are directly applicable to them. We posit dependent self-employment as a contractual mechanism through which employers transfer the risk of the social costs of employment onto the individual worker, crucially removing access to employment rights. This has resulted in a number of legal cases contesting the status of dependent self-employed workers. In the case of parcel delivery 'self-employment' reconfigures both job and work quality; while collective regulation has protected the job quality of the directly employed workers (arguably at the expense of those they work alongside), there is evidence of that both groups of workers experience compromised work quality, particularly in terms of their autonomy.

The degradation of parcel delivery work has attracted growing media and public policy interest in the UK. Field and Forsey's report (2016) describes the typical experience of self-employed home couriers who deliver from home in their own cars and are sometimes referred to as 'life-style' couriers as work is promoted as having the capacity to be organised around their other commitments. One such respondent exposed the myth that as 'self-employed' workers they have control over their work:

> As 'lifestyle' couriers we are supposed to be able to work around our home commitments. In the past, yes. But not now, although the company still perpetuates this myth. We now have to give a delivery ETA at the beginning of the day. Failure to meet these times incurs the wrath of a compliance manager, the loss of your bonus and even your job. It is impossible to plan anything as you do not know how many parcels you will receive each day. You are expected to attempt to deliver every parcel given to you on the day of receipt, regardless of how many there are.
>
> (Field and Forsey, 2016)

The extract graphically reveals the contradiction between the status of 'self-employment' and the high level of dependency and surveillance that increasingly dominates the experience of parcel delivery work where service provision in an increasingly competitive market is time critical.

The chapter consciously locates the job and work quality of parcel delivery workers as an outcome of not only contestation within the workplace but also of the dynamics of wider supply chain and sector pressures. In the wider literature, the escalation of consumption through e-retailing has increased the demand for home delivery services. The capacity to satisfy growing consumer demands is built upon the transformation of the once relatively hidden domain of logistics, distribution and parcel delivery. The necessary 'revolution' of the logistics function, predicated upon pressures from retailers, is dedicated to securing more exacting, demanding and time critical levels of service delivery and provision. The resulting movement of commodities through inter-linked and integrated supply chains and logistics networks is increasingly regarded as the key arena for securing competitive advantage in contemporary capitalism, a process referred to as 'supply chain capitalism' (Tsing, 2009). Whilst there are signs of a growing interest in logistics workers within global value chains per se, to date little qualitative research attention has focused on the experience of parcel delivery workers, operating in the 'last mile of delivery' at the end of the supply chain. In response this chapter firstly looks at the increase in dependent self-employment and the legal cases that challenge self-employed status and expose the institutional context. It then explores the political economy of the parcel delivery sector before moving on to outline research methods. The chapter then considers the job quality of parcel delivery workers and particularly the fiction of self-employment. Finally it explores the quality of work in the context of supply chain pressures, in particular incursions on autonomy, before drawing some tentative conclusions for measures of job quality.

The rise of dependent self-employment

Dependent self-employment in parcel delivery is part of a wider expansion in self-employment in the UK where in most years from the early 2000s, the numbers of self-employed grew more rapidly than the numbers of employees and, following the 2008–9 recession, self-employment was a main source of employment growth. Tomlinson and Corlett (2017) estimate from the UK Labour Force Survey data that it accounted for 45 per cent of the growth in total employment from March-May 2008 to the end of 2016 when it totalled 4.6 million (5 million including those self-employed in a second job) or one in seven of the workforce (15 per cent). The ILO (2015, p. 2) has described dependent self-employment as a situation in which 'workers perform services for a business under a civil or commercial contract but depend on one or a small number of clients for their income and receive direct instructions regarding how the work is to be done'. Here the 'independent contractor' would seem to be in the equivalent position of an employee in terms of economic dependence on a main employer and subordination to the management's authority. However, contractual status means that the dependent self-employed do not have the employment protection rights of an employee. Eurofound (2013) conceived of bogus (sham or false) self-employment as 'subordinate employment relations which are disguised as autonomous work, usually for fiscal reasons, or in order to avoid the payment of social security contributions and thereby reduce labour costs, or to circumvent labour legislation, such as provisions on dismissals' (Eurofound, 2002, p. 2). Employers may insert 'substitution clauses' into workers' contracts to imply self-employment. Bogus self-employment is sometimes discussed as presenting issues distinct from those relating to dependent self-employment: it is a relatively straightforward matter of misclassification whereas the concept of dependent self-employment combines two issues that may each need to be addressed to establish the employment relationship (subordination in addition to economic dependence). However, analyses that present the distinction also emphasise how the 'two aspects are strongly intertwined, not least because the emergence of the latter 'ambiguous' forms of employment' (i.e. dependent self-employment) 'makes the disguise of 'bogus self-employment' easier' (Eurofound, 2013). Eurofound's analysis of the European Working Conditions survey data found that economically dependent workers are financially in a less favourable position in comparison with the self-employed on the one hand and employees on the other. The incomes of the economically dependent worker group 'lie in the lowest tertile of their country disproportionately often' and their households 'have a correspondingly high level of difficulty making ends meet' (Eurofound, 2013). Similarly the UK Citizen's Advice (2015) estimated that the median weekly income for the self-employed in 2013/14 was £209, or just 54 per cent of that for employees. Around half (49 per cent) of the self-employed are low paid (below two thirds of median earnings) compared to 22 per cent of employees, according to Broughton and Richards (2016). They see the UK labour market as now highly bifurcated as a consequence of discriminatory employment law and tax and national insurance regimes for the self-employed and employees. The regulatory framework 'is making it artificially cheaper for firms to move to a model of firm-contractor, and away from the employer-employee model of working' (2016, pp. 6–7).

A series of legal cases have challenged self-employed workers' status. In October 2016 an Employment Tribunal ruled that a group of Uber drivers were not self-employed, but workers and entitled to receive the National Minimum Wage and holiday pay (Employment Tribunal, 2016a). The decision of the Tribunal was based upon Uber's exertion of significant control over and direction of its drivers (Uber subsequently lost an appeal against the decision). This control included recruitment and also the setting of prices, instructing them in their work and controlling their duties and performance as well as their terms and the absence of any contract with the customer. Uber drivers were in a dependent work relationship and an unequal bargaining position. A further ET ruling in November 2016 also ruled that a CitySprint bicycle courier should be classed as a worker and entitled to holiday pay, with CitySprint's assertion of couriers as self-employed described as 'window dressing' (Employment Tribunal, 2016b). Here the control exercised by the company, the fact the claimant was tracked by GPS technology and wore a company uniform, along with her lack of control over pay, were considered germane. She was considered to have no real right to appoint a substitute (to take her place when she was not available for work) in practice, with little autonomy over the performance of the services performed. A third judgement in February 2017 against Pimlico Plumbers also ruled that a plumber, apparently self-employed, had worker status because he was subject to a range of controls through the company: he had to wear a uniform, be available for work full-time, and conform to rules and standards (Royal Court of Justice, 2017). However, in November 2017 a claim for union recognition with collective bargaining rights for Deliveroo riders failed on the basis that they were judged to be 'self-employed' because of their apparent freedom to 'substitute', allowing other riders to take their place on a job (CAC, 2017). The General Secretary of the Independent Workers' Union of Great Britain, Dr Jason Moyer-Lee, responded to this defeat by stating that,

> It seems that after a series of defeats, finally a so-called gig economy company has found a way to game the system. . . . On the basis of a new contract introduced by Deliveroo's army of lawyers just weeks before the tribunal hearing, the Central Arbitration Committee decided that because a rider can have a mate do a delivery for them, Deliveroo's low paid workers are not entitled to basic protections.

In contrast Dan Warne, Managing Director for Deliveroo in the UK and Ireland commented:

> This is a victory for all riders who have continuously told us that flexibility is what they value most about working with Deliveroo. As we have consistently argued, our riders value the flexibility that self-employment provides. Riders enjoy being their own boss – having the freedom to choose when and where they work, and riding with other delivery companies at the same time.

The case exposes the tension over 'preference' for self-employment, cast in terms of work autonomy as a trade-off for employment rights and reflected in our case studies of parcel delivery workers, but also the subjective dimensions of job satisfaction and quality (Muñoz de Bustillo et al., 2009).

Parcel delivery and supply chain pressures

The increasing demands of e-retailing and 24/7 consumption within the retail sector have been much documented in recent academic debates. To satisfy these changing patterns of consumption the 'logistics mix' of storage, transportation and ultimately delivery has inescapably been reconfigured sending vibrations into the supply chain. Within the mainstream management literature this transformation of relations within the supply chain between retailers, producers and logistics companies is predicated upon two main drivers: cost and service delivery. The movement and delivery of goods/products within retail supply chains is increasingly time critical. The necessity for delivery companies to implement increasingly complex IT systems which track and trace the movement of products often under the electronic gaze of the final customer is paramount. These cost and service-delivery pressures have transformed retailer's/clients' strategy regarding 'goods in motion'.

With the increasing geographical fragmentation of production from consumption, logistics provides the necessary capacity to integrate the movement of goods under the tutelage of dominant retailers/clients (Coe, 2014). Bonacich and Wilson (2008) and Cowen (2014), referring to the politics of circulation, highlight the capacity for logistics to transform 'space-time' and reduce to a minimum the time commodities spend in motion. At a more concrete level, retailers (or clients) thus encourage competition amongst contractors as a mechanism to maximise efficiency and drive down costs. Contracts between retailers and logistics (parcel delivery) providers are contingent on delivering cost savings and securing high levels of service delivery with the power dynamic firmly in favour of the client organisations (Harvey, Quilley and Beynon, 2002). Coe (2014) highlights the contested territory between logistics firms and their clients, indicating that logistics organisations become contributors to 'value creation and capture' in their client organisations, as well as being concerned with the protection and mobilisation of their own interests of value capture. Newsome (2015) similarly argues logistics is uniquely positioned as central to the process of realising value generated through the exercise of labour power in production through speed-up in circulation. She highlights the critical role of logistics in the 'preservation of value' within the circuit of capital. The concurrent process of 'value capture' within the parcel delivery companies themselves presents the possibility of significant impact on job quality and the degradation of work.

There is a growing body of research evidence that explores the impact on both the job and work quality of this 'contested terrain' between retailers and logistics companies embedded within a context of fragmented global production networks and new logistics technologies (Coe, 2014; Haidinger, 2012; Newsome, 2015; Gregson, 2017). In terms of job quality diverse employment contracts in parcel delivery including temporary workers, self-employed owner-drives and home-based couriers are increasingly in evidence. The evidence from a recent European study exploring employment change in the sector highlights that growing liberalisation and de-regulation has resulted in far-reaching deterioration in employment conditions. Hermann's 2013 study reveals that increases in atypical employment, growing precarity and increasing numbers of self-employed drivers paid by piece-rate are evident within the sector (Hermann, 2013). This deterioration in work and employment is attributed to the increased levels of outsourcing and changing supply relations coupled with acute cost pressures, whereby global players contract service providers who in turn hire self-employed drivers. In terms of work quality the study correspondingly highlights increased work intensification, and increased delivery routes culminating in a reduction in autonomy and discretion. The critical literature on new logistics technologies highlights the capacity of IT systems to offer coherence to fragmented supply chains. These not only track the movement of products in a seamless flow from production to points of passage, gateways and ports finally to distribution and delivery; but also track the movement of labour. Gregson (2017), referring to the growth in self-employment in lorry drivers (a useful comparator to parcel delivery workers in terms of atomised and isolated work), juxtaposes the once nomadic lorry driver as 'king of the road' with the current tracing of repetitive spatial movements via GPS tracking with the opportunity for real-time surveillance and monitoring. These algorithmic tools and routing software accelerate circulation through the annihilation of space by time, but also offer the possibility of closer and tighter performance management for these atomised workers. The measurement of real-time labour performance creates the capacity for labour optimisation, removing the porosity of the working day and thus reducing costs.

To date there is limited research evidence, which explores the impact of supply chain pressures on the job quality of parcel delivery workers in the UK. The UK provides an insightful regulatory environment to explore job quality for postal delivery workers. The liberalisation of the postal services has involved a change in the regulatory regime and ultimately the privatisation of the state postal provider. Concurrently, the parcels delivery market has expanded in response to the revolution of e-commerce' with the UK operating the third largest e-commerce market in the world in 2015. In 2015, roughly 80 per cent of UK internet users did online shopping, the highest online shopping penetration rate in Europe (www.statista.com/topics/2333/e-commerce-in-the-united-kingdom/, 2017).

This chapter will consider how these supply chain pressures impact upon job quality in terms of contractual arrangements, collective representation and employment rights; and in terms of work quality, autonomy and discretion and work pressures. It emphasises that it is the absence of autonomy that exposes that parcel delivery workers are de facto workers and not self-employed. Finally, in conceptual terms the paper will seek to contribute to growing debates concerned with supply chain pressures and job quality.

Research methods

The chapter reports on a qualitative research project exploring the impact of supply chain pressures on the work and employment of parcel delivery workers. Initial interviews were undertaken with key stakeholders within the sector. Following these initial 'scoping' interviews, case studies of three parcel delivery companies were undertaken. Company A is a nationally based parcel delivery provider; it is unionised with terms and conditions of employment regulated by collective agreements. Within Company A, 12 interviews were undertaken with depot managers, first line managers, supervisors, trade union representatives and directly employed drivers and owner-drivers. The second case study, Company B, is part of a US multinational. Eight interviews were conducted with full-time union officials as well as directly employed and self-employed workers. This company was also unionised, with terms and conditions of employment regulated by collective agreements. Finally, six interviews were undertaken in Company C, a national organisation which operates with 'home-based couriers'. Interviewees from all case studies captured changes in the delivery labour process, the nature of work and the contractual status of employees. Owner-drivers and home couriers are necessarily difficult to locate – their working hours and time pressures mean in-depth interviews are problematic. In addition to these case studies, five in-depth interviews were conducted with owner-drivers working for a range of national parcel delivery companies with most having worked for at least two.

Supply chain pressures and job quality: mixed resourcing, owner-drivers and home couriers

The research evidence highlights the key role of supply chain pressures in the reconfiguration of the contractual status of workers. As one union officer stated, 'it is the supply chain that dictates from the retail side'; another confirmed the pressures placed on parcel delivery contracting arrangements by large retailers:

> Their customers are putting pressure on them to reduce the price . . . their customers are exercising pressure – if you've got a contract coming up they will say 'you do the job for us at that price, if you don't do it there is enough spare capacity in the market' – these (parcel delivery) companies are effectively price takers rather than price setters – that puts pressures on the companies to reduce their costs and they look at the outsourcing model.
>
> (Union Officer)

These pressures are intensified by apparent customer expectations for next and/or the same day delivery with the time when customers can order pushed back further and further to the end of the day.

Our research findings point to the subsequent emergence of a three-tier system of employment status driven by this transformation of the logistics supply chain. The first tier covers directly employed workers covered by collective agreements and with a history of collective regulation. Directly employed parcel delivery workers in these companies may have terms and conditions renegotiated in the context of the pressures brought by service level agreements, but they have some guarantee of direct permanent employment supported by collective organisation. The second tier involves the introduction of technically 'self-employed' owner-drivers generally paid by delivery, but based in depots and working alongside directly employed drivers. A third tier is of home-based couriers, also technically self-employed, using their own vehicles and with limited organisational relationships.

These three typologies were evident across the case study organisations. Company A was characterised by a balance between directly employed and owner-drivers with limited evidence of using home couriers. The ratio between directly employed and self-employed was negotiated by the union and was part of the collective agreement. Union officials highlighted that maintaining the ratio had to be 'policed' to ensure depot managers adhered to the agreed targets. In Company B the emphasis was on service delivery as a competitive strategy and as a result this organisation did not use home couriers, but was increasingly dependent upon owner-drivers incentivised by piece-rate with a higher rate per drop. In Company C all drivers are self-employed home couriers. Working from home, workers in this organisation had parcels delivered daily which they sorted and loaded onto their own vehicles prior to delivery. Respondents reported that often the number of parcels to be delivered varied considerably, as a result they often felt anxious that they would not have enough work to secure at least minimum wage rates of hourly pay.

While directly employed drivers had fixed hours and hourly rates, self-employed drivers are paid by delivery or drops. The key advantage of owner-drivers for the companies is the removal of the costs of non-delivery. In Company A directly employed drivers had a target of 70–80 drops per day; by contrast, owner-drivers were expected to achieve in the region of 120–130 drops per day. Owner-drivers in Company A were reported to receive £1.65 per parcel delivery stop and £2 for collections or pick-ups. By contrast, rates per drop for home couriers in Company C varied from 85p to £1. Couriers highlighted that they were meant to be paid more if parcels were heavier than a standard package, but that often the extra payment did not occur.

Dependent self-employed workers were only paid for deliveries, yet their working day included failed deliveries, with no extra payment for reattempts to deliver or timed deliveries or the sorting and loading of vans ready for delivery. In addition, self-employed respondents highlighted that if they were sick, wanted to take a holiday or were faced with any family emergency, they would be required to provide substitute cover for their route or they would be charged the costs to the company of an agency worker and may also be fined. Respondents in Company C highlighted that failure to deliver the required parcels (often within specified delivery slots) could result in the immediate removal of work. One respondent highlighted her insecurity;

> You live in threat of them saying, no parcels, that's it. It's awful to think, that after doing ten years for them, doing all the hard work, building a round up for them they go 'see you later'. You've got nothing, and that's what they threaten you with. All the time, 'we'll just take your parcels'. Everything you do wrong now, they say, 'oh well you know we can suspend your parcels'.
>
> (Company C, Home Courier)

Reconfigured contractual status in parcel delivery is integral to cost cutting, the speed-up of delivery and, crucially, the removal of non-delivery costs. Dependent self-employment facilitates the excision of these costs, while the social costs of labour – holiday and sick pay and pensions – are transferred to the worker. For owner-drivers while the demand for delivery work might mean that work is not necessarily insecure and the capacity to earn could be relatively attractive, it depends upon long and intensive hours and once the cost of vans, insurance, petrol and maintenance were excluded, hourly rates could be near to the National Living Wage (NLW). Yet as self-employed workers, delivery workers are not entitled to the NLW or other employment rights even though the quality of their work strongly questions their contractual status.

Work quality – autonomy and discretion: 'the industrial engineer in the cab'

For both directly and self-employed delivery workers, logistics technology not only provides the capacity to electronically track and trace the movement of goods, but also the movement of labour. The organisation of a vanload of parcels into a delivery route reflecting timed deliveries demands considerable mental as well as physical labour from drivers. All drivers highlighted the vital importance of local knowledge, indicating that this insight was crucial. The introduction of SMS messaging to notify customers that a parcel was on the way introduced the need for further anticipation and route planning in accordance with a 'manifest' or schedule that might change at any moment.

GPS navigation systems facilitated the remote monitoring of drivers. Increasingly parcel delivery companies are using telematics technology which has the capacity to dictate more effective delivery routes through Satellite Navigation. The use of navigation systems and route planners was starting to remove drivers' discretion to plan their daily routes, effectively constraining their autonomy in the labour process. ORION, the On-Road Integrated Optimisation and Navigation system, used by Company B in the US can continually evaluate routing options up to the moment a Company B driver leaves the depot making 'tens of thousands of route optimisation calculations each minute', reconfiguring a driver's pick-ups and drop-offs in real time. Company B claims 'a reduction of just one mile per day per drive would save it $50m a year in costs', including savings on fuel (Company B to save millions with ORION route optimising system, Post & Parcel, November 1st, 2013). Company B was trialling its telematics system in the UK with data from drivers' handheld mobile devices and vehicle telematics systems producing algorithms which then define the labour process; drivers are given an iPad dictating optimal routes in terms of time and mileage and texting anticipated delivery times to customers. Recalling Gregson's proposition that algorithmic optimisation and routing software accelerates circulation through the annihilation of space by time, a Company B union rep described the use of metrics to calculate delivery times:

> Every route in this country is timed. There's a time element put on every route. So, every route you would have a certain time allowance for this area around here and they base it on the last 13 weeks of what he's done over there as an average and then they time it by whatever they do. So that's how they work – on how many stops per hour you should be doing, how many miles you should do, and they can also look at the way that you can do the route. The new system they're trying to bring in will actually put it so that you basically are a robot. 'This is your first call and that's where you're going next'. What it's replacing is the driver's brain because at the moment it's the driver who works out his route. At the moment he dictates where his first stop is going to be, what road to go down. This will replace all that and tell you 'This is the way'. It's got a SatNav on that shows you which roads to take.
>
> (Company B, Union Rep)

As the union rep indicates, telematics has the potential to reduce the autonomy of drivers and there was a fear that telematics would remove discretion in a way which might not better local knowledge. Company B was primarily differentiated by its technology, which could sort parcels into a route for drivers, determine their schedule and then automatically text customers with a delivery time within a one-hour delivery slot. Telematics does not just track the location of drivers but monitors the entire driving labour process with the aim of controlling costs and with implications for driver discretion, as a national officer described:

> The track and trace, effectively you've got an industrial engineer in the cab, not only it measures what you do in terms of driving, how

> much fuel you use – if you are heavy on the pedal. It takes away discretion from the driver in terms of route planning they will come in and the van's loaded, so they just drive to the route that has been set, (for example) they do it to eliminate all right turns as they take longer.
>
> (Union Officer)

The technology monitors right turns, if the van doors are open (a security issue), when the engine is 'idling' and excessive reversing, although the latter provided opportunities for resistance:

> I know that they brought up excessive reversing, but that was just quite funny because what they discovered was when you actually put the vehicle into reverse you didn't have to move, but it just registered on the Telematics. So, a lot of my guys just sit there with the lights going like that in reverse and when they get back they go 'You put it in reverse 98 times!!'
>
> (Company B, Union Rep)

For the drivers in our sample the loss of autonomy and the potential for technology to determine the labour process was experienced and anticipated as a threat to the quality of their work.

Work pressures: micromanaging seconds and performance management

The research evidence also highlights that employers were increasingly using the capacity of the new IT systems to monitor the performance of these remote workers. This monitoring and surveillance also offered the possibility of rendering more transparent the expected daily tasks and targets of delivery workers and monitoring their completion more closely. Personal Digital Assistants (PDAs) or Hand-Held Devices (HHDs) are used throughout all stages of the supply chain; managers are able to track on-screen the precise location of parcels in real time through GPS, whilst drivers capture customer signatures providing automated proof of delivery for both parcel delivery companies and their clients (with phone technology built in to prove delivery in some cases).

Importantly technology mitigates against non-delivery and loss, since local depot budgets bear the cost of claims for loss:

> It's very much to protect our business because if we can turn round to the customer and say 'Well, do you know what, on the balance of probability we've got a GPS that says he was at your front door. We've got a signature that's got your name. The driver has confirmed in a recorded interview that he delivered the parcel to your house. I'm really sorry,

> but we're not going to accept your claim'. So, it actually does protect our business and our revenue; and actually protecting our revenue in this sort of day and age when competition is so fierce is really, really important.
>
> (Company A, Depot Manager)

For some drivers the technology provided safeguards for them since it proved that they had made the delivery in instances where customers claimed they had not received the item. However, the PDA also allows communication between depots and the drivers, facilitating management control over the labour process and crucially, non-delivery, through text messages. This was seen by union reps as tantamount to bullying:

> You don't need to move into direct threat on the text, you can send one 'Are you going to clear today?' Now to an outsider that seems like a reasonable request, doesn't it, but it doesn't when you've been told back in the depot 'I don't want any missed. I don't want this, I don't want that, I don't want that'. So, when you get that question 'Are you going to clear today?' there's a different inference to that, isn't there? When we challenge them about bullying and intimidating messages they say to us 'That's not bullying. I only asked. I'm the manager, I need to know', which is fair comment, but it's the micro-management and that's the pressure, as we said, they're forced to stay out – go back to ones that you haven't been able to deliver, and you have to keep going back and back until it's done.
>
> (Company B, Union Rep)

For unions the frontier of control is the potential of management to use information gathered on the PDA in disciplinary procedures and collective agreements defended against management's ability to do so. In Company A strong union organisation meant that attempts to use this information for disciplinary purposes had been rejected – at least for the directly employed drivers they represented. However, across logistics companies drivers felt subject to the managerial and customer gaze even if the data could not be used directly against them and this was not as clear-cut for drivers on probation. Another manager confirmed that the system tracked non-deliveries by driver with 'red' alerts:

> In the morning the first thing that we do is we come in at half past six and the drivers don't start till seven, so we'll be having a look already at the day before's performance, so we'll be dealing with that straightaway in the morning. 'Why did you bring back this many parcels? Why didn't you deliver that? Why is there a red here?' and then we'll go in the meeting and go through all that again.
>
> (Company A, Manager)

The PDA can be used to monitor not only non-deliveries, but also 'down time' or apparently unproductive working time, as a Company A union rep reported:

> 'Going back probably six months, certain guys used to come back at a certain time. Now they know here what time your last delivery is by these handheld (devices). They know what time you've done your last collection or last delivery. So every now and again on these (PDAs) it brings up what they call down time. If you have more than 10 minutes/15 minutes down time on your (PDA) where you haven't done a drop or a collection it comes up showing on the thing saying you've had down time, there. Now if you come back and you haven't done as many collections they'll look at your down time and say 'Well, you've come back early and you've had down time here', if you say 'Well, I finish at five', and you say 'Well, I haven't enough time. I want to finish at five and that's it. I've got ten drops left that I've brought back that I couldn't do', then they'll look at the down time and say 'Well, you've had 15 minutes here where you've done nothing'.
>
> (Company A, union rep)

For directly employed drivers PDAs can ensure drivers are taking statutory breaks in terms of whether the vehicle is stationary, but the pressure to deliver meant drivers could get round this, again increasing the porosity of the working day, as a national officer reported:

> One of the questions we've asked our members is 'An honest answer. How many of you physically work through your lunch break?' And we've been taken aback by the response. They feel obliged to either go on the back of their van and sort the packages out or maybe go on and deliver while the van's parked up because they need to catch up with their working day and that defeats the object of what a lunch break's about.
>
> (Union Officer)

One directly employed driver reported parking up and delivering on foot in a shopping centre whilst he was supposed to be on his lunch hour. For owner-drivers breaks are not monitored.

In Company B metrics were increasingly being used to measure, in terms of seconds, every aspect of the labour process:

> There's 2,300 delivery drivers in the UK and two people timed the routes for the whole of the UK – two people in an office.
>
> (Company B, Union Rep)

This was linked by union reps to shareholder demands at multinational level, 'instead of being a service related industry it became production' (Company

B, Union Rep). Measurement includes the time taken from the doorstep to return to the van with drivers being questioned if they took extra seconds and similarly the time taken from placing the key in the ignition to pulling away.

The wider context to the calibration of worker movements through metrics and in terms of speed-up in the supply chain was captured by a Company B rep as 'micromanaging seconds'. The concern of the Company B reps was the potential for managers to 'take this data and apply it to the workforce in a bullying way'.

In company C home couriers similarly reported increasing levels of monitoring and surveillance coupled with heightened performance management regimes. The micro-management of how and when they delivered their parcels as well as the notifications they were required to send to customers was of growing concern. All highlighted that Company C managers monitored their activities daily to ensure that they adhered to the required time slots for delivery. One respondent stated that he was aware of the daily monitoring, suggesting that it was like being watched by big brother. Failure to adhere to the required timings could result in being placed on 'improvement notices' for up to six months. Respondents in this company were eager to highlight that the growing levels of monitoring and surveillance allied to punitive measures employed by the company were seemingly at odds with their self-employed status. Overall the surveillance of self-employed drivers and home couriers through technology, along with the control exercised by the companies through depot managers, appears to be consistent with worker status as declared in the Employment Tribunal judgements outlined earlier. Work relationships are dependent and, with limited access to union representation, self-employed drivers were in an unequal bargaining position.

Conclusion

The research evidence has highlighted the impact on both job and work quality of supply chain pressures for parcel delivery workers. In terms of work quality the evidence highlights the significant role of technology in providing coherence to the supply chain. Technology tracks the seamless movement of products, from producer to consumer, thereby protecting retailer value and minimising loss. In response to retailer control over the supply chain and increasing competitive pressures technology also serves to speed up the velocity of circulation. Within this context the autonomy and discretion drivers may have once enjoyed, determining their own routes, deploying local knowledge, offering what they regarded as a service to a community, is eroded. In turn the routing software plots their working day, effectively removing their discretion and their capacity to make decisions and commodifying delivery.

Technology has the capacity to not only specify drivers' daily routes but also to monitor every moment in the driving labour process. As highlighted previously, Gregson's (2017) argument that algorithmic tools and routing software accelerate circulation through the annihilation of space by time, but also offer the possibility of closer and tighter performance management for these atomised workers, is highly pertinent in this context. Drivers are subject to increasing work pressures resulting from the daily targets, levels of monitoring and the possibility of constant surveillance. Both a managerial and customer gaze extends over the labour process and in Company C in particular, a low-cost model resulted in the most pernicious performance management regime.

While the erosion of autonomy impacts on directly employed drivers, the level of surveillance and organisational control exposes the fiction of 'self-employment' for owner-drivers and home couriers. The mixed resourcing model, in the form of directly employed workers, owner-drivers and home couriers, allows logistics companies to cut the costs of non-delivery. Where there is existing union recognition, collective agreements allow unions to have some control over the ratios of self-employed workers used by companies and ensured that technology could not be used for disciplinary purposes against drivers – this is the frontier of control for unions. Our case studies provided no evidence of mainstream trade unions organising the self-employed workers that their members work alongside, although the unionisation of Citysprint, Deliveroo and Hermes drivers, involving legal cases against these companies, shows that it is possible.

The high demand for home delivery means owner-drivers had some limited power in the labour market and could move from company to company – (self-)employment rather than job security (Chapter 1). Yet pay could be variable, with delivery rates subject to cuts and income dependent upon long hours. Home-based couriers particularly referred to their daily apprehension as to whether sufficient parcels would be dropped off at their homes for delivery, which could result in them effectively working for less than minimum rates of pay once hours were taken into account.

The evidence presented in this chapter has highlighted the importance of understanding the dynamics of job quality, as an outcome of the labour process and the frontier of control reflecting power dynamics within the employment relationship (Simms, 2015; Hoque et al., 2017) – a fluid and permeable concept. Yet it is also clear that dependent self-employment is located within the political economy of logistics, but also a national institutional framework that legally and fiscally promotes self-employment (Behring and Harvey, 2015). In conclusion the evidence demands that contractual status – namely 'disguised employment relationships' (ILO, 2014) – is a key dimension of job and work quality, particularly in the way that it facilitates unpaid working time and removes what is insufficiently asserted in the job quality literature: employment rights.

References

Behring, F. and Harvey, M. (2015). The evolution of false self-employment in the British construction industry: A neo-Polanyian account of labour market formation. *Work, Employment and Society*, 29(6), pp. 969–988.

Bonacich, E. and Wilson, J. (2008). *Getting the Goods: Ports, Labor and the Logistics Revolution*. Ithaca, NY and London: Cornell University Press.

Broughton, N. and Richards, B. (2016, March). *Tough Gig: Low Paid Self-Employment in London and the UK*. Social Market Foundation.

Central Arbitration Committee. (2017). *Independent Workers' Union of Great Britain (IWGB) V Deliveroo*. Available at: www.gov.uk/government/uploads/system/uploads/attachment_data/file/663126/Acceptance_Decision.pdf [Accessed 10 December 2017].

Coe, N. (2014). Missing links: Logistics, governance and upgrading in a shifting global economy. *Review of International Political Economy*, 23(1), pp. 224–256.

Cowen, D. (2014). *The Deadly Life of Logistics Mapping Violence in Global Trade*. Minneapolis, MN: University of Minnesota Press.

Employment Tribunals. (2016a) *Aslam and Farrar V Uber*. Available at: www.judiciary.gov.uk/wp-content/uploads/2016/10/aslam-and-farrar-v-uber-reasons-20161028.pdf [Accessed 10 December 2017].

Employment Tribunal. (2016b). *Dewhurst V City Sprint*. Available at: www.bwbllp.com/file/judgment-pdf [Accessed 10 December 2017].

Eurofound. (2002, June 13). *Economically Dependent Workers*. Employment Law and Industrial Relations. Available at: www.eurofound.europa.eu/observatories/eurwork/comparative-information/economically-dependent-workers-employment-law-and-industrial-relations

Eurofound. (2013). *Self-Employed or Not Self-Employed? Working Conditions of 'Economically Dependent Workers'*. Background Paper. Dublin: European Foundation for the Improvement of Living and Working Conditions.

Field, F. and Forsey, A. (2016). *Wild West Workplace Self-employment in Britain's 'Gig Economy' Report*. Available at: www.Frankfield.co.uk.

Findlay, P., Kalleberg, A. L. and Warhust, C. (2013). The challenge of job quality. *Human Relations*, 66(4), pp. 441–451.

Gallie, D. (Ed.) (2007). *Employment Regimes and the Quality of Work*. Oxford: Oxford University Press.

Gregson, N. (2017). Logistics at work: Trucks, containers and the friction of circulation in the UK. *Mobilities*, 12(3), pp. 343–364.

Haidinger, B. (2012). *On the Move in Global Delivery Chains: Labour Relations and Working Conditions in the Parcel Delivery Industries of Austria, Germany, the Czech Republic and Hungary*. SODIPER Synthesis Report. Vienna: FORBA-Working Life Research Centre.

Harvey, M., Quilley, S. and Beynon, H. (2002). *Exploring the Tomato: Transformations of Nature, Society and Economy*. Cheltenham: Edward Elgar Publishing.

Hermann, C. (2013). *The Liberalisation of European Postal Markets and the Impact on Employment and Working Conditions*. FORBA Research Report 3/2013. Available at: www.forba.at/data/downloads/file/911-FB_03_2013.pdf

Holman, D. (2013). Job types and job quality in Europe. *Human Relations*, 66(4), pp. 475–502.

Hoque, K., Earls, J., Conway, N. and Bacon, N. (2017). Union representation, collective voice and job quality: An analysis of a survey of union members in the UK finance sector. *Economic and Industrial Democracy*, 38(1), pp. 27–50.
ILO. (2015). *Non-Standard Forms of Employment*. Report for Discussion at the Meeting of Experts on Non-Standard Forms of Employment. Geneva: ILO.
International Labour Office. (2014). *World Social Protection Report 2014/15: Building Economic Recovery, Inclusive Development and Social Justice*. Geneva: ILO. Available at: www.ilo.org/public/libdoc//ilo/2014/485584.pdf.
Kalleberg, A. (2011). *Good Jobs, Bad Jobs: The Rise of Polarized and Precarious Employment Systems in the United States, 1970s to 2000s*. New York, NY: Russell Sage Foundation.
Muñoz de Bustillo, R., Fernández-Macías, E. and Antón, J. (2009). *Indicators of Job Quality in the European Union*. Study of the Directorate General for Internal Policies. Policy Department A: Economic and Scientific Policy IP/A/EMPL/ST/2008-09. Brussels: European Parliament.
Muñoz de Bustillo, R., Fernández-Macías, E., Antón, J.-I. and Esteve, F. (2011). E pluribus unum? A critical survey of job quality indicators. *Socio-Economic Review*, 9, pp. 447–475.
Newsome, K. (2015). Value in motion: Logistics, labour and contemporary political economy. In Newsome, K., Taylor, P., Rainnie, A. and Bair, J. (Eds.) *Putting Labour in Its Place; Labour Process Analysis and Global Value Chains*. London: Palgrave Macmillan.
Osterman, P. (2013). Introduction to the special issue on job quality: what does it mean and how might we think about it? *ILR Review*, 66(4), pp. 739–752.
Royal Court of Justice Employment. (2017). *Pimlico Plumbers Limited V Charlie Mullins and Gary Smith*. Available at: www.judiciary.gov.uk/wpcontent/uploads/2017/02/pimlico-plumbers-v-smith.pdf [Accessed 10 December 2017].
Simms, M. (2015). Unions and job quality in the UK extending interest representation within regulation institutions. *Work and Occupations*, 44(1), pp. 47–67.
Tomlinson, D. and Corlett, A. (2017). *A Tough Gig? The Nature of Self-Employment in 21st Century Britain and Policy Implications*. London: The Resolution Foundation.
Tsing, A. (2009). Supply chains and the human condition. *Rethinking Marxism*, 21(2), pp. 148–176.

6 For the sake of quality of care

Nurses' struggles for job quality in the context of flexibility arrangements: the case of Poland

Julia Kubisa

Introduction

The era of flexibility refers to different sectors of economy and segments of labour market. The public services such as healthcare experience changes and challenges such as new technologies and the ageing of society that poses new questions around care. In this sector labour costs make up a significant part of the budget. The Polish healthcare sector faces struggles to keep consistency of the budget that is chronically underfinanced, so the cuts in labour costs are seen as an opportunity for healthcare units. A variety of flexibility practices have been introduced since the late 1990s, but their impact on care work performed in the healthcare system has not been debated. This chapter aim is to study what happens to care work in the context of flexibility practices introduced in the healthcare system. This broad question will be answered by looking at the job quality of nurses – the biggest occupational group in the sector, crucial for performance of care work. The position of nurse is between employer and hospital hierarchy on one side and the patient on the other. Changes in job quality under flexibility practices are shaped in the dynamics of social dialogue both by management and the trade union of nurses and midwives. Their outcome directly relates to the experiences of patients. This can be viewed as a three-party relationship uneven in terms of roles, since patients' well-being is related to the quality of work and employment offered in the healthcare system.

This chapter presents the decisions and actions undertaken by hospital managements as a response to healthcare system reform that justified the introduction of flexible employment arrangements, and the reactions of the All-Poland Trade Union of Nurses and Midwives. In this chapter I examine the changes in the Polish healthcare system with a special attention to flexibility practices from the perspective of job quality – understood as the combination of work quality and employment quality – following the index offered by Muñoz de Bustillo, Fernández-Macías, Esteve and Antón (2009, 2011), presented in the Introduction chapter. Then I present the views and strategies of the trade union, focused on linking job quality with the quality of care provided to patients. The aim of the chapter is to analyse job quality experienced by nurses in order to examine the character of flexibility introduced in the healthcare system – if and for whom was it really flexible? Following Jonsson's theoretical model presented in the Introduction chapter of this volume, I will study whether the flexibility in the healthcare sector is desired by any of the parties – management and nurses and what happens to job quality of nurses. Next, I will study the relationship between job quality and care work in the framework offered by the trade union of nurses and midwives.

The chapter is organised as follows: the first part presents an overview of changes in the Polish healthcare system; the second part presents previous research on nurses and job quality, the third part presents methodology, the fourth part is focused on an analysis of the experience of job quality by nurses; the fifth part describes the collective agency of nurses applied to try to influence their job quality by establishing the connection between it and the quality of care; and the sixth part presents the chapter's conclusions.

The healthcare system in Poland

Flexibility and restructuring have often been viewed as a solution for increasing the competitiveness of companies by a swift response to changing conditions. From the private sector the idea was transmitted to the public sector in the form of "New Public Management" – the idea of introduction of market-driven mechanisms in order to make public services more efficient, less expensive, and client-oriented. One of its main elements – along with pressure for effectiveness and individual responsibility (unlike in traditional bureaucracy) – is flexibility in work arrangements, employment and work organisation (Zawicki, 2002). The healthcare systems in various European countries have undergone changes under a general framework of "rationalisation" and "economisation" of public expenditures (see Verschuren, de Groot and Nossent, 1995), which are mainly a result of budgetary cuts. Certain forms of privatisation followed, with private healthcare operators competing for public funding. The market-inspired approach emphasises the need to decrease labour costs, since their share in general hospital expenses is relatively large (Kozek and Radzka, 2011). Cuts in employment are typically followed by an intensification of work – ostensibly in order to better use the remaining human capital (Buchan and O'May, 2002). Generally, on the level of practices, this translates into changes in employment arrangements (fixed-term contracts, part-time, various other forms of contracts and self-employment), presented in managerial discourse as flexibility practice that aims at productivity and effective use of resources.

Since the beginning of the 1990s, the Polish healthcare system came to be viewed as malfunctioning, with hospitals struggling with the problem of constant debts as they tried to provide medical services with insufficient budgets (Domagała, 2004; Kozek, 2011). The system underwent a major reform in 1999–2001, which can be interpreted as a flexibility and restructuring paradigm. The introduced changes aimed to resolve these problems through a rapid downsizing of the labour force, whereas in the 2010s the flexibility of contracts with employees was increased and the self-employment of nurses introduced. The reform of 1999 also introduced a financing system based on an insurance fund (Włodarczyk, 1999, 2010) that replaced government budget financing with contributions collected as taxes. Currently, the National Health Fund does not provide the financing of hospitals, but orders and pays for specific services: medical treatment, operations, and patients' stay in hospitals. The hospitals were transformed into "independent public healthcare units", while directors became hospital managers responsible for the division of the means obtained through the contracts: wages, repairs and purchases of equipment. This reform was based on the processes of decentralisation, rationalisation and introduction of market mechanisms into public services and institutions, according to the principles of New Public Management for the calculation of the costs of delivery and organisation of healthcare (Hardy and Stenning, 2005; Hardy, 2009; Kozek, 2011). In order to speed up the restructuring process, the government launched the Restructuring Programme, which was supposed to accelerate the changes and at the same time ease the effects of layoffs. In years 1999–2001, 87000 were laid off in the public healthcare units and some of them found new employment in the newly formed private sector healthcare that could also compete for contracts with the National Health Fund (Domagała, 2004). The newly introduced practices that were supposed to improve working conditions were: contracting of medical services (both for public and non-public units), introduction of managers' contracts in the public units, civil law contracts for medical workers, privatisation and outsourcing. The change to the system of contribution and financing was supposed to introduce beneficial solutions for healthcare workers, such as higher financing of the system and a better adjustment between finances and services; depolitisation of medical services in the form of disconnecting the services from the state budget; rationalisation of expenses and therefore productive use of the resources; higher wages for workers, in direct connection to their workloads; higher satisfaction and higher social prestige of the occupations; and access to objective criteria to rationalisation of employment. The latter was widely debated and much hope was put into the idea of flexibility practices in terms of employment – under the framework of flexible wages, flexibility of forms of contracts, and functional and numerical flexibility (Domagała, 2004). Productivity and rationalisation became the main goals of healthcare management. In order to achieve it, the work performed in the healthcare sector became recognised as "ordinary work", and its special status of public service, connected to public interest, faded.

Restructuring and new forms of employment

The public healthcare system reform included the restructuring of employment. However, the numbers of patients did not change. Since 2000, when wage negotiations were transferred to the level of the individual healthcare units (hospitals, clinics etc.), the level of wages has depended on various factors: the level of wages on the local labour market, managerial policy (are investments in technology or in human capital?), on the workers' representatives and on the decisions of hospital nursing departments (Ostrowski, 2003; Kubisa, 2014). The market-inspired approach introduced into the healthcare system encouraged head administrators to seek different cost-cutting solutions, including so-called flexible employment arrangements. The reform brought the option of civil law contracts to nurses. The discourse around the introduction of civil law contracts concentrated on the effective use of the nurses' workforce according to the needs of the healthcare unit. The financial incentive was also raised. It was also argued that in the end, the civil law contracts will strengthen the prestige and social position of the occupation (Domagała, 2004). It is quite common for hospital managers to offer "contracts of mandate" regulated by civil law as a cheaper addition to regular employment contracts instead of creating new permanent job vacancies. The "contract of mandate" is:

> a civil law agreement characterised by the freedom to shape the contents of the contract; the lack of a minimum wage requirement; lack of obligation to determine daily and weekly working time limits; the freedom to introduce paid sick leaves and holidays; the freedom to set the date//time and place of work performance. . . . In case the 'contract of mandate' too many elements of employment, the contract is converted into *an employment contract. It may be terminated at any time. . . . The termination takes effect immediately.
>
> (Centrum Informacyjne Sluzb Zatrudnienia, 2016)

The freedom of choice between a full-time employment contract and self-employment in the healthcare sector was confirmed by a set of healthcare Acts voted into law by the Polish Parliament in 2011 and promoted by the government coalition of the Civic Platform party and the Polish People's Party (Trappmann, 2011).

Flexibility in the healthcare system

The introduction of flexibility solutions to the healthcare sector should be seen in a broader context, as a part of the New Public Management approach. The role of the public sector is changing as NPM provides sort of a new narration based on norms related more to the private sector that is becoming a main point of reference. Generally, if NPM is treated as one of the trends of privatisation of the state, it should not be analysed only in economic terms: there are new rules of management, new capital, new qualifications, new technology, and also a change in power relations (Hibou, 2004). The processes of liberalisation and privatisation can be traced in public sector change relations between capital and the state, which includes cultural change and institutional change (Connell, 2009). The very idea of public sector and public services is deeply changed when rules of NPM are being applied. As Connell (2009) points out, the changes are introduced on an organisational level, where each part of an organisation must function as a profit-making firm, with its managers held accountable for the income/expenditure balance, down to the lowest level of organisation. Individual workers are treated as firms and expected to follow a profit-making logic. Their work is being evaluated through "performance management" (Connell, 2009; Selberg, 2013; van Thiel and Leeuw, 2002).

The healthcare sector is one of the examples of public services that cannot produce profit. Therefore the pursuit for cost reduction is much more visible, even though the character of care should be beyond such pursuits (Kozek, 2011). Public services are being restructured in forms of concentration and outsourcing, with the emphasis on reduction of labour costs – in form of employment cuts, lower wages, intensification of work and also in form of changes in employment arrangements – reductions, non-standard forms of employment, new groups of employees (temporary contracts, temporary agency workers) and introduction of numerical and functional flexibility (Hermann and Flecker, 2012).

For many years self-employment was regarded in Poland as a flexible means to decrease unemployment, especially in the time of its highest levels – in the beginning of the 2000s. The "entrepreneurial spirit" was praised especially in case of women, who were encouraged to form one-person companies in order to create jobs for themselves instead of being unemployed. The discourse was combined with work-life balance arguments that presented flexibility arrangements as opportunities for the combination of work tasks and family obligations, with a little bit of self-independence both in terms of the choice of the business niche and control over time (see critical assessment by Trawińska, 2010). Self-employment of women is seen as a potential for development in rural areas (Szepelska, 2014). This means that the negative aspects of self-employment – precariousness, long hours, delays in payments, and lack of permanency, usually pointed out in the literature (see Kalleberg, 2011; Kalleberg, Reskin and Hudson, 2000; Cranford, Vosko and Zukewich, 2003) were not that much debated.

In order to understand the character of flexibility in the healthcare sector in Poland, I will follow the theoretical debate presented in the Introduction chapter in the volume (Kubisa and Mendonca) that shows that flexibility is always "flexibility for somebody" (Furåker, Håkansson and Karlsson, 2007; Karlsson, 2007). This will be supported by Jonsson's framework of flexibility, inflexibility, stability and instability in order to determine if the solutions introduced in the healthcare sector can be characterised as flexibility or rather instability (Jonsson, 2007).

Previous research on nurses' job quality

The work performed by nurses is a multi-dimensional combination of high-level skills, dirty work (Wolkowitz, 2006) and emotional labour (Hochschild, 2012). They perform physical work, deal with high levels of stress and critical situations, and all the while are responsible for the administration of medicines. Various aspects of the job quality experienced by nurses have been widely studied. Their work combines long shifts, physical, emotional and intellectual tasks performed as teamwork, and the need to constantly balance the pressures exerted by management and to establish good contact with patients (Gordon, 2006). The aspect of control over place and working time is crucial in healthcare. The work is always unpredictable as there can always be medical emergencies that disrupt planned schedules. Nurses learn early how to cope with the unpredictability of their working time by combining a planned schedule with a large amount of flexibility that allows them to adjust to unexpected tasks. Their working schedules are arranged differently from the "standard" 9-to-5, with frequent night-shifts and 12-hour shifts, and their regular working time is often exceeded by periods of overtime.

Nurses' control over ways of using time at work can be organised differently. The choice to work full-time, overtime or less than full-time, and the relation of this to wages, as well as provisions for time spent outside of work (vacations and sick leave) – all of this has consequences for nurses in terms of valuing and keeping their jobs (Gerstel and Clawson, 2014). Nurses value the social environment at work, understood as workplace integration, which together with pay and autonomy are the most important job factors (at least in the case of Norwegian nurses). Also further education, such as one day or more reserved for professional development is a factor positively related to the intent to stay employed at a hospital (Bjørk, Samdal, Hansen, Tørstad and Hamilton, 2007). The social environment in nursing work refers to the relationship between nurse and patient. Nurses point out that the dialogue between them and patients should evolve towards partnership, both to support the recovery of the patient and to resist the tendency in contemporary health service delivery towards a purely technical form of nursing practice, in order to protect the relational core of professional nursing practice (Jonsdottir, Litchfield and Dexheimer Pharris, 2004; Gordon, Buchanan and Bretherton, 2008).

The work quality experienced by nurses is also studied in terms of physical conditions. Their work, especially when not supported by technology, requires assuming strenuous positions and sometimes the lifting of considerable weights. However, the availability of research, especially in form of statistical data on working conditions, is very scarce and fragmented so it has to be interpreted more as exploratory than representative. For example, in a recent survey of 100 nurses in Poland, 60 respondents rate their job as physically hard; 28 – very hard; 10 – moderately difficult, and only two evaluate it as physically easy. Seventy-nine think that, over time, their work is becoming more and more difficult physically, with 13 saying that working conditions have not changed over the years, and for eight, it has been getting easier. Asked about equipment for moving patients, 29 say they have it, but 69 do not have such equipment, with two nurses not specifying. The nurses also state they seldom take sick leave (Wyderka and Niedzielska, 2016).

The New Public Management-driven changes impact the working conditions and work intensification of nurses. Selberg (2013) delivers a broad overview of research in the field of changes in the Swedish healthcare sector caused by neoliberal pressures. Growing workloads combined with restructuring and organisational changes cause stress, anxiety, burnout and breakdowns at work (Glasberg, Norberg and Söderberg, 2007). The emphasis on cost-cutting and increased efficiency affects ward nurses' tasks that are the most time-consuming but directly linked to patient care (Blomgren, 2003). Selberg's (2013) own research points out the direct connection between the New Public Management-inspired restructuring paradigm and growing workloads, causing both physical and emotional consequences, while the creative altruism embedded in nurses' care work is repressed.

The following section presents outcomes of the research conducted among nurses in Poland, in the context of changes in the Polish healthcare sector. The aim is to investigate the "flexibility for whom?" question that casts light on the character of changes in job quality in this particular case. Therefore, my research questions are as follows – what is happening to job quality of nurses when the flexibility solutions are introduced and what is the response of nurses to those changes?

Research methods

The chapter is based on a qualitative research comprised of semi-structured interviews, non-participant observation, analysis of the documents, media coverage and secondary data (see Denzin and Lincoln, 2011; Silverman, 2013). The main part of the research – 43 interviews and observations – was conducted in 2009 and 2010 for the purpose of a PhD project about the trade union activity of nurses and midwives in Poland, which was initially more oriented towards women's activity patterns in trade unions. The issue of the relation between job quality and quality of care emerged from the research material and brought a new angle to the analysis. In the years 2012–14 the author participated in a research project on the migrations of healthcare-sector workers which made it possible to study the relation between job quality and quality of care further in the form of 10 interviews. The author established a trustful relationship with the nurse community and is in frequent contact with them, which allows her to update the research material. The author regularly meets with the nurses, their representatives of the trade union and the official chamber, in order to gather updated information, in the form of workshops, debates and lectures. The meetings, debates, workshops and interviews that took place every several months from 2010 to 2017 broadened her knowledge and understanding of the tensions between job quality and quality of care as experienced by nurses.

Findings

This section presents findings of the multimethod research set in the context of the statistical data that has been referred to by the nurses in the interviews. It first presents the situation of employment quality, describing changes in contracts and extreme prolongation of working time, both closely related to wages. Then it presents issues of work quality – intensification, autonomy and social work environment. Finally, it characterises options of participation in the form of the trade union and its agenda that combines work and employment quality issues that result in the creation of strategies for shaping job quality.

Nurses and employment quality: contracts, working time and wages

Nurses represent the largest occupational group in the Polish healthcare system. They are also a highly feminised group. According to the database of the National Chamber of Nurses and Midwives (2015), in 2014 there were 277 334 women and 5188 men certified to work as nurses, 199 188 of whom – according to Poland's Central Statistical Office – were actually working with patients (GUS, 2015). The National Chamber of Nurses and Midwives annually publishes statistics on Polish nurses in European comparisons. The number of employed nurses and midwives per one-thousand citizens is 8,1 in the Czech Republic, 7,5 in France, 9,6 in Germany and 9,2 in the United Kingdom, while in Poland it is 5.

Low wages has been one of the major problems experienced by nurses in Polish healthcare, creating pressure on them to seek additional jobs. In the early 2000s nurses usually worked additionally as cleaners. Currently, since the number of nurses is decreasing and more retire from than start careers (according to National Chamber of Nurses and Midwives data), additional work within the occupation is increasingly possible part-time. Depending on the local labour market offer, nurses work part-time in at-home care, public and private clinics, and on hospital wards, where intensive teamwork is necessary.

> My colleagues work on double shifts, and they organise their family lives around that. There are not enough jobs and approximately 20% of nurses are sole breadwinners because their husbands were laid off.

> So when they have an opportunity to work fulltime and additionally three-quarter time, they take it and the husbands take care of the house. Nurses do not have free time; they only have a little time to get some sleep. It was not like that in the past, but now everyone has a second job.
>
> (Nurse and trade union activist, Lublin region)

In one regional capital, a new academic hospital employed only three full-time nurses on its neurosurgery ward. The rest of the nurses worked on contracts of mandate in addition to their full-time jobs in other hospitals. Hospital managers do not often create new full-time jobs and do not increase wages, but offer instead additional, fragmentary contract jobs, which enables them to achieve a labour-cost reduction. The head managers did not compete for nurses by increasing wages to attract (e.g.) nurses with rare specialisations.

With regard to the contractual conditions in the healthcare sector, the time and place of work performance cannot be freely chosen. As a result nurses work full-time on a permanent employment contract plus overtime at one location, and additionally work on contracts of mandate at another location or even at the same one. Thus their overall working time is not supervised and they are not discouraged from taking extra hours. On the contrary, with their relatively low regular wages, the overtime and contracts of mandate are regarded as the only solution to improving their home budgets. In 2015 the Polish National Labour Inspectorate conducted a random check of 29 ER wards in the country. In 31% of cases the weekly norm of working time per worker was exceeded; 28% of workers (mostly nurses and paramedics) were not allowed a proper 24-hour rest. There were cases discovered of persons working 14 hours or even 24 hours straight without rest. The National Labour Inspectorate concluded that contracts of mandate very much fostered non-compliance with regulations on working time.

> I am on a 24-hour shift – that makes about 10–11 shifts per month. I sleep between the shifts: we have a bed in the office for taking naps there. Because of the service contracts we now have more staffing on the wards.
>
> (Self-employed nurse, Silesia region)

Nursing work on the basis of self-employment as a one-person business means that, in signing a contract with a hospital, nurses are not under the protection of Polish Labour Law provisions, such as working-time restrictions. Self-employed nurses are obliged to pay their own social security and tax, and usually they need to hire a bookkeeper to do their accounting. The self-employed social security contribution, as for all self-employed, is a low flat-rate, which poses a threat to their future retirement income level. The self-employed are not entitled formally to paid holiday, and their sick leave is less beneficial compared to that of those on full employment contracts.

The self-employed nurses work many more hours than the Labour Law regulations permit, sleeping between work shifts in staff rooms. There are no state regulations that limit their work time or monitor if they take holidays. According to Polish trade union law, the self-employed cannot be organised by trade unions, so that the cost-cutting strategy is, as well, an anti-union strategy. According to the interviews with nurses who work in the Western Pomerania region, the self-employed nurses work 300 hours per month – with a regular full-time job being 160 hours.

Nurses' work quality: work intensification, autonomy and social work environment

The major issue raised by Polish nurses is the rapid decrease in staffing levels on wards. The nurses have attempted to publicise the issue of nurse/patient ratios, which is regulated by official minimum staffing standards on wards. The strategy of cost-cutting came to be focused on nurses, who were assessed as being a too-numerous group of employees. The resulting work intensification for nurses was accompanied by the systematic shortening of time spent at hospital by patients.

> Our colleagues work one nurse per 40 patients; sometimes they are alone on the ward on night shift and the ward is located on two floors. We have been fighting for new regulations because a nurse should not be responsible for 40 patients at the same time. But as it is now, she is fully responsible for them.
>
> (Trade union leader, regional level)

Intensification of work, jointly with a lack of material possibilities for good-quality care, results in high frustration levels among nurses, out of anxiety that they cannot take care of their patients properly. In Poland the cuts in full-time nurse employment and low nurse/patient ratio is resulting in even more dangerous situations for patients, with one nurse often responsible for 20 to 30 patients. In the case of long-term care, one nurse is often alone on a ward on the night shift.

There have been several attempts to regulate the nurse/patient ratio, first in 1999 based on a very complicated algorithm that was hardly practiced. In 2012, after a very long process of consultations with the National Chamber of Nurses and Midwives and the All-Poland Trade Union of Nurses and Midwives, the Ministry of Health proposed a new scheme, which was supposed be based on proposals made by both nurses' organisations. Nonetheless, the Ministry's proposal does not solve the basic problem of determining the minimum number of nurses on wards. The regulation currently in force transfers the responsibility for defining the adequate number of nurses to the head manager of the hospital. Therefore in each case the ratio can be different and is actually dependent on the hospital's budget. What is more, another key aspect emphasised by nurses lies in the norms included in the contracts offered by the National Health Fund. In the case of doctors, the NHF requires a certain obligatory number of different specialists. However there is no required minimum of nurses. Therefore it is up to hospital managers to decide whether they will invest more in technology or in human capital – and, in the latter case, in which occupational groups.

> Our input into the realisation of the contracts with the National Health Fund is really significant. . . . Work with machines should not be worth more than work with a human: what is more important – the skill needed to press a button, or to work with a sick person who is in deep crisis? Here in Poland it is always the technicians who are more important because they work with precious machines. But it is the nurse who supports the patient in getting back to health and life.
>
> (Nurse on a hospital ward, trade unionist)

As nurses often point out, the valuation of job importance in hospitals is crucial, with workers' responsibilities in diagnostic technologies usually being valued higher than nurses' care work. There is consequently relatively more investment in medical technologies than in care technologies that support nurses' work (e.g. man lifts, levers, rotators).

As one of the leaders of the nurses' trade union indicated, in 2015 the All-Poland Trade Union of Nurses and Midwives conducted a survey among working nurses and midwives about their experience of working conditions. The problem of nurse staffing and the ageing of this occupational group is widely acknowledged among nurses. They point out that there is a clear connection between these issues and the excessive intensification of work. Another relatively common problem related to the deficits in staffing and budgets are one-person shifts. Twenty-five per cent of nurses and midwives interviewed had worked such shifts in the last three months, and among them, most had worked such shifts more than once per week. In hospitals, almost one-third of nurses had worked one-person shifts, and more often than once per week. Almost 95% of respondents claim that they cannot fulfil all their work duties on their shifts due to extra tasks that are actually not in their job description, e.g. filling out medical documentation (the parts that should be filled out by doctors) (21%), writing reports of routine medical examinations, writing out doctors' prescriptions (14%), transport of patients between wards (13%) and cleaning (10%). Generally nurses and midwives say they have too much bureaucratic work that keeps them away from patients.

The lack of control over the pace of work and increasing intensification of work results in very low work autonomy. As nurses are overloaded with tasks, their influence over the scope of their responsibilities is much lower. They may also lose control over the procedure of distribution of medicines (formally, one nurse should be responsible for the preparation and distribution of medicines). In reality, due to work overload, one nurse prepares medicines and another who is available administers them to the patients, which creates many opportunities for mistakes.

Nurses are trained to work in teams – with other nurses, technicians, doctors and cleaners. The traditional hierarchical system, still visible in Polish hospitals, frames nurses into a "feminised servant group", and this along with low staffing rates results in the deterioration of the nurses' social work environment because they find it difficult to find social support within the workplace. What is equally important, they do not have time to establish proper contact with patients and their families; for example, they lack time to pass on information to patients about proper diet and healthy lifestyle that are important parts of the process of regaining health.

Strategies and problems of collective action

Nurses and midwives have attempted to counteract the unwelcome changes in the healthcare system by introducing their point of view and experience into the public debate. The most-recognised worker representation organisation is the All-Poland Trade Union of Nurses and Midwives (OZZPiP) with 20 years' of activity history. All workers in the healthcare sector face the dilemma of choosing a form of protest that will not harm patients and yet be visible. The union seeks to form a model of resistance that can publicise members' problems and demands without posing any risk to patients.

The OZZPiP's agenda is focused on a new vision of a healthcare system that provides good-quality care and opposes the "race to the bottom". OZZPiP has tried to take up the "politisation of care" approach (Briskin, 2013) that can alert public opinion about the worsening job quality that in turn affects the quality of care. However, the decision to organise a widely visible protest or strike is usually difficult because nurses want to avoid any harm thereby to patients. Their main rule therefore has been to organise protests, which will have minimal negative impacts on patients and the routine activity of hospitals – quite a paradoxical assumption for a workers' protest in the form of a work-stoppage. In terms of protest, over the last 20 years nurses have organised demonstrations, blockades of streets and border crossings; they have become known for occupying public buildings such as Ministries, the Prime Minister's Office and visitors' gallery in the Polish Parliament, as well as for organising "protest camps" in front of public administration buildings, with the 2007 "White Village" the most prominent among these. They often use the method of the hunger strike, while trying to minimise the risk of any harm to patients.

> 'We always left the head ward nurse, we organised an ER team and on the hour, two of us went through the wards to check the patients and the number of doctors. If anything serious happened, they called us on the phone and we immediately went to the wards.
>
> (Nurse, trade union leader, regional level)

During strikes the work is provisionally distributed among doctors and nursing management. Nurses admit that they have had to strongly restrain themselves from taking care of patients. Therefore during a strike they usually create a strike method that enables them to participate in the protest and take care of their patients at the same time. The nurses gather in one room and refrain from performing work. However in case of emergency they answer the call and take up tasks on their wards. Combining striking and working effectively is the ultimate realisation of the "no harm to patients" doctrine, but it places an additional burden on the striking nurses. It also weakens their bargaining position, as the employer is aware that in case of emergency nurses will work anyway. The strike scheme described also discourages employers from covering any vacancies resulting from a strike by hiring external nurses.

The decentralised model of the healthcare system has in the past hindered coordination of collective protests that could put pressure for change on the Ministry of Health (and not only on the heads of hospitals). This changed in 2015 when trade union leaders managed to convince shop floor leaders to coordinate their activities in order to enter into collective disputes with the hospitals all at the same time. This level of coordination would enable them to launch a general strike of nurses in hospitals all over Poland. Meanwhile the leader of the trade union, in collaboration with the leaders of the National Chamber of Nurses and Midwives, continued talks with the Ministry of Health, negotiating for a stable mechanism of wage increases to be built into the financing system and independent of the individual decisions of hospital managers. In autumn of 2015, one month before parliamentary elections, nurses organised massive demonstrations in Warsaw and threatened a general strike. After intense negotiations, the Ministry signed an agreement called "4 x 400" that guaranteed nurses wage increases to be introduced in four parts over 4 years from a special fund created by the Ministry to be transferred to the National Health Fund. However, the same agreement limits nurses' protest activities – they are prohibited from organising similar coordinated protests at the national level. The wage increase after tax is approximately 50 euros monthly, which was considered a bitter victory. The problem of understaffing of nurses that causes work-related stress and pressure and endangers patients was not addressed.

Discussion

The outcomes of union activity, despite its having shown the crucial relation between changes in job quality and of care quality, are ambiguous. The union has managed to initiate the discourse of job quality, resulting in public awareness of the nurse/patient ratio problem that translates into higher work intensity and in the end prevents the optimal performance of care work. However, union bargaining achievements in terms of wage raises never reached a point that would allow nurses to stop taking extra jobs in healthcare, although in 2015 the first built-in, regular and independently funded wage increases were achieved.

Nor did this development stop the transformation of traditional employment to self-employment of nurses. The Civic Platform Party and Polish People's Party liberal-conservative coalition government presented self-employment in terms of the freedom of choice over the form of contract and prioritised this higher than the risk of the potential harm to the performance of care work. The flexibility discourse prevailed over that of the value of care. The employers' and the government's perspective fragments job quality into its aspects and detaches the issues of contracts and wages from those of work intensification and task discretion. Flexible employment arrangements dressed up as "freedom of choice" are simply more attractive than cost-cutting explanations.

The nurses acted collectively as a trade union in order to show the relation between various job quality aspects and the influence of changes that are deteriorating care quality. The index provided by Muñoz de Bustillo et al. (2009) proves to be instructive in understanding the agenda of the nurses' trade union of showing interlinks between different dimensions that all contribute to job quality – the interrelations between employment quality aspects such as types of contracts, wages and working time and work quality aspects – autonomy and pace of work. The nurses still do not have any control over working time and shifts and therefore hardly enjoy any autonomy or control over the pace of work due to work overload. Their low wages create pressure on them to take on extra work often far beyond the amount of a full-time job. The legal arrangements in the healthcare sector make it possible to use other so-called flexible forms of contracts regulated by civil law (instead of labour law), or as self-employment. The working time regulations of labour law do not apply to these contracts and therefore the extent of working time is set only between the contract parties. The employees' position is thereby significantly weaker since they lose the possibility to influence the extent of flexibility. This disadvantage is made worse by deficiencies in the legal procedures: the fact that contracts with the National Health Fund do not stipulate the minimum staffing of wards with nurses, or regulate the use of non-labour law types of contracts.

With reference to the theoretical model on flexibility and stability by Jonsson (2007), nurses hardly experience flexibility, as their working lives are unstable in terms of forms of contracts, lack of control over working time and lack of autonomy over tasks and pace of work. By using collective action they try to show that the instability is directly connected to the lowering quality of care work – therefore it transfers instability to patients. Although the appearance of the new forms of contracts and work intensification brings savings to hospital budgets, they strongly affect the quality of care work, which may turn out to be more expensive for the healthcare sector in the long run. Instead of being seen as a cost-cutting strategy in hospitals, it should be rather interpreted as a strategy of postponing important costs – individual and social. Low staff levels on wards increase the possibility of mistakes by nurses and in the end is potentially dangerous for the health and life of patients. The same applies to higher work pressures and the lack of control over working time of self-employed nurses. Theoretically they should enjoy more control over time and the pace of work, but in practice they work much more than in a regular full-time job; the chronic fatigue they suffer again increases the risk of serious mistakes.

Conclusion

This chapter aimed to answer what is happening to the job quality of nurses when flexibility solutions are introduced. The response is hardly positive from employee perspective, with employment and work quality being deteriorated. However, the second question that focused on nurses' responses to changes enabled the debate on the relationship between flexibility and job quality to move further. The nurses' trade union shows that changes in job quality such as the lack of control over working time and pace of work of nurses pose a general threat both to the quality of care and to the healthcare units in the long-term perspective. If so, what does it tell about the character of flexibility that was introduced into the healthcare sector? The practices introduced in the domain of forms of contracts and level of employment did not bring more flexibility to the hospitals. Therefore, this is neither positive for employer nor employee – it is a situation of instability for both parties – or simply bogus flexibility. This can be seen when job quality is used as a proxy to understand the complex relations between employers, employees and patients in the healthcare system.

References

Bjørk, I. T., Samdal, G. B., Hansen, B. S., Tørstad, S., Hamilton, G. A. (2007). Job satisfaction in a Norwegian population of nurses: A questionnaire survey. *International Journal of Nursing Studies*, 44, pp. 747–757.

Blomgren, M. (2003). Ordering a profession: Swedish nurses encounter new public management reforms. *Financial Accountability & Management*, 19(1), pp. 45–71.

Briskin, L. (2013). Nurse militancy and strike action. *Workers of the World – International Journal on Strikes and Social Conflicts*, 1(2), pp. 105–134.

Buchan, J. and O'May, F. (2002). The changing hospital workforce in Europe. In McKee, M. and Healy, J. (Eds.) *Hospitals in Changing Europe*. Buckingham and Philadelphia, PA: Open University Press.

Centrum Informacyjne Sluzb Zatrudnienia. (2016). Available at: http://zielonalinia.gov.pl/web/zielona-linia [Accessed 18 July 2016].

Connell, R. (2009). Good teachers on dangerous ground: Towards a new view of teacher quality and professionalism. *Critical Studies in Education*, 50(3), pp. 213–229.

Cranford, C., Vosko, L. and Zukewich, N. (2003). The gender of precarious employment in Canada. *Relations Industrielles/ Industrial Relations*, 58(3).

Denzin, N. and Lincoln, Y. (2011). *The Sage Handbook of Qualitative Research*. Sage Publications.
Domagała, A. (2004). *Wpływ reformy ochrony zdrowia na zmiany w strukturze i warunkach za- trudnienia kadr medycznych*. praca doktorska, IZP Collegium Medicum UJ, Kraków.
Furåker, B., Håkansson, K. and Karlsson, J. Ch. (Eds.) (2007). *Flexibility and Stability in Working Life*. Basingstoke: Palgrave Macmillan.
Gerstel, N. and Clawson, D. (2014, September). Class advantage and the gender divide: Flexibility on the job and at home. *American Journal of Sociology*, 120(2), pp. 395–431.
Glasberg, A., Norberg, A. and Söderberg, A. (2007). Sources of burnout among healthcare employees as perceived by managers. *Journal of Advanced Nursing*, 60(1), pp. 10–19.
Gordon, S. (2006). *Nursing Against the Odds: How Health Care Cost Cutting, Media Stereotypes, and Medical Hubris Undermine Nurses and Patient Care (The Culture and Politics of Health Care Work)*. Ithaca, NY and London: ILR Press.
Gordon, S., Buchanan, J. and Bretherton, T. (2008). *Safety in Numbers: Nurse-to-patient Ratios and the Future of Health Care*. Ithaca, NY and London: ILR Press.
GUS Główny Urząd Statystyczny. (2015). *Statistical Yearbook of the Republic of Poland 2015*. https://stat.gov.pl/en/topics/statistical-yearbooks/statistical-yearbooks/statistical-yearbook-of-the-republic-of-poland-2015,2,10.html
Hardy, J. (2009). *Poland's New Capitalism*. London: Pluto Press.
Hardy, J. and Stenning, A. (2005). Public sector reform and women's work in Poland: 'Working for juice, coffee and cheap cosmetics!'. *Gender, Work and Organization*, 12(6).
Hermann, C. and Flecker, J. (2012). *Privatization of Public Services Impacts for Employment, Working Conditions, and Service Quality*. Routledge.
Hibou, B. (2004). *Privatising the State*. London: C. Hurst and Co.
Hochschild, A. (2012). *The Managed Heart: Commercialization of Human Feeling* (3rd ed.). Berkeley, CA: University of California Press.
Jonsdottir, H., Litchfield, M., Dexheimer Pharris, M. (2004). The relational core of nursing practice as partnership. *Journal of Advanced Nursing*, 47(3), pp. 241–250.
Jonsson, D. (2007). Flexibility, stability and related concepts. In Furåker, B., Håkansson, K. and Karlsson, J. Ch. (Eds.) *Flexibility and Stability in Working Life*. Basingstoke: Palgrave Macmillan.
Kalleberg, A. L. (2011). *Good Jobs, Bad Jobs: The Rise of Polarized and Precarious Employment Systems in the United States, 1970 to 2000s*. New York, NY: Russell Sage Foundation.
Kalleberg, A. L., Reskin, B. F. and Hudson, K. (2000). Bad jobs in America: Standard and nonstandard employment relations and job quality in the United States. *American Sociological Review*, 65, pp. 256–278.
Karlsson, J. Ch. (2007). For whom is flexibility good and bad? An overview. In Furåker, B., Håkansson, K. and Karlsson, J. Ch. (Eds.) *Flexibility and Stability in Working Life*. Basingstoke: Palgrave Macmillan.
Kozek, W. (Eds.) (2011). *Gra o jutro usług publicznych w Polsce*. Warsaw: Wydawnictwa Uniwersytetu Warszawskiego.
Kozek, W. and Radzka, B. (2011). Wpływ liberalizacji i prywatyzacji usług publicznych na zatrudnienie. In Kozek, W. (Eds.) *Gra o jutro usług publicznych w Polsce*. Warsaw: Wydawnictwa Uniwersytetu Warszawskiego.

Kubisa, J. (2014). *Bunt białych czepków. Analiza działalności związkowej pielęgniarek i położnych*. Warsaw: Wydawnictwo Naukowe Scholar.

Muñoz de Bustillo, R. M., Fernández-Macías, E., Antón, J.-I. and Esteve, F. (2011). E pluribus unum? A critical survey of job quality indicators. *Socio-Economic Review*, 9, pp. 447–475.

Muñoz de Bustillo, R. M., Fernández-Macías, E., Esteve, F. and Antón, J. I. (2009). *Indicators of Job Quality in the European Union*. Employment and Social Affairs. European Parliament.

National Chamber of Nurses and Midwives (2015). *Raport Naczelnej Rady Pielęgniarek i Położnych. Zabezpieczenie społeczeństwa polskiego w świadczenia pielęgniarek i położnych*. Warsaw.

Ostrowski, P. (2003). Deregulacja rynkowa w procesie reformy ochrony zdrowia a protesty pielęgniarek i położnych. In Kozek, W. (Ed.) *Instytucjonalizacja stosunków pracy w Polsce*. Warszawa: Wydawnictwo Naukowe Scholar.

Selberg, R. (2013). Nursing in times of neoliberal change: An ethnographic study of nurses' experiences of work intensification. *Nordic Journal of Working Life Studies*, 3(2).

Silverman, D. (2013). *Doing Qualitative Research*. Sage Publications.

Szepelska, A. (2014). Bariery przedsiębiorczości kobiet zamieszkujących obszary wiejskie. *Zeszyty Naukowe Ostrołęckiego Towarzystwa Naukowego*, 28, pp. 290–300.

Trappmann, V. (2011). *Precarious Employment in Poland: A Legacy of Transition or an Effect of European Integration?* Employment and Economy in Central and Eastern Europe, EMECON 1/2011. http://www.emecon.eu/fileadmin/articles/1_2011/emecon%201_2011Trappmann.pdf

Trawińska, M. (2010). Samozatrudnienie – lekiem na całe zło? In Łapniewska, Z. and Czerwińska, A. (Eds.) *Kobiety na zielonej wyspie*. Warszawa: Feminoteka.

Van Thiel, S. and Leeuw, F. L. (2002). The performance paradox in the public sector. *Public Performance & Management Review*, 25(3), pp. 267–281.

Verschuren, R., de Groot, B. and Nossent, S. (1995). *Working Conditions in Hospitals in the European Union*. Dublin: European Foundation for the Improvement of Living and Working Conditions.

Włodarczyk, C. (1999). Reforma opieki zdrowotnej. In Kolarska-Bobińska, L. (Ed.) *Druga fala polskich reform*. Warszawa: Instytut Spraw Publicznych.

Włodarczyk, C. (2010). *Wprowadzenie do polityki zdrowotnej*. Warszawa: Wolters Kluwer.

Wolkowitz, C. (2006). *Bodies at Work*. London: Sage Publications.

Wyderka, M. I. and Niedzielska, T. (2016). Ergonomics in nurse' work. *Pielegniarstwo Polskie*, 2(60).

Zawicki, M. (2002). New Public Management i Public Governance – zarys koncepcji zarządzania publicznego. In Hauser, J. and Kukiełka, M. (Eds.) *Studia z zakresu zarządzania publicznego*. Kraków: Wydawnictwo AE.

7 Job quality dynamics at the call centre

Workers' strategies in Poland[1]

Justyna Zielińska

Introduction

In this study I depict the call centre industry in Poland, precisely in Warsaw, with reference to job quality.[2] The call centre industry was chosen for two reasons. Firstly, it is part of the service industry and the private sector in which the highest percentage of workers in Poland are employed nowadays compared to the industrial, agricultural and public sectors, and as in other countries, the increase in employment in the service sector has coincided with the weakening of the position of the employees towards the employers (e.g. significant increase in unemployment, deregulation of the labour law, substituting contracts of employment with flexible forms of employment). Secondly, the call centre is a relatively new and rapidly growing sector in Poland, characterized by a dynamic growth of job vacancies. The work organization, working conditions and job quality in call centres have been studied in Western social sciences (i.e. Russell, 2008; Scholarios and Taylor, 2011; Stevens, 2014; Woodcock, 2017), but not in Poland, where the management approach analyses prevail. Poland often is presented as a country that is good for investors and according to outsourcingportal.eu, Poland is one of the key outsourcing destinations in Europe (Łukasik, 2016). The data provided by A. T. Kearney Global Services Location Index indicates that Poland is among the 20 most attractive offshoring destinations in the world, and it is the first such country in Europe (Kearney, 2016). What does it mean for workers, in this case for call centre workers?

Job quality is understood as a set of components (i.e. type of contract, wage, working hours, work autonomy, physical working conditions, participation, skills development; see: Kubisa and Mendonca in this volume) which contribute to the level of satisfaction and the level of well-being of workers in the workplace, and in their other spheres of life. Job quality affects not only the level of satisfaction and the well-being of workers, but also the background in which they live (i.e. their families, the local communities). This chapter focuses on the access to skills development, work autonomy and employment quality components (type of contract, working hours, distribution of working hours, wage, social benefits) in call centres.

These three dimensions have emerged as the key ones during research, and they will form the basis for the study of job quality in this chapter.

Previous research, aim of this chapter and theoretical framework

In Western social sciences there is a plethora of lot of research on call centres. This branch has been studied in detail for years, focusing on issues like: classifying call centres, researching the organization of work and working conditions and making comparisons among different types of call centres. Next, the relocation of call centres, segmentation in relation to gender (e.g. call centre as a 'female ghetto', Belt, 2002), the growing relevance of emotional labour, workers' influence on the working and employment conditions and studying work-life balance among the call centre workers have been studied. According to the purpose of this study, I distinguish the three most interesting areas of research, which I will briefly present. These are: classification of call centres according to the work design, organization of work and job quality, and resistance of workers with reference to the working and employment conditions.

Types of call centres

In the public discourse the call centre is often a synonym of a bad quality job. On the other hand, researchers point out that the call centre sector is diverse in terms of the customer service quality and the working and employment conditions (e.g. Taylor, Hyman, Mulvey and Bain, 2002; Taylor and Bain, 2007). Over the years of research, different classifications of call centre types have been proposed, and the most important ones relate to quantity and quality trade-off. As Bob Russell writes, it 'refers to the rival objectives of transacting the maximum number of calls with the lowest staffing ratios while delivering a level of customer service that will not only retain, but will win over, the public' (2008, p. 198). For example, Korczyński (2002) divides call centres into cost efficiency orientation and customer orientation, and Batt and Moynihan (2002) into Taylorized mass-production, professional services and mass customization. The more quantity-oriented call centres are focused on mass processing that results in standardization and routinization of work, intensive work processes (high call volume), relatively short job cycle and rather low job discretion. In turn, in the more quality-oriented call centres there is more attention paid to individualization and more complex professional tasks, longer call handling times (low call volume), higher job discretion and customization of services. Quality and quantity workflows represent a continuum and they can be located according to the combination of different quality/quantity dimensions (e.g. mass customization) (compare: Taylor et al., 2002) and most of the call centre managers attempt to combine quantitative and qualitative objectives. However, according to the international comparative research conducted in 2500 call centres in different parts of the world, 75% of the call centres predominantly serve mass-market customers compared to 25% that serve business customers, and job quality significantly varies between them (Holman, Batt and Holtgrewe, 2007). In mass-market centres workers work in worse conditions, have less autonomy and lower wages than in business-to-business centres (Holman et al., 2007).

Organization of work and job quality

High managerial control and technological surveillance which are the effects of the computerized development of Taylorist management principles (Woodcock, 2017, p. 50) are a common topic in research regarding work organization and job quality in call centres. The managerial focus on high intensification of work and productivity (which is often called effectiveness) results from the pursuit of competitive advantage (Taylor and Bain, 1999, p. 102). Taylor and Bain use the notion 'assembly-line in the head' with reference to the intensification of work in call centres. It means that workers always feel constant pressure and they are aware that once a task is completed, it is immediately followed by another one (Taylor and Bain, 1999, p. 109). Productivity linked with the pressure to achieve targets imposed by the management and new technologies of surveillance facilitate the control over the operational processes for the management. The organization of work is compared to the panopticon where 'workers are subjected to an audible, visual and even electronic 'field of visibility" (Woodcock, 2017, p. 84; see also Fernie and Metcalf, 1997). Thus, it is highlighted that managerial control and technological surveillance are high and they mostly apply to women. According to the Global Call Center Report, 70% of the workforce are female (Holman et al., 2007) and women usually occupy the lower-level positions (see Scholarios and Taylor, 2011). The same research shows that only 12% of the operators work in high- to very high-quality jobs, which is a combination of high job discretion with low performance monitoring. Call centres that operate in countries where the institutional framework is relatively deregulated and more liberal, and where trade unions are rather weak (e.g. UK, USA, Brazil, India, Poland), offer worse quality jobs, higher wage dispersion and higher turnover comparing to coordinated economies (e.g. Germany, France, Denmark, Sweden). Finally, the combination of high managerial control over work and the deregulation of economies influences precarious working and employment conditions.

Resistance of workers

According to Weinkopf (2009), the research on call centres in Germany shows that the existence of collective agreements and work councils have a key impact on pay, working conditions and work organization (see also

Bain and Taylor, 2000). Some researchers focus on studying the forms of resistance in the workplaces where there is no collective representation, and on the prospects of unionization of the call centre workers (e.g. Taylor and Bain, 2001; Mulholland, 2004; Woodcock, 2017). For example Jamie Woodcock attempted to establish a trade union in one call centre in UK, and he was studying and analysing examples of successful unionization in some other call centres (Woodcock, 2017, pp. 118–147).

Aim, assumptions and research questions

The aim of this chapter is to describe and explain job quality for call centre workers and their strategies to improve job quality. As the previous research subsection shows, the call centre sector often tends to have attributes of quantity-oriented workplaces and it may foster the organization of work and job quality which can be detrimental for workers (i.e. high managerial control and intensification of work, low job discretion, precarious working and employment conditions). Moreover, Poland is a semi-peripheral country where the institutional framework is deregulated and liberal, and trade unions are relatively weak. On the other hand, researchers indicate that workers take up acts of resistance against poor-quality jobs in call centres, even if these acts are latent. For example Kate Mulholland observed within the Irish call centre that workers' resistance can take forms of slammin', scammin', smokin' an' leavin', which means: cheating, work avoidance, absence and finally resignation from work (Mulholland, 2004, pp. 709–724). I adopt the assumption that workers are active actors who 'negotiate' their position on the labour market and in the social distribution of goods, and tend to improve their situation (i.e. Tronti, 1964; Cleaver, 2011). Therefore, despite disadvantageous changes on the labour market and the weakening of workers in comparison to capital, workers are not passive recipients of capital's activity and they take actions in order to improve their situation. Hence, the research questions are: how do workers try to influence job quality in their workplaces? What strategies do they undertake to improve their situation?

Strategies: individual and collective

Strategies are defined as a type of agency and a recipe for action which support the realization (rather long-term, but also every day) of goals (compare: Hyman, Scholarios and Baldry, 2005). Choosing strategies depends on the resources available to the people and on the cultural, social and economic context in which they are embedded. First of all, we can distinguish the two most general types of strategies: collective and individual. A prerequisite for using collective strategies is a sense of identification with the group and a sense that people can act and influence the reality – they have a sense of collective agency (i.e. Lister, 2007, p. 159). Collective strategies are especially useful for people who lack bargaining power and have a weaker position on the labour market. Individual strategies indicate actions undertaken by individuals 'separated from each other' and they are especially effective among workers who have a strong bargaining power on the labour market, and thus can successfully negotiate their working conditions with employers.

Exit, voice and loyalty

I use the concept of Albert Hirschman who determined three strategies which reflect the responses of organization members to decrease the quality or the benefit: exit, voice and loyalty (Hirschman, 1970). I apply this typology to the analysis of workers – the management relations – because it synthesizes the peoples' reactions to conflicts in organizations. Exit denotes withdrawal from the relationship, which means leaving the organization (i.e. it can be manifested in frequent job changes or emigration). Voice is a form of critique and an attempt at changes within the organization (i.e. negotiations, complaints, grievances etc.) and loyalty signifies remaining in an organization and accepting the conditions and rules established there. Beverly Silver points out that loyalty can sometimes be forced or fictitious (2009, pp. 243–244). As she writes, forced loyalty is the effect of a weak position of employees in comparison to employers and it can take forms like intentionally refraining from making critical remarks or practicing indirect forms of protest. Finally, these three types of actions do not have to be mutually exclusive options (e.g. it is possible to use exit and voice strategies simultaneously).

Summary of previous research and theoretical framework

As Peter Bain and others write, 'since the mid-1990s, call centres have provided the most dynamic area of growth in white-collar employment internationally' (Bain, Watson, Mulvey, Taylor and Gall, 2002, p. 172) and Jamie Woodcock calls them 'factories of our times' (2017, p. 1) where organization of work is based on 'computerised Taylorism' (2017, pp. 49–52). Although there are different kinds of call centres, the poor-quality job in this sector is a recurring motif. Researchers emphasize that this is an effect of the 'Taylorization of white-collar information job' in the context of the increasingly deregulated national economic orders and the rise in global competition (Russell, 2008, p. 197). It can be clearly seen that technology is not neutral and that the development of new technologies and automation, instead of improving working conditions and job quality, often results in the deterioration of the latter ones. Lack of institutionalized forms of employees' influence of the job quality in many call centres causes workers to take up different forms of resistance, which are often individual and covert. However, these forms could be used in order to create collective forms of resistance and to improve the working conditions and job quality (see Woodcock, 2017).

Development of call centres in Poland

According to the 'call center news' (ccnews.pl), the first call centre company in Poland started operating in the mid-1990s, almost 20 years later than in Western countries. There can be distinguished three main factors explaining the emergence and the development of the call centre sector in Poland after the collapse of communism in 1989. These are: the semi-peripheral position of Poland in the international division of labour, the shift from industry and the public sector to a service industry and the private sector, the opening of borders and the reinforcement of relations with the West and other regions outside the CMEA countries (Council for Mutual Economic Assistance; that is, countries in the Soviet sphere). The first component relates to the divisions of labour which are rooted in the 16th century, whereas the two latter ones relate to the transition of Poland from a state-owned means of production to private-owned means of production (Burawoy, 2000), which are typical for Central Eastern European (CEE) countries.

Semi-peripheral position of Poland

One of the factors that facilitated the development of call centres in Poland is its position in the global division of labour. Poland is often described as a semi-peripheral or dependent market economy (e.g. Nolke and Vliengenthart, 2009; Sommer, 2015). Development in Poland is based on the transfer of technological innovations within transnational companies and the provision of Western capital and Western investments, while competitiveness is raised by cheap labour (Nolke and Vliengenthart, 2009, p. 672; Sommer, 2015, p. 62). It is emphasized that cheap and skilled labour is the main advantage of the Polish economy (Sommer, 2015, p. 62; Orenstein, 2014). For example, the authors of the 'Outsourcing sector in key CEE markets' report identify the factors that attract foreign investors from different sectors to Poland and other CEE countries: the operating costs, in other words, employees' salaries and the rent for office space are lower than in the West which is called a 'competitive advantage'. Next are the access to an educated workforce and improvements in the business environment – improvement in transparency and the ease of business activity and the increasing supply of office space (Żuchniewicz et al., 2014). The aforementioned four factors often make the semi-peripheral countries more attractive business destinations than the core Western countries, where employees have higher salaries, and more attractive than peripheral countries, where there is lower transparency and more difficulties in business activity in some regions.

Transition from state-owned means of production to private-owned means of production

The 1990s were a period of intensive political and economic changes in Poland. Very shortly after the collapse of communism, the new Polish authorities focused on fast democratization and 'rationalization' of economic activity (i.e. Dunn, 2008). The aim of the new governments was to catch up with Western capitalist societies. Likewise in other countries, the shift to service and private sectors was one of the most important factors which enabled the creation and development of call centres. With the development of these sectors, the internal and external markets for different kinds of services provided by call centres appeared. An additional factor for Poland and other CEE countries is the reinforcement of the political and economic relations with Western countries and concentration on entrepreneurship and profit-driven activity. It is worth noting that the process of transformation which took the form of free-market reforms has atomized and weakened the workers' position (i.e. Hardy, 2010; Ost, 2007). For example, the level of unionization has dropped significantly and right now it amounts to 11%. Moreover, the rate of people who have ever had any contact with trade unions has been dropping (CBOS, 2015).

Labour market instability

As in other countries, the idea of flexibility understood as a 'desirable variability' (Jonsson, 2007) in conducting business and in the expected workers' behaviour has also gained importance in Poland. On the one hand, what is emphasized is the importance of entrepreneurship, rationality, creativity and fast adaptation to changes in order to gain a competitive advantage in conducting business, and on the other hand, what is stressed is the importance of these factors for workers. An important issue in the context of the Polish labour market is the deregulation of contracts concluded between employers and employees. As I will present, the deregulation of contracts increases employers' flexibility, but it results in workers' instability at the same time (see Jonsson, 2007).

From permanent contracts to 'junk contracts'

Among the EU countries, Poland has the highest proportion of employees with temporary contracts (27,9%, Eurostat, 2016). According to Polish law, the employer should sign a 'contract of employment' with each employee who performs work under supervision, in place and time indicated by the employer – for an unspecified period or a specified period. Such a contract provides workers safety of work and employment such as: specified notice period in the event of dismissal, paying social contributions, insurance, the right to paid holiday leave, sick leave, parental leave and obtaining statutory minimal wage. It also determines the amount of working time and breaks at work. The Labour Code relies on the assumption that the position of employees is weaker in relation to the employers and hence the Labour Code is there to safeguard the employees' rights. However, the Labour Code has been changed many times since the transformation; the regulations are less beneficial now, and hence protect workers to a lesser extent. Additionally, employers have been more and more often substituting contracts of employment by temporary contracts, which are very often called 'junk contracts' in the public discourse. Most of these contracts are based on the Civil Code, which is predicated on the assumption that employers and employees have the same position, and they determine the arbitrary conditions of work between themselves. Therefore, these contracts, compared to the contracts of employment, do not obey the laws that would protect employees. The main instability aspects present in the temporary contracts based on the Civil Code are: the ease of employee dismissal, the lack of maximum working time and the lack of minimum wage.[3] These contracts allow the employers to reduce their costs, which simultaneously means reducing the profits of the employees. Apart from the lack of the minimum wage, employees also do not obtain paid holidays, paid sick leave and parental leave, additional payment for overtime, work at night, etc. Finally, workers who have had temporary contracts based on the Civil Code were not allowed to join trade unions until 2015.

Instability of employment in call centres

There is a lack of statistical data about the types of contracts among the call centre workers in Poland. Nevertheless, it can be assumed that the percentage of operators who obtain temporary contracts based on Civil Law can be significant due to weak or non-existent structural, associational and discursive powers within this group of workers (Wright, 2000; Silver, 2009). Most of call centre operators are not sought for their specialist knowledge and scarce skills (i.e. Holman et al., 2007), so they have rather weak position on the labour market (lack of structural power). Next, lack of trade unions or other collective representatives (associational power) in call centres may facilitate lowering the employment standards by employers. I also assume that widespread neoliberal individualist discourse and lack of workers' representatives in call centres may result in the lack the awareness of workers' common interests and the belief that one can influence the improvement of labour relations (discursive power).

Presentation of call centre industry in Poland

The call centre sector in Poland (as well as in other Central East Europe countries) has been rapidly developing – in terms of the call centre number, revenue and job vacancies – since the mid-1990s (i.e. Datamonitor, 2002; Małachowski and Małachowski, 2015; Newseria Biznes, 2016).

Size of call centres

The research of the Polish Marketing Association indicates that call centres in Poland deliver services for companies both in Poland and all over the world (SMB, 2015). In terms of the number of call centres in Poland, small centres that employ up to nine people prevail (Bera, 2012). On the other hand, in terms of the number of employees, large call centres that engage at least 50 to over 1000 people predominate – they employ 66% of all operators in Poland (Małachowski and Małachowski, 2015).

In-house centres vs. subcontractors and localization

Although there are companies which have their own call centres (in-house centres), at the same time the number of companies which specialize in delivering call and contact centre services have been growing significantly: from 48 in 2004 to 1930 in 2012 (Bera, 2012). There are estimates which indicate that most call centre services will be outsourced – from 20% at the beginning of this decade to 80% at its end (Małachowski and Małachowski, 2015). Almost half of the major operating locations are situated in Warsaw and also in other big cities. However, there are plans to relocate the call centres offices to smaller cities and towns in order to reduce office space and salaries costs (SMB, 2015, pp. 18–21).

Number of employees

The Polish Marketing Association estimated the number of job posts in the call centre sector in Poland to have been 24,548 in 2015. According to this association, it was 12% higher than in 2014, and it is likely to increase in the next years. However, it is often noted that the total number of job vacancies is much higher than provided by the Polish Marketing Association, and it amounts 200,000–250,000 employees (i.e. Małachowski and Małachowski, 2015; ccnews, 2017).

Salaries

Unfortunately, there is a lack of studies regarding wages and working conditions in this sector. It is known that the call centre is a segmented sector. According to Sedlak&Sedlak, the highest salaries are among the workers of customer service departments in IT, services for business, heavy engineering, energy production, district heating, media and banking (Bancerz, 2016). However, Sedlak&Sedlak (2016) points out that the average hourly wage for a telephone consultant is 10,35 PLN gross (around 2,36 EUR gross). Other research also conducted online by Sedlak&Sedlak (2015) indicates that the median of monthly earnings among operators in call centres in Poland is 2659 PLN gross (around 605 EUR gross).[4]

Methodology

The study is based on two qualitative research projects conducted in call centres (2013–2016) in Warsaw. Firstly, 11 individual in-depth interviews (with narrative elements) were conducted with call centre workers who work in different call centre companies.[5] Next, another research was carried out which consisted of two participatory observations in two different companies which deliver call centre services, and five individual in-depth interviews (semi-narrative) with operators who have worked in different call centres for at least six months.[6]

Participatory observations

Two researchers (Justyna Zielińska and Antoni Rokicki from the Institute of Sociology at University of Warsaw) worked as telephone consultants in two big (in terms of their revenue) in-house companies in Warsaw. Each fieldwork lasted from 5 to 7 weeks. The first company operates in the finance sector in Poland and in some other CEE countries. It is a Polish company, which employs more than 23,000 employees and it has its own call centres where over 2000 people work (in Poland). The second one is an international market research company which employs over 13,000 workers worldwide. It also has its own call centre in Poland, where over 200 operators work. These call centres operate in non-specialized segments, where there is low demand for highly specialist knowledge and skills as far as call centre operators are concerned, which means that it is easy to start working as an operator in these companies.

Profile of the interviewees

The interviewed call centre workers work as operators and some of them as low-level management (supervisors, trainers). They belong to the 'young' category of employees (20–34); they often study and women predominate among the interlocutors (12 women and four men). These attributes of the research group reflect employment in the call centres, where the sector is young and feminized (i.e. Holman et al., 2007; Woodcock, 2017, p. 162). It can be clearly seen that some of the interviewees migrated from other Polish cities and towns to Warsaw, which is the biggest city and labour market in Poland, also in terms of educational and professional career opportunities (see i.e. Mroczkowska, forthcoming). For the youngest interlocutors the work in the call centre is often their first job experience.

Use of the research material

In this chapter the aforementioned research material is used in order to follow the chosen dimensions of job quality in the studied call centres and to analyse how workers try to influence job quality in their workplaces. However, it is important to highlight that this research is an exploratory study and the collected data do not allow for a generalization of the results on the whole call centre sector in Warsaw or in Poland.

Job quality in call centres

In this subsection I present how the organization of work in the examined call centres influences the work autonomy, access to skills development and employment quality. Firstly, I explain my choice of the aforementioned job quality dimensions and consider the types of call centres where the research was conducted. Then, I analyse the impact of the work organization on the job quality for call centre workers.

Access to skills development, work autonomy and employment

I focus here on the access to skills development, work autonomy and employment quality components (type of contract, working hours, distribution of working hours, wages, social benefits) in call centres. These three aspects of job quality were chosen due to particular research findings. During the research on the call centre workers, there were two key expressions that the interviewees kept saying when they told their story about the work and other spheres of their lives. These are 'development' and 'independence' and they represent important values for interviewed call centre workers. Development has a twofold meaning for them: primarily, it denotes gathering knowledge and experience, which will be reflected as assets to workers' curriculum vitae. Thus, this is market-oriented development with the focus on expanding the professional career. Secondly, development means gathering knowledge and experience, i.e. doing something interesting, related to individual interests, without calculating whether and how it could be useful in relation to the professional career. Independence signifies autonomy, i.e. self-reliance and self-sufficiency in terms of financial resources, time and organizational resources (e.g. taking care of the children). Skills development and work autonomy, as well as employment quality, seem to reflect the values that are important for the interviewed call centre workers.

Types of call centres

The interviewees (and researchers) work(ed) as operators and some of them as low-level management in different kinds of call centres: outbound and inbound, in-house and in call centres, which operate as subcontractors. They work in research agencies, as telemarketers and in customer service, where in the latter case the duties involve answering phone calls from clients and giving them information, resolving their problems concerning a product or service etc. In relation to the working conditions, the research was conducted in call centres that are more quantity oriented, which influences the job quality.

Work autonomy

In the researched call centres one can distinguish the same organizational attributes as in other countries: high intensification of work, standardization and managing by control and stress. High intensification of work was a leitmotif which regularly occurred in the interviews. The interviewees kept talking about the pressure exerted by their supervisors in order to work faster and more effectively, for example to sell as many products and services as possible in the shortest time. The same was observed during participatory observations. A popular tactic is introducing competition among the co-workers by disclosing information at the workplace about the so-called effectiveness (that is productivity) of particular workers. This involves sharing information about the people who have the highest effectiveness (they can obtain some benefits) as well as information about the people who have the lowest effectiveness (they can be punished).

> They [supervisors – J.Z.] take you to talk to you, they say what you do wrong, they push you. They say: 'push, push, you have to sell until the end of the day, there have to be 3 sales or it would be bad'.
>
> (Interview no 6, male, 22)

> I was thinking about my effectiveness all day. I did 4 or 5 surveys/questionnaires on Tuesday, it gave me green colour [it means that effectiveness was assessed as high – J.Z.]. However, I was afraid that if today I don't keep up the high level [of effectiveness – J.Z.] they [management – J.Z.] would not take me on the job next week.
>
> (Participatory observation no 2)

Work is highly standardized and the process of work is put under strict control in terms of skill utilization and task discretion. The workers have a clear delineation of how to behave towards clients and what formulas they have to use during contact with them. Phone calls are made automatically, which generally means that the time between successive calls and conversations with clients is reduced to the minimum. Conversations with clients are recorded and some of them are evaluated by the management. Moreover, whenever workers want to take a break, for example go to the bathroom, they have to ask for permission.

> Work your buns off, work your buns off, all the time. Pick the phone calls, pick the phone calls, because people [clients – J.Z.] are waiting, there is a line of people. After 4 hours [of work – J.Z.] one was allowed to take a break. In my opinion it is a real massacre, such a

> labour camp. . . . There was a horrible rigour placed on everything, you couldn't exceed your break, you couldn't be late, because it was subtracted from your premium. So, massacre. Thus, one didn't want to go to this work.
>
> (Interview no 16, female, 22)

The high intensification of work, standardization and managing by constant control and stress contribute to the low or even the lack of work autonomy by workers. The style of management is designed in such a way so as to deprive the workers of control over the work they perform.

Access to skills development

The management does not require specific education, knowledge or skills from the new operators. On the other hand, the call centre operators do not have access to skills development. The only trainings they have are induction trainings and meetings which concern the evaluation of their performance – effectiveness at work. The interviewees mentioned that they have a feeling that they do not learn and do not gain new skills at work – especially skills which could influence their professional career and improve their situation on the labour market. As a result, the only skills they think they have acquired are those related to emotional labour, i.e. concerning the contact with clients.

> You have to be very firm at this work. You can't let client ensnare you. I thought I would not know how to do this, and right now I'm one of the best.
>
> (Interview no 7, female, 34)

The only exception are workers who work with foreign language clients, and workers who have been promoted in their companies. The first group can practice foreign languages everyday and the second one – the low-level management are the only ones who are offered some trainings (e.g. within the area of employee or rather 'human resources' management).

Employment quality: type of contract and social benefits

The interlocutors usually obtain temporary contracts based on the Civil Code (researchers who worked in the call centres were offered the same contracts). The people who have contracts based on the Labour Code usually have been working in one company for a few years, their work is more specialized or they have been promoted to low-level managers. As I wrote in the labour market instability subsection, temporary contracts based on the Civil Code deprive workers of social benefits, like paid holidays, paid sick leave and parental leave, additional payment for overtime etc. The only ones who get social benefits are the workers who have contracts based on the Labour Code, who are mostly managers.

Distribution of working hours

The interlocutors' working time in the call centres varies significantly – some of them work full-time – it means 160 hours per month, some work part-time and others work irregularly. It sometimes happens that there is no work for all operators in certain periods and work is canceled day by day and workers are sent home without payment. Low-level managers are those who have to mostly adapt their time to the requirements of the companies in which they work and their working time often exceeds 160 hours per month.

Working hours

As the study shows, although workers can determine the distribution of their working hours, they must take into account that there are employers who do not pay for breaks at work or who even do not pay for breaks between consecutive telephone connections. In turn, an employee who has no paid breaks at work has to work more if they want to earn the same amount of money as if they had paid breaks.

> There was such an effective working time. Ineffective was for example a break. They didn't pay me for breaks. . . . And when I was doing nothing, it means I finished telephone conversation [with a client – J.Z.] and I for example was doing nothing for 2 minutes, it was also subtracted [from salary – J.Z.].
>
> (Interview no 4, female, 22)

Moreover, the management try to motivate workers to work more, and different hourly rates – depending on the number of hours worked in a given month – are often introduced. When a person works fewer hours than the management determines, they receive a lower hourly rate, and when they work as many hours or more than was set, they obtain a higher hourly rate.

Wages

A declared hourly rate among the interlocutors amounted from 10 PLN gross (about 2,25 EUR) to 14 PLN gross (3,16 EUR). These hourly rates mean that when one works full-time they receive a salary between 1600 and 2240 PLN gross (about 361–505 EUR) per month and these wages oscillate around the minimum wage in Poland. The level of salary depends on the working time, but also on the effectiveness – for high effectiveness a worker can receive additional money and for low – a punishment. The system of calculating a commission is not clear for the interviewees, and they do not know how much money they will receive exactly after every month of work.

Summary

It is hard to say that job quality in the researched call centres enhances the realization of the values that are important for the workers (namely development and autonomy). On the contrary, the workers are in fact treated as 'expendable', with the management not investing in workers' professional development, and the lack of workers' autonomy coincides with their exploitation. The management have broad freedom in setting up the working and employment conditions and they can quite freely redefine salaries, employment, working time – and try to extend it to the maximum. It can be clearly seen that the management treat the contracts based on the Labour Code as a form of an award or a privilege that is available for people who have gotten promoted or have been working in one company for a long time.

Workers' strategies regarding job quality in call centres

The aim of this subsection is to analyse how the call centre workers try to influence job quality in their workplaces and what strategies they undertake to improve their situation. It starts from examining the perception of workers regarding job quality in call centres. Then I analyse the strategies which the call centre workers undertake in their workplaces using Albert Hirschman's categories (loyalty, exit, voice).

Perception of job quality in call centres

Bad job quality within the aforementioned dimensions makes the workers perceive call centres as a non-progressive, stressful and low-paid job. Jamie Woodcock who names this sector factories of our times, combines call centres more with 'chain work' than with 'brain work' (2017, p. 56). Referring to F. Berardi, Woodcock writes that

> whereas 'brain workers' are harnessed for their 'communication, invention and creation', the 'chain workers' are those 'people who sit at their terminals in front of a screen, repeating every day the same operation a thousand times', and 'relate to their labour in a way similar to industrial workers.
> (Woodcock, 2017, p. 56)

If we look at how flexibility affects job quality, it turns out that temporary contracts based on the Civil Code cause instability of employment and they deprive workers of their labour rights. Moreover, the organization of work in call centres causes workers to lack a sense of control over their work and salaries and it hinders workers to plan in a long-term perspective. These characteristics cause call centres to be regarded by the interviewees and their social background as a job which is not right for serious and adult people, as a junk job (i.e. Kozek,

Kubisa and Ostrowski, 2005). It is perceived as a job suitable for young people – students, for whom it can be the first job experience and a source of some extra money (compare Klein, 2004, pp. 249–276). If call centres are valued so low, it is worth answering why people take up work there. As the research shows, the first reason was its working time flexibility, which means the possibility of tailoring work in the call centre to other duties. Secondly, working as an operator is a job which is easy to get and indeed young people treat the availability of those jobs as an occasion for gaining the first job experience.

Agency and strategies of workers at the workplace

As I will show next, workers do not do much to influence job quality in their workplaces. It is mainly the organization of work in call centres that deprives workers of influence. Management sets up rules and has significant power in their hands, as some researchers write – management is the 'frontier of control' (i.e. Hyman, 1975, p. 26). Secondly, high turnover is an effect of treating this job as 'temporary' by workers. Therefore, the most commonly used strategy by them is exit (Hirschman, 1995, pp. 27–35). As long as it is worthwhile for workers, they use a loyalty strategy, but this is rather forced or fictious loyalty (Silver, 2009, pp. 243–244). In turn, voice is the least frequently used strategy. All these strategies are individual and collective strategies are not practiced.

Exit

Bad job quality often results in high staff turnover – that is, an exit strategy. The conviction that this work is non-developmental and non-prestigious strengthens this strategy. High turnover in the call centre is characteristic for this sector, especially in countries, like Poland, where the institutional framework is deregulated and more liberal, and where trade unions are rather weak (Holman et al., 2007). Jamie Woodcock remarks that

> quitting the job as a form of unorganised resistance – and on that is not that different from striking – is key to understanding that call centres are not workplaces devoid of any form of struggle, despite their low levels of unionisation and officially sanctioned industrial action.
>
> (2017, p. 111)

However, it is worth pointing out that researched call centre workers often exchange jobs within the same sector or similar sectors, where the job quality is comparable.

Loyalty

Albert Hirschman writes that loyalty is the strategy that is chosen in the face of crisis when people are attached to an organization (Hirschman, 1995, pp. 77–78). As we could see in the previous subsection, the call centre management does not do much to retain their workers, and those who do stay at work are those who have to, for example people who cannot find another job, people who need to have a flexible distribution of working hours (for example single mothers) etc. Thus, one can ascertain that the loyalty strategy is fictitious or forced and eventually it will be converted into the exit strategy. For example, students are a group that plan to work in call centres until they finish their education, and in their everyday life they focus on the studies. Here they place their agency – they 'invest' in their future professional career. Nonetheless, what is visible is their consternation concerning the studies. They know that graduating does not guarantee them a good position on the labour market. This situation is connected with the devaluation of university diplomas in Poland. I claim that it relates to the semi-peripheral position of the Polish economy, where there is no vast need for workers with higher education. On the contrary, there is a vast need for lower-skilled workers. For example, there are ideas of creating particular classes at secondary schools in Poland where students would learn how to perform the profession of call centre operator (i.e. Turlej, 2016), and the Polish Ministry of Development positively commented on this proposal.

Voice

The voice strategy is not often used. Those ones who use voice belong to the older group of the researched workers or have been working in one workplace for a long time and have higher bargaining power there. These workers usually focus on making attempts in order to negotiate with the management salary raises. They take up individual attempts to improve the job quality in their workplaces and the collective voice strategy is not practised. There is a lack of institutionalized channels in the call centres which could facilitate the articulation of the workers' interests and the fight for improving job quality. There are no trade unions or other workers' representatives. Moreover, the researched workers have never had any contact with trade unions in their lives and they do not think about trade unions as potential partners who could support them. Next, treating work in instrumental and temporal categories also prevents workers from influencing job quality in call centres. When work is regarded as temporary, the effort of involvement ceases to be sensible. If a worker encounters difficulties, they will rather choose the exit strategy.

Conclusion

In this chapter I was following the results of an exploratory research focusing on job quality and on the strategies of workers in the call centres in Warsaw, in Poland. As the research shows, job quality is rather poor and call centre workers do not have much opportunity for skills development or work autonomy, and they often are deprived of worker's rights and have a low salary. Moreover, workers do not do much to influence job quality in their workplaces, mostly because management is the 'frontier of control', and the most commonly used strategy is exit.

The workers are subjected to strict control, their workers' rights are violated and actually they often experience exploitation. Although the work in call centres has at least one attribute of the employee-driven flexibility (a wide range of freedom regarding the distribution of working hours in case of the operators), the employer-driven flexibility prevails. Next, Taylorization of production, depriving workers of control over their work and the separation of conception from execution results in deskilling.

Job quality in the studied call centres causes workers to treat their work in instrumental and temporal categories, and the loyalty strategy sooner or later becomes the exit strategy. All workers' strategies are individual, young workers do not know the patterns of collective actions and perhaps to some degree they associate cooperation with dependence, which they do not value. Young workers seem to accept the capitalist values, such as entrepreneurship, individualism and they often think of themselves in market terms. Neoliberalism can be defined as a lack of collective awareness without which workers hardly can improve their situation, especially in sectors like the call centre.

What would have to happen to invert the exit strategy into the voice strategy? Certainly the collective voice is needed, creating strong workers' organizations at workplaces which would articulate the workers' interests and defend their rights. Perhaps it is a good moment for introducing collective representation in call centres, because there are signals that call centres are starting to lack workers (GazetaPraca.pl, 2017), thus workers may have more workplace bargaining power now (Wright, 2000; Silver, 2009).

Notes

1 This chapter was written with funding from the National Science Centre, Poland. Project registration number: 2016/20/T/HS6/00406.
2 Although I use here the term call centre industry and call centre sector, it is worth highlighting that call centres have emerged across different kinds of industries, rather than as an industry itself (Woodcock, 2017, p. 16). What distinguishes call centres is the particular organization of work, not being a sector of the economy itself.
3 There are two widespread temporary contracts based on the Civil Code: contract of mandate and contract for a specified task. Since January 2017 the minimum wage in relation to the contract of mandate has been introduced.
4 At the end of 2014 the median of salaries in Poland amounted to 794 Euro gross per month (GUS, 2015).
5 This research was conducted within the framework of a seminar for students led in the Institute of Sociology, University of Warsaw by Wiesława Kozek and Marianna Zieleńska.
6 This research was conducted within the framework of a research grant for young researchers (DSM, no.107700) led by Justyna Zielińska.

References

Bain, P. and Taylor, P. (2000). Entrapped by the 'electronic panopticon'? Worker resistance in the call centre. *New Technology, Work and Employment*, 15(1), pp. 2–18.
Bain, P., Watson, A., Mulvey, G., Taylor, P. and Gall, G. (2002). Taylorism, targets and the pursuit of quantity and quality by call centre management. *New Technology, Work and Employment*, 17(3), pp. 170–185.
Bancerz, K. (2016). Ile zarabiamy w obsłudze klienta. *Ccnews* [online]. Available at: http://ccnews.pl/2016/03/01/ile-zarabiamy-w-obsludze-klienta/ [Accessed 14 April 2016].
Batt, R. and Moynihan, L. (2002). The viability of alternative call center production models. *Human Resource Management Journal*, 12(4), pp. 14–34.
Belt, V. (2002). A female ghetto? Women's careers in call centres. *Human Resource Management Journal*, 12(4), pp. 51–66.
Bera, A. (2012). Aktualna sytuacja na rynku pracy w branży call/contact center. *Rynek – Społeczeństwo – Kultura*, 3/2012, pp. 32–38.
Burawoy, M. (2000). Marxism after communism. *Theory and Society*, 29, pp. 151–174.
CBOS. (2015). *Opinie o związkach zawodowych i protestach górników*. Komunikat z badań CBOS. Centrum Badań Opinii Społecznej. Available at: www.cbos.pl/SPISKOM.POL/2015/K_066_15.PDF [Accessed 28 April 2016].
ccnews. (2017). *Oda do telemarketera* [online]. Available at: http://ccnews.pl/2017/02/06/oda-do-telemarketera/utm_source=ccnews.pl&utm_campaign=855f92d45anewsletter_2017_02_07&utm_medium=email&utm_term=0_ca3296545a-855f92d45a-327127013 [Accessed 7 February 2017].
Cleaver, H. (2011). *Polityczne czytanie Kapitału*. Poznań: Oficyna Wydalnicza Bractwa Trojka.
Datamonitor. (2002). *Poland: Call Centres*. Industry Profile.
Dunn, E. (2008). *Prywatyzując Polskę. O bobofrutach, wielkim biznesie i restrukturyzacji pracy*. Warszawa: Wydawnictwo Krytyki Politycznej.
Eurostat. (2016). *Employment Statistics* [online]. Available at: http://ec.europa.eu/eurostat/statistics-explained/index.php/Employment_statistics [Accessed 20 December 2016].
Fernie, S. and Metcalf, D. (1997). *(Not)Hanging on the Telephone Payment Systems in the New Sweatshops*. London: Centre for Economic Performance, London School of Economics.
GazetaPraca.pl. (2017). *Na rynku brakuje telemarketerów. Na słuchawce zarobisz nawet 15 tys. zł.* [online]. Available at: http://gazetapraca.pl/gazetapraca/7,90438,21252610,na-rynku-brakuje-telemarketerow-na-sluchawce-zarobisz-nawet.html [Accessed 15 March 2017].
GUS. (2015). *Struktura wynagrodzeń według zawodów w październiku 2014 r.* [online]. Available at: https://stat.gov.pl/obszary-tematyczne/rynek-pracy/pracujacy-zatrudnieni-wynagrodzenia-koszty-pracy/struktura-wynagrodzen-wedlug-zawodow-w-pazdzierniku-2014-r-,5,4.html [Accessed 21 December 2016].
Hardy, J. (2010). *Nowy polski kapitalizm*. Warszawa: Instytut Wydawniczy Książka i Prasa.
Hirschman, A. (1970). *Exit, Voice and Loyalty: Responses to Decline in Firms, Organizations and States*. Cambridge, MA: Harvard University Press.
Hirschman, A. (1995). *Lojalność, krytyka, rozstanie. Reakcje na kryzys państwa, organizacji i przedsiębiorstwa*. Kraków: Wydawnictwo Znak.

Holman, D., Batt, R. and Holtgrewe, U. (2007). *The Global Call Centre Report. International Perspectives on Management and Employment (Executive Summary)*[pdf]. Ithaca, NY. Available at: http://digitalcommons.ilr.cornell.edu/cgi/viewcontent.cgi?article=1011&context=reports [Accessed 11 March 2016].

Hyman, J., Scholarios, D. and Baldry, Ch. (2005). Getting on or getting by? Employee flexibility and coping strategies for home and work. *Work, Employment & Society*, 19(4), pp. 705–725.

Hyman, R. (1975). *Industrial Relations: A Marxist Introduction*. London: Palgrave Macmillan.

Jonsson, D. (2007). Flexibility, stability and related concepts. In Furåker, B., Håkansson, K. and Karlsson, J. Ch. (Eds.) *Flexibility and Stability in Working Life*. London: Palgrave Macmillan, pp. 30–41.

Kearney, A. T. (2016). *Digital Transformation. On the Eve of Disruption. 2016 A.T. Kearney Global Services Location Index* [online]. Available at: www.atkearney.com/digital-transformation/article?/a/2016-global-services-location-index- [Accessed 7 January 2017].

Klein, N. (2004). *No Logo*. Izabelin: Świat Literacki.

Korczyński, M. (2002). *Human Resource Management in Service Work*. Basingstoke: Palgrave Macmillan.

Kozek, W., Kubisa, J. and Ostrowski, P. (2005). Bliżej junk job niż working poor. Nisko kwalifikowana nisko płatna praca w usługach w Polsce. *Polityka Społeczna*, 10/2005, pp. 1–8.

Lister, R. (2007). *Bieda*. Warszawa: Wydawnictwo Sic!

Łukasik, M. (2016). *Polish Market Call Centre Forecast*. Outsourcing Portal [online]. Available at: www.outsourcingportal.eu/en/polish-market-call-center-forecast [Accessed 8 February 2017].

Małachowski, A. and Małachowski, J. (2015). Outsourcing call centre w działalności przedsiębiorstwa. *Zeszyty Naukowe Uniwersytetu Szczecińskiego. Ekonomiczne Problemy Usług*, 117, pp. 241–255.

Mroczkowska, J. (forthcoming). Podlaski 'Słoik' – mobilna grupa społeczna i mobilne medium tożsamości lokalnej. *Studia Socjologiczne* [in print].

Mulholland, K. (2004). Workplace resistance in an Irish call centre: Slammin', scammin', smokin', an' leavin'. *Work, Employment & Society*, 18(4), pp. 709–724.

Newseria Biznes. (2016). *Polska jednym z liderów branży call contact center. Firmy z branży świadczą coraz bardziej wyspecjalizowane usługi* [online]. Available at: www.biznes.newseria.pl/news/polska-jednym-z-liderow,p1164683495 [Accessed 11 February 2017].

Nolke, A. and Vliengenthart, A. (2009). Enlarging the varieties of capitalism: the emergence of dependent market economies in East Central Europe. *World Politics*, 61(4), pp. 670–702.

Orenstein, M. A. (2014). Six markets to watch: Poland. From tragedy to triumph. *Foreign Affairs* [online]. Available at: www.foreignaffairs.com/articles/140336/mitchell-a-orenstein/six-markets-to-watch-poland [Accessed 31 November 2015].

Ost, D. (2007). *Klęska "Solidarności". Gniew i polityka w postkomunistycznej Europie*. Warszawa: Warszawskie Wydawnictwo Literackie MUZA SA.

Polskie Stowarzyszenie Marketingu SMB. (2015). *Badanie branży outsourcing call/contact center. Edycja lipiec-sierpień 2015 roku*. Available at: www.smb.pl/badania_smb [Accessed 12 January 2016].

Russell, B. (2008). Call centres: A decade of research. *International Journal of Management Reviews*, 10(3), pp. 195–219.

Scholarios, D. and Taylor, P. (2011). Beneath the glass ceiling: Explaining gendered role segmentation in call centres. *Human Relations*, 64(10), pp. 1291–1319.

Sedlak&Sedlak. (2015). *Moja płaca. Raport premium dla stanowiska konsultant call centre* [pdf]. Available at: https://wynagrodzenia.pl/moja-placa/ile-zarabia-konsultant-call-center [Accessed 10 December 2015].

Sedlak&Sedlak. (2016). *Ile kosztuje koszyk wielkanocny w 2016?* wynagordzenia.pl [online]. Available at: http://wynagrodzenia.pl/dla_mediow_1.php/wpis.456-ile-kosztuje-koszyk-wielkanocny-w-2016-roku [Accessed 5 April 2016].

Silver, B. J. (2009). *Globalny proletariat. Ruchy pracownicze i globalizacja po 1870 r.* Warszawa: Instytut Wydawniczy Książka i Prasa.

Sommer, M. (2015). Unia solidarna, liberalna czy . . . żadna (interview with T. G. Grosse). *Nowy Obywatel*, 17, pp. 54–63.

Stevens, A. (2014). *Call Centres and the Global Division of Labor: A Political Economy of Post-Industrial Employment and Union Organizing*. New York, NY: Routledge.

Taylor, P. and Bain, P. (1999). 'An assembly line in the head': Work and employee relations in the call centre. *Industrial Relations Journal*, 30(2), pp. 101–117.

Taylor, P. and Bain, P. (2001). Trade unions workers' rights and the frontier of control in UK call centres. *Economic and Industrial Democracy*, 22(1), pp. 39–66.

Taylor, P. and Bain, P. (2007). Reflections on the call centre: A reply to Glucksmann. *Work, Employment & Society*, 21(2), pp. 349–362.

Taylor, P., Hyman, J., Mulvey, G. and Bain, P. (2002). Work organization, control and the experience of work in call centres. *Work, Employment & Society*, 16(1), pp. 133–150.

Tronti, M. (1964). *Lenin in England*. Available at: www.marxists.org/reference/subject/philosophy/works/it/tronti.htm [Accessed 18 February 2017].

Turlej, E. (2016). *Ministerstwo Rozwoju chce klas o profilu call center. Po co uczniom nauka obsługi klientów?* Polityka [online]. Available at: www.polityka.pl/tygodnikpolityka/spoleczenstwo/1684782,1,ministerstwo-rozwoju-chce-klas-o-profilu-call-center-po-co-uczniom-nauka-obslugi-klientow.read [Accessed 30 March 2017].

Weinkopf, C. (2009). Job quality in call centres in Germany. *International Labour Review*, 148(4), pp. 395–411.

Woodcock, J. (2017). *Working the Phones: Control and Resistance in Call Centres*. London: Pluto Press.

Wright, E. O. (2000). Working-class power, capitalist-class interests, and class compromise. *American Journal of Sociology*, 105(4), pp. 957–1002.

Żuchniewicz, M., Colquhoun, A., Wykrota, K., Przesmycka, B., Cihova, K., Boucek, V., Simonyi, B. and Cojocoru, M. (2014). *Outsourcing Sector in Key CEE Markets*. outsourcingportal.eu [online]. Available at: www.outsourcingportal.eu/pl/userfiles/image/raporty/2014/12/17/Outsourcing_sector_in_key_CEE_markets.pdf [Accessed 28 November 2016].

8 Voice and its implications for employment quality in temporary agency work in Sweden and Belgium

Kristina Håkansson, Valeria Pulignano, Tommy Isidorsson and Nadja Doerflinger

Introduction

This edited volume discusses job quality in the era of flexibility. Temporary agency work (TAW) can be seen as the exponent of flexibility in today's working life. It provides flexibility for employers while offering some stability to the agency workers through a sequence of different (short-term) assignments, not necessarily with the same client organization. Current research has critically shed light on the insecurity characterizing temporary agency work, which is considered as likely to entrap individuals in precarious work conditions (Standing, 2011; Kalleberg, 2009; Håkansson, Isidorsson and Kantelius, 2012; Håkansson and Isidorsson, 2015). It is argued that structural contexts and social policy differences across, and within, diverse national institutional settings contribute to the insecurity of agency workers by differentiating social policy and benefits (e.g. pensions, childcare, sickness, unemployment) as well as working conditions, wages and types of employment contracts between agency and regular workforces (Burroni and Carrieri, 2011; Emmenegger, Häusermann and Palier, 2012). Further, institutional settings are important in the understanding of how temporary agency workers' conditions could be improved.

Access to collective voice (worker participation according to Bustillo's terminology described in the introduction chapter) as well as job security are two dimensions of job quality. The institutional framework is, according to Muñoz de Bustillo et al. (2009, 2011), affecting job quality but should not be included in the concept. Thus, the influence of the institutional framework is recognized, but how this influence works is left out. In this chapter, we will shed light on the link between the institutional framework and two dimensions of job quality: job security and voice. Both dimensions could be referred to as employment quality.

Although several studies point to the insecurity of agency work, only a few have focused to date on understanding how different regulatory contexts concur to shape such insecurity (Forde and Slater, 2005; Pulignano and Doerflinger, 2013; Doerflinger and Pulignano, 2015). In particular, these studies show that employment and industrial relations institutions can deepen or relax the security divide between different groups of workers. For example, institutional settings where unions are stronger (Chung, 2016) and where bargaining structures are more encompassing (Pulignano and Doerflinger, 2017; Benassi, Doellgast and Sarmiento-Mirwaldt, 2016) can provide workers with security. Similarly, different employment systems can influence security by fostering or hindering employers to balance their flexibility preferences, thereby enhancing or reducing security and affecting the employment quality for workers (McKenzie et al., 2010).

This chapter aims at explaining how institutional settings interplay with employment quality for temporary agency workers. The focus for our study is how national and sectoral regulation on employment and representation influences job security for temporary agency workers at the workplace level, thereby contributing to shaping those workers' employment quality. By comparing two similar Belgian and Swedish workplaces, the chapter assesses how different social arrangements for TAW, including both regulatory settings at the national (industry) level and the collective practices of representation and voice of agency work at local levels, can explain agency workers' experience of job security. As the two countries differ in terms of employment relations systems, regulation of TAW and representation structure, a comparative analysis is appropriate.

The research in context

Temporary agency work is based on the triangular relationship consisting of the 'employment' relationship between the agency worker and the agency, the 'management' relationship between the agency worker and the client organization and the 'business' relationship between the client organization and the temporary work agency (Bergström and Storrie, 2003, p. 9; Storrie, 2007, p. 106; Håkansson et al., 2012) (Figure 8.1). The 'employment' relationship deals with employment conditions like contract, wages or training. The 'management' relationship concerns factors in the day-to-day working situation, for example, job characteristics and agency workers' integration with the client organization's employees. The 'business' relationship is such

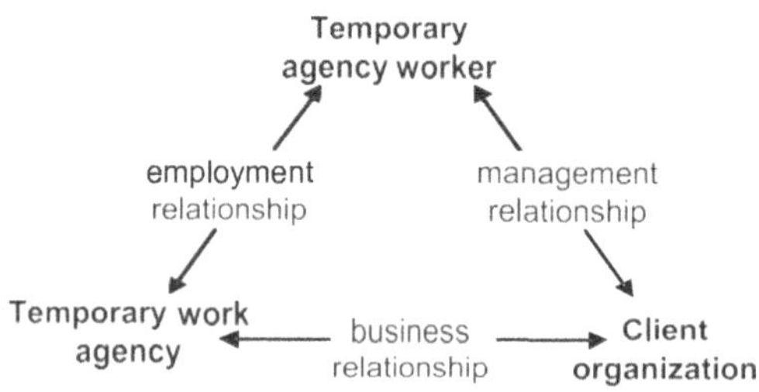

Figure 8.1 The triangular relationship within the temporary agency work industry

that the client organization buys labour from the temporary work agency temporarily or until further notice. In sum, workers are employed by (contractually linked to) the agency, but they work at the client organization.

The 'employment', the 'management' and the 'business' relationships are all considered important when examining how temporary agency workers' experiences of security are shaped in workplaces. Several studies illustrate that agency workers experience lower job security compared to the permanent workforce at the client organization. This is also when the traditional sociological categories of age, gender, educational level and occupational group are taken into consideration (Aletraris, 2010, p. 1144; De Cuyper, Notelaers and De Witte, 2009; de Graaf-Zijl, 2012; Forde and Slater, 2005; Håkansson et al., 2012; Morris, 1999; Sheikh, 2017). The business relationship entails possibilities for the client organization to dictate the terms and conditions, which could include demands regarding who will (not) be contracted for the assignment. This lead to employment protection in practice that is weaker in the TAW sector than in other industries (Björkemarken, 2012).

Aside from the contractual differences that naturally attain a lower level of security for temporary agency workers vis-à-vis the client organization employees, literature shows that the employment contract, together with age and training, accounts for the perceived job security of the agency workers (Håkansson et al., 2012; Hall, 2006). However, empirical results in Sweden reveal that differences exist across professions, with nurses employed by temporary work agencies experiencing the highest level of security (Allvin, Jacobsson and Isaksson, 2003).

Håkansson, Isidorsson and Strauss-Raats (2013) illustrate that lack of job security is a major psychosocial issue for the TAW industry. Job security can be defined as 'the certainty of retaining a specific job with a specific employer' (Leschke, Schmid and Griga, 2007, p. 340). Gazier (2007, p. 102) draws on this definition but formulates it as 'granting the continuation of the same job'. Accordingly, job security connects to the actual employer and the possibility of remaining in the job with that employer. Even though open-ended contracts for temporary agency workers are feasible from a legal point of view in several countries, temporary contracts are widespread (OECD, 2013, p. 89). The lower perceived job security in the temporary agency industry is therefore hardly surprising. Regalia (2013) discusses different kinds of security for employees with non-standard work, offering a classification of interventions that aim to ensure security for these employees. One type entails a gradual transfer to a standard employment contract, thus reaching job security in the end. This transfer implies a pact between union and client organization employer where also employment conditions for the ordinary staff might be affected. According to Regalia (2013), another way of gaining security is by being engaged by different employers, which corresponds to the idea of TAW. However, agency workers are assigned to different client organizations but employed by one employer, the temporary work agency. Theoretically, this type entails high job security in case the agency worker has an open-ended contract at the temporary work agency and the agency can provide for new assignments.

Aside from contractual differences, research also emphasizes that temporary agency workers may lack voice and workplace representation. This is partly because trade unions experience difficulties in organizing agency work, which may be the result of unions not addressing issues relevant for this particular group of workers (Holst, Aust and Pernicka, 2008; Croucher and Brewster, 1998). Specifically in this regard, Heery (2004) proposes a typology of union responses towards TAW. By rejecting the simplistic categories of union inclusion and exclusion, he elaborates a more in-depth classification, distinguishing between exclusion, regulation, replacement and engagement. *Exclusion* means a rejecting attitude towards temporary work agencies and an excluding attitude towards temporary agency workers/consultants. Accordingly, unions oppose temporary work agencies and do not see agency workers as legitimate union members, denying them possibilities for participation. *Regulation* entails the union having an accepting attitude towards the temporary work agency industry but an excluding attitude in relation to agency workers. This response safeguards and defends the core workforce's interests. *Replacement* implies a dismissive attitude towards temporary work agencies but an including attitude towards agency workers. *Engagement* entails an accepting attitude towards temporary work agencies and an including attitude towards agency workers. Hence, unions aspire to improve the agency workers' conditions by giving them possibilities of voice.

Likewise, in a case study of a Swedish company, Bergström and Styhre (2010) show how the union can simultaneously be against using temporary agency workers in principle but accept them in practice. This could be understood as the unions attempting to protect their political influence when negotiating on labour market policies and employment dismissals for workers at the macro level (Davidsson and Emmenegger, 2013). Thereby, when this occurs, they may engage less in retaining membership at the micro level (Schmitter and Streeck, 1999). This is in line with Olsen's (2005) claim that unions' different responses at local and national levels are worth looking at to develop a better analysis of responses to agency work.

Overall, these studies illustrate that the unions at national and local levels might have different agendas for how to deal with TAW and their possibilities to voice and participation. This is relevant to understand how job security via the union channel is guaranteed to agency workers, since at a national level, the unions could influence regulation, while at a local level, works councils and trade unions may adopt different strategies in dealing with agency workers. These strategies are often the response to the corporate strategy of using temporary agency work (Pulignano and Signoretti, 2016) either as a buffer in case of a downturn or for extensive long-term use (Purcell, Purcell and Tailby, 2004; Elcioglu, 2010; Kalleberg and Marsden,

2005). Holst, Nachtwey and Dörre (2010) also discern a new way of using agency workers, whereby assignments have no fixed termination date.

As illustrated earlier, temporary agency workers may experience low employment quality in regards to lack of security at work and lack of collective voice. What is less known is how the national regulatory system and union representation practices interact at workplace levels and how these practices impact agency workers' employment quality. Trade unions are the traditional channel for employees' voices. Since agency workers have dual (or split) employment and management relationships, the traditional form of representation at work, which entails that workers are represented in one workplace and organized by the same union, might not be accessible to them.

In this chapter, we aim to go beyond the obvious link between type of contract and job security and focus on how employment quality is shaped by access to voice and representation in different regulatory contexts. This approach entails a multi-dimensional understanding of security where job security and representation security are intertwined.

The regulation of agency work in Sweden and Belgium

Sweden and Belgium feature a different regulation and system for collective representation of TAW. Although the working conditions in the agency industry are regulated via sectoral collective agreements in both countries, there are remarkable differences in the way agency work is used and represented.

Sweden

Since 1993, it has been legal in Sweden to run private work agencies for profit-making purposes (Swedish Code of Statutes, 1993:440). The number of employees in the temporary work industry increased from some 5,000 in 1994 to 76,000 in 2016 (Bemanningsföretagen, 2006, 2009, 2011–2017). This increase has been steady with the exception of the first half of the 2000s and in conjunction with the economic crisis during 2008–2009, but recovered soon after. Data from Statistics Sweden (SCB, 2014, p. 252) shows that about 1.6 per cent of all employees are agency workers. According to the International Confederation of Private Employment Services (CIETT), long contract periods prevail in Sweden, as almost all contracts last a month or longer, and 70 per cent of all assignments are longer than three months (Ciett, 2013).

The operations of temporary work agencies are regulated by the Private Employment Agencies and Temporary Labour Act (Swedish Code of Statutes, 1993:440, 2012:854). There are no restrictions regarding motives for using temporary agency workers, in neither the length of time nor the cumulative duration of assignments. Although the regulation of the agency work industry is weak in Sweden (OECD, 2013), there is legislation protecting the employees in the agency industry (Swedish Code of Statutes, 1993:440, 2012:854). This legislation emphasizes that employees may not be prevented from being employed by the client organization to which they are assigned. Working conditions in the Swedish agency industry are regulated via collective agreements as in other industries. Although there is no legislation regarding minimum pay for agency workers, according to the 2016 collective agreement between Swedish Staffing Agencies and the 14 blue-collar unions of the Swedish Trade Union Confederation, temporary agency workers must have an hourly wage corresponding to the average hourly wage for comparable groups at the client organization (Staffing Agreement, 2016, Section 3, Subsection 2). The collective agreements also state the right to pay for temporary agency workers between assignments. This compensation payment is approximately 80–90 per cent of the regular salary. This compensation is possible in a few other countries, although sometimes at a low level (OECD, 2013). Moreover, the Swedish Employment Protection Act (Swedish Code of Statutes, 1982:80) prescribes that the normal form of employment contract is open-ended (i.e. permanent position), applies also to agency workers. Hence, an agency worker can have a permanent employment contract with a temporary work agency.

Trade union density in Sweden is high from an international perspective. Although there was a substantial membership drop in the mid-2000s, due to raised fees for union unemployment funds (Kjellberg, 2011), union density is still 70 per cent (Kjellberg, 2016). However, unionists estimate that union density is significantly lower in the temporary staffing industry, and it is uncommon to find local branches at temporary work agencies (Björkemarken, 2012). Even if there are local unions at the temporary work agency, it is difficult to organize activities since members are on assignments at different client organizations (Håkansson and Isidorsson, 2014). When it comes to union membership, agency workers are organized according to where they have their employment relationship, which is the work agency. The union branch organizing agency workers depends on the work agency's business focus. If the focus is logistics, the temporary work agency would be organized by the transport workers union, and if its focus is manufacturing, the metal workers union would normally be the organizing trade union. Since agency workers are assigned to workplaces in different industries, it is not obvious which union that should organize agency workers. Furthermore, agency workers and client organization employees working in the same workplace sharing the same work tasks may be organized by different trade unions.

Workplace representation for employees in Sweden is regulated along a single channel of representation, which means that it is through the local union at the employing organization, i.e. the temporary work agency – not the client organization. In work agencies where there is no local union branch, the organized agency worker can turn to the regional ombudsman. Legislation requires the employer to inform and negotiate with the unions at the workplace before making major changes at the workplace including termination of employment contracts, and many of the practical arrangements for doing so, which elsewhere in Europe are fixed by law, are left to local negotiations.

Moreover, in accordance with the Co-determination at Work Act (MBL), unions at a workplace have the right to negotiate with an employer on any matter relating to the relationship between the employer and any member employed by the organization, which in a client organization does not include agency workers on assignment. The Trade Union Representatives Act (Swedish Code of Statutes, 1974:358) states that the appointed union representative has the legal right to represent employees employed by the employer at the workplace (Section 1). This implies that it is difficult for the client organization's union representative to represent agency workers, as agency workers are not employed by the same employer (see Figure 8.1). To secure union representation, there must be a local union at the temporary work agency or a regional union ombudsman, representing the agency workers.

Belgium

Temporary work agencies are the prevalent type of private employment agencies in Belgium. They are often part of international groups offering their clients so-called 'one-stop-shopping', whereby they can get diverse services at one agency. Nonetheless, various other employment agencies exist, such as recruitment agencies, selection agencies, outplacement agencies and head-hunters. The conditions for private employment agencies are regulated by both federal and regional authorities.

The penetration rate of agency work was 2 per cent in 2011 (CIETT, 2013). According to CIETT (2014) statistics, in comparison with 2013 the activity in the temporary agency work industry in 2014 in Belgium grew by 9.22 per cent, resulting from a rise in the blue-collar segment.

The Belgian legislation for temporary work agencies is restrictive (OECD, 2013). Even if not headquartered in Belgium, agencies need a licence to be active, which is not necessary for other private employment agencies. The 1987 Act regulates the use and conditions of temporary agency workers. When a temporary work agency sends a worker to a client organization, the agency nevertheless remains responsible, together with the client, for paying the wages, indemnities and social security contributions. The law prohibits the agency from conducting any other activity parallel to placing workers at the disposal of client organizations. Agencies can only contract workers, and not self-employed persons, to perform temporary work. The recognition of temporary work agencies falls within the competence of the regions (the Flemish, Walloon and Brussels regions). Accordingly, each of the regions has an advisory committee on which the trade unions and employers have several representatives and on which they have an advisory capacity concerning the recognition, suspension or withdrawal of agencies' licences. The conditions for recognition are similar in the three regions. Each region is also responsible for the implementation of the EU Directive on Agency Work.

Belgium is one of the most regulated markets for agency work in Europe. Agencies employ temporary workers, with all of the national obligations of labour law and social security law that this involves. Moreover, the Act of 1987 is to a large extent complemented by national-, sectoral- and firm-level collective agreements in both private and public sectors. Accordingly, conditions for hiring out employees to another enterprise or recruiting temporary workers are strictly defined by law, while working conditions of the temporary workers are guaranteed by law to be similar to any other workers executing the same job in the same company (equality principle). However, open-ended contracts are not possible for temporary agency workers in Belgium.

Sectoral bargaining involving trade unions and employers' associations of work agencies exists in Belgium. In particular, agency work is formally recognized as an industry in Belgium, with a joint committee (number 322). The law foresees specific conditions and procedures regulating the use of agency work, particularly in the situation of a temporary increase in workload. The maximum assignment duration is generally defined by law and depends on the legal motive for using temporary agency work (Federale Overheidsdienst Werkgelegenheid, Arbeid en Sociaal Overleg, 2017). Generally, only six motives are allowed (according to the Labour Agreement 108): to replace a client organization employee particularly in the case of sickness; to accommodate a temporary increase of work volumes; to meet exceptional/seasonal work needs; to achieve a predefined employment trajectory, for example, reintegrating the long-term unemployed; to allow for the intake of new staff; and for occasional artistic work.

Recently, new regulations have been enforced to improve working conditions, increase employment opportunities and prevent abuses of agency work. At a time when the EU Directive encourages European governments to remove unnecessary restrictions, the Belgian legislation generates additional responsibilities for employers using agency workers. Accordingly, from 2013 onwards temporary agency work is to be used by client organizations as a 'stepping stone' to directly hire the agency worker (on a fixed-term or permanent basis) after six months.

As in Sweden, Belgian unions are involved in social security management through handling unemployment funds as part of the 'Ghent system' (Vandaele, 2006). This contributes to the high union density (53%), particularly among agency workers, who are unionized at a rate of about 64 per cent in Belgium (Arrowsmith, 2006; Delbar and Léonard, 2002). Belgian unions have a strong presence in the workplace, especially in large firms, via union-dominated works councils and trade union delegates. Workplace representation in Belgium runs through two separate channels: the works council (*Comité d'enterprise* or *Ondernemingsraad*) within larger workplaces (above 100 employees) and the trade union delegation in companies with at least 50 employees. Only trade unions are able to nominate members to the works council and negotiate key issues with management. The works council has extensive information and consultation rights, and although it is a joint body with an employee majority, it has decision-making powers in some areas, such as restructuring. The 1981 national collective agreement allows the establishment of a trade union delegation in work agencies to represent the rights of their workers within the agency. Moreover, agency workers have representation rights at the client organization, too, where their numbers are taken into account to determine the necessary threshold of employees to the settlement of works councils.

Comparing Sweden and Belgium

Both countries differ in several aspects. In Sweden, the use of agency work is of a 'permissive' (liberal) form, since it is possible to use temporary agency workers for any reason and for unlimited time, while in Belgium the use is strictly regulated (restrictive). However, while job security is regulated by the Employment Protection Act in Sweden, which prescribes permanent employment contracts for agency workers, this is not the case in Belgium, where job security is not guaranteed by law as a way to make the use of agency workers something temporary. In addition, union representation of agency workers in Sweden is formally regulated through the agency firm where they have their employment relations; in absence of a local union organization at the agency workers are represented by a regional union ombudsman. Conversely, in Belgium, agency workers have representation rights at both the client organization and the agency.

Table 8.1 summarizes the features of the regulation of agency work in Sweden and Belgium. It incorporates the regulation for the use of agency

Table 8.1 Regulation of agency work in Sweden and Belgium

	Sweden	*Belgium*
Regulation of the industry	Liberal	Restrictive
Regulation of working conditions	Collective agreements, stating e.g. equal pay and pay in between assignments	Collective agreements
Representation by union at temporary work agency	Yes	Yes
Representation by union at client organization	No	Yes
Representation by work councils at temporary work agency	Not applicable	Yes
Representation work councils at client organization	Not applicable	Yes
Maximum length of assignment	No limits	Dependent on the motive for using agency work
Possibility of permanent contract at the agency	Yes	No

work as well as its local regulation through the collective structures of workplace representation.

The empirical questions this paper engages with are how these different institutional configurations turn out at a workplace level and in representation practices, and how these practices in turn affect the employment quality of agency workers. The following sections present the findings of a cross-national study in Sweden and Belgium highlighting the experiences regarding agency workers' insecurity within two similar workplaces in the manufacturing industry.

Research design and methodology

The article is based on a cross-national comparative case study methodology. Two similar cases in Sweden and in Belgium were examined to understand how differences regarding the regulatory and representation structures of agency work in two similar workplaces affected workers' employment quality. Case study research is suitable in this respect, because it allows for examining social processes in a particular setting (Eisenhardt, 1989). The selected cases (see Table 8.2) belong to the manufacturing sector; they share a similar nature of the production process and technology, and they both make use of agency work. Moreover, the workplaces are highly unionized.

The Swedish case is part of a multinational corporation within the automotive industry and has operations worldwide. It is a medium-sized production unit with some 500 employees, with day-to-day operations consisting of assembly work as well as some R&D. Most employees have a long

Table 8.2 Workplace characteristics in the two cases

	Swedish case	*Belgium case*
Total workforce	500 workers (about 340 blue-collar)	1600 workers (about 1000 blue-collar)
Agency workers	37%	5% (15% flexibility quota 10% fixed-term, 5% agency work)
Union representation for agency workers	Regional ombudsman If Metall	Dual: union delegation and works council in both agency and client organization
Overall unionization rate (client organization employees)	99.5%	95%
Trade unions in the client organization	If Metall	Christian union (ACV-CSC), socialist union (ABVV-FTGB), liberal union (ACLVB-CGSLB)

tenure. Production is organized into separate flow systems, where each flow consists of a number of workstations with up to four workers per workstation. Production is based solely on customer demand, entailing that demand can fluctuate on short notice. Agency workers need one week of on-the-job training for one work task; thereafter, they gradually learn more tasks to be able to take part in job rotation.

The Belgian case belongs to a US multinational company operating as an automotive supplier. The company manufactures low-tech products, using highly automated production processes involving many low-skilled tasks at the assembly line. The workplace – employing 1600 staff (about 1000 in production) – thus needs to offer quality products at low cost, delivered just-in-time. Customers can specify demand volumes on a weekly basis, which causes high flexibility needs on short notice, which are partially covered by using agency workers. Agency workers are trained on the job, and they learn different tasks so as to work in job rotation.

Data were collected mainly through semi-structured interviews. Regarding the Swedish case, we performed interviews with key actors at four times: 2008, 2011, 2015 and 2016. We interviewed union representatives, HR manager, production managers, employees, the manager at the temporary agency, agency workers and the ombudsmen at the regional union office. Hence, we talked to all key actors involved in issues about agency workers' assignments, job security and union representation. Interviews lasted 60–120 minutes and were recorded, then summarized and the summaries were sent to the interviewees for approval. In total, we conducted 17 interviews.

For the Belgian case, we conducted 30 semi-structured interviews in total during the period 2008–2013 with European HR managers, local HR managers, works councillors and trade unionists as well as the manager at the temporary agency, temporary agency workers and ombudspersons at the regional union office. As all major actors involved in workplace regulation of agency work were interviewed, a comprehensive picture regarding local policies and practices as well as corresponding negotiation processes evolved. In addition, we also interviewed specialists for agency work at the sector level to get a better view on overall developments in the agency work sector and the regulation of this form of work at different levels. All interviews took between 60 and 120 minutes and were transcribed and subsequently analysed with the help of NVivo. The analysis also involved documentary materials (e.g. collective agreements at different levels, company and union documents) collected during field work.

Temporary agency work in Swedish and Belgian workplaces

Evidence from the Swedish case

The plant has been using temporary agency workers on a fairly regular basis ever since 2004. During the economic crisis of 2008, the client organization had to reduce staff, and agency workers were the first ones to leave. Thereafter, the company had to give notice to approximately 10 per cent of its own employees. In January 2010, the client organization's sales started to recover and demand continued to grow, reaching higher production levels than during the years prior to the crisis. In the wake of the financial crisis, the corporate executive board forced local plants to provide for 30 per cent flexibility. This was achieved mainly by using agency workers. They constituted a buffer, easy to terminate in case of a downturn.

> When this [hiring of agency workers] started again, it was a way to avoid dismissals.
>
> (HR manager SE)

In spring 2011, agency workers constituted about one third of the blue-collar workforce. The long-term strategic use of them allows first-line managers to handle day-to-day short-term absences in the entire workforce by deploying both regular and agency workers where there is a gap in the production line. To fill the needs at different workstations, the client organization has to maintain and develop the agency workers' skills and competences, which means that they can keep up or develop their competences and thus increase their employability. Since 2011, some 50 temporary agency workers have been employed by the client organization. Such an employment contract is highly attractive; the client organization's manager can pick and choose among agency workers. Some of the agency workers have been at the client organization for 6 years. The HR manager describes the situation when announcing 13 jobs openings.

> All [agency workers] want to have this employment [at the client organization]; 80 people applied. Individuals who did not get the job were crying; there were many emotions involved. . . . We gave very much importance to personal characteristics, we do a lot of changes, and we want people who easily deal with changes. And we also looked for individuals with leadership traits. . . . We did not employ those with the longest assignments, nor those who were most multi-skilled.
>
> (HR manager SE)

There is no career path from the agency to being employed by the client organization. The union has no say in these decisions and the local union representative complied with this and did not consider intervening in these issues with references to the employer prerogative to freely choose who to employ. In June 2016, the share of temporary agency workers reached 37 per cent. The union's response to temporary agency workers was ambiguous, demonstrating both positive and negative attitudes. The union expressed a positive attitude to using temporary agency workers during production peaks. However, the union criticized that national regulation allows for hiring agency workers for any reason, making extensive hiring possible. According to the union, the client organization's use of agency workers was too extensive, and the union would prefer direct hiring. However, the union's attitude to the agency workers was supportive.

> We don't make any distinction. For me, they [temporary agency workers] are union members as much as the others [client organization employees].
> (Union representative SE)

The supportive attitude is evident in that agency workers can take part in union meetings, although they cannot – as client organization employees – claim working time for these meetings. Furthermore, the local union at the client organization represents them in issues related to the work during the assignment. However, when it comes to questions about wages, the assignment duration or dismissals, the local union has no discretion as according to legislation, it has no mandate to represent staff from temporary work agencies in issues concerning the employment relationship. Therefore, issues on job security cannot be dealt with by the local union at the client organization, but at the agency (Swedish Code of Statutes, 1982:80, Section 29). However, in the agency used by the client organization there is no local union representing the agency workers at the agency, and hence, the agency workers have to turn to the union representative at the regional level.

The close cooperation between the client organization and the agency entails some stability for the agency workers; most agency workers' assignments are long term. This could be called assignment security. However, when interviewing the agency's manager in 2016, the client organization's need for agency workers was decreasing, and one third of them were to leave the client organization, which illustrates the buffering function of agency workers. So when demand decreases, the client organization can easily reduce the buffer. The agency workers leaving the client organization are still employed by the agency; they have open-ended contracts providing job security. Thus, the agency has to find new assignments at other client organizations, and the agency workers should be mobile. However, client organizations can choose whom they want and change agency workers at will:

> In case the client organization is not satisfied [with the agency worker], we have to listen to that. Because they decide who they want to hire.
> (Manager at the work agency SE)

The trade unions do not have any say in these decisions. From their perspective, this entails a feeling of insecurity for agency workers:

> The temporary agency workers are terrified not to behave properly. They know that they are just a phone call away [from being replaced].
> (Union representative at regional level, If Metall SE)

At the time of the interview there was increased demand in the business, and the agency's manager was quite confident about finding new assignments for those leaving the client organization. However, during recessions the demand for agency workers decreases, making it difficult to find other assignments. Accordingly, long tenure at the agency hardly produces security. In case of staff cuts, the employer has to provide notice and call for negotiations. According to Swedish legislation, tenure is the main principle when deciding on dismissals. The union representatives interviewed claim that the principle of 'last hired, first fired' is difficult to maintain in the temporary agency sector in general due to the business relation, as the client organization decides whom they want to hire independently of their tenure at the work agency. The investigated agency has not made any staff cuts since the crisis of 2008.

This case illustrates that although the temporary agency workers have open-ended contracts with the agency, their function as a buffer makes them vulnerable in downturns. Also, despite a positive attitude from the local trade union at the client organization towards temporary agency workers, they have no possibility to represent the agency workers when it comes to where they should have their assignment or whether they are to be dismissed from their agency.

Evidence from the Belgium case

The Belgium case organization produces low-tech parts for the automotive industry. As a supplier of the big automotive groups, high levels of flexibility – especially in terms of just-in-time delivery and flexible volumes (changeable week by week) – are required. Although legislation guarantees equal treatment – which means that wages and working conditions of regular and agency staff are almost the same (the only differences are voluntary benefits given by the Belgian case organization) – local unions started to actively engage in local bargaining to improve the agency workers' situation. This was possible because of the specific status of the agency workers; that is, on the one hand, they are covered by a Joint Committee establishing regulation. On the other hand, regulation foresees that as soon as agency workers leave the agency and are sent to an assignment, they are represented in their client organization, too. Hence, local unions have a mandate to represent not only the client organization's staff, but also the agency workers. Moreover, and this corresponds to the unions' general policy, they want to avoid competition between different groups of workers at any price, implying that wages, working conditions and voluntary benefits need to be the same.

> We need to make sure that agency and regular workers have the same rights. This also includes voluntary benefits, such as meal vouchers or the yearly Christmas present. We achieved an agreement with management on that – every agency workers who has worked here for three months has the same benefits as regular workers.
>
> (Local unionist BE)

Management agreed to the local unions' demands, as assignments tended to be shorter than three months, which limited the number of agency workers entitled to voluntary benefits. When flexibility pressures mounted in 2002, management started hiring high numbers of blue-collar agency workers to deal with fluctuations in production. While assignments tended to be short in the beginning, the duration got longer and longer, sometimes even up to 2 years without clear prospects of contractual upgrades. At the same time, management felt challenged by the situation, because the sheer number of agency workers adversely affected the efficiency of production and administrative processes.

At first in late 2003, local unions demanded a quota to limit the use of agency contracts to avoid an abuse of this flexible form of work. In their view, the situation particularly got out of control in terms of pressure at work and stress for the whole workforce, as production volumes steeply increased. Specifically, the huge number of agency workers entering the company meant that not all of them were skilled for the job, which led to quality issues and the need for regular workers to train them during their working hours. Since no compromise was found locally, and the dispute regarding the quota became severe, management and local unions had to go into mediation. As a result of the mediation in 2004, a 15 per cent flexibility quota was implemented, consisting of 10 per cent fixed-term and 5 per cent agency workers. Management accepted the agreement mainly because it feared an even stronger regulation of agency work, since

> There are companies in Belgium in which agency work cannot be used at all due to the unions and their strength.
>
> (Local HR manager BE)

While this represented another step in terms of workplace regulation on agency work, in the following years local unions pushed further to achieve higher levels of security for agency staff, regarding both job security and training. On the one hand, they demanded a system of subsequent contractual upgrades in accordance with the (nowadays) collectively negotiated stepping-stone motive of using agency work. On the other hand, an arrangement regarding training was demanded. This would limit potential differences between regular and agency staff and improve the skills and thus the employability of agency workers. After the previous dispute and mediation, and considering the fact that the negotiated agreement worked well in practice, management was open to negotiate about these issues, especially because of the need to retain skilled workers.

> Obviously, you want to retain your skills, so you cannot constantly have your skills go out, and then you maybe don't get the right skills anymore.
>
> (Local HR manager BE)

Furthermore, management also saw the potential benefits of an agreement on formalized employment trajectories with contractual upgrades. On the one hand, this had positive effects on the motivation and commitment of agency workers due to the prospect of being hired by the client organization. On the other hand, the agency contract represented a trial or probation period that could be used to identify potentially good workers for contractual upgrades. Due to such shared interests, an agreement stating that agency contracts would be upgraded to fixed-term (after 6–12 months) and permanent contracts (after 2 years) was reached, giving clear career prospects to agency workers in the client organization. In terms of training, there was no formal workplace agreement, since this was handled based on the company's and workers' individual needs. In any case, each agency worker would receive a safety briefing and on-the-job training before starting the assignment.

> At first, agency workers get relevant information from their agency. Then they directly go into the on-the-job training program that is set up in the department they work for. They get training, but to a limited extent because they are the most flexible group of people in our plant which means that in theory, they can go from one department to another pretty quickly. But we also have agency workers with very stable working patterns. Those are mostly well-trained and of a high added-value for us.
>
> (Plant manager BE)

Overall, the fact that agency workers in the client organization were represented by the local unions was crucial for their security. Although regulation set equal treatment between agency and regular workers, local unions' used their mandate to limit competition and increase equality between different groups of workers by extending voluntary benefits to agency workers and by negotiating a system of formalized employment trajectories. This remarkably increased agency workers' security and offered prospects of being hired by the client organization in the long run.

Discussion

Previous research shows that temporary agency workers perceive lower employment quality in terms of job insecurity and lack of collective voice compared to others (Aletraris, 2010; De Cuyper et al., 2009; de Graaf-Zilj, 2012; Forde and Slater, 2005; Håkansson et al., 2012; Morris, 1999; Sheikh, 2017). This chapter's main contribution is to explain how this low employment quality is produced by taking the institutional settings on voice and representation into account. Further, it shows how the two dimensions of job quality, i. e. voice and job security are intertwined. In particular, it emphasizes how regulation on national and sectoral levels as well as practices for collective voice shape how agency workers are used at the workplace level, which in turn produce insecurity.

National regulation shaping workplace practices

In Sweden, the national regulation permits indefinite length of assignments; accordingly, extensive hiring at the workplace level is possible. The Swedish case illustrates such extensive use where the agency workers prevalently are used on long-term assignments to constitute a buffer that increases the client organization's flexibility. This entails stability for the directly employed staff at the expense of instability for agency workers. However, the termination of an agency worker's assignment should not entail job insecurity, as the Swedish regulation admits open-ended contracts for agency workers, so in case an assignment ends, the agency should assign the agency workers to other firms. Hence, in principle agency workers should have the same job security as other employees. This is in line with Regalia's (2013) classification – sharing the work between employers (i. e. client organizations in the case of agency workers) entails job security for the employee.

However, our analysis reveals that when agency workers are used in large proportions as a buffer, the client organization has no incentives to transfer the agency workers to ordinary staff. Hence, the agency workers remain employed by the agency. In case of a recession, redundancies at the agency may result from the difficulty of finding other client organizations. According to the Swedish employment protecting legislation, the last employed should be the first to leave. Nevertheless, the business relation between the temporary work agency and the client organization puts pressure on the agency to withdraw from this legislative principle. If the agency does not comply with the request from the client organization, they can turn to another temporary work agency. They can even inform the employee to apply for a position in another agency and return to the same position at the client organization employed by another agency. Thus, negotiations about redundancies at the work agency require strong union power.

The Swedish case also illustrates that the client organization employed some of the agency workers, implying increased job security because of no longer being part of the buffer. In contrast to the Belgian case, the union at the Swedish client organization has no say on this issue, since agency workers according to regulation are not represented at the client organization. Thus, client organizations can easily pick and chooses whom to employ. This path-way to job security differs from Regalia (2013), because there is no pact between union and client organization employer. On the contrary, the client organization union accepts that recruitment is solely an employer prerogative, and agency workers' assignment tenure is not taken into account when recruiting from that pool. For agency workers, this may negatively affect job security.

According to the Belgian regulation, conversely, it is not possible to achieve job security in work agencies, because agency workers are per se hired on fixed-term contracts, as agency work is considered to be something temporary. Job security can thus only be achieved by transforming the contract with the agency to an employment contract with the client organization. As the Belgian case illustrates, a strong union at the client organization, with an inclusive stance towards agency workers, is a prerequisite. However, our comparison shows that this is not sufficient, as also in the Swedish case, the local union was strong and had a positive stance towards agency workers. The transformation to improved employment quality presupposes voice and collective representation rights for agency workers in the client organization, and the local union or works council at the client organization needs the possibility to represent agency workers on assignment.

Employment quality and representation intertwined

The Swedish case illustrates the ambivalence in the local union's attitude to agency workers. The union's strategy is to accept extensively using temporary agency workers in peak periods, but limit their use as a buffer. This two-sided strategy corresponds to Bergström and Styhre's (2010) work, illustrating the local union's efforts to safeguard its own members (client organization employees) while trying to embrace agency workers in the union's work. Relating this response to Heery's (2004) model, we find similarities to both 'replacement' and 'restriction'. Accordingly, the union is striving to improve the agency workers' job security, but at the same time, they accept that agency workers safeguard the regular workers' stability in case of a downturn.

In Belgium, the inclusive union's response to temporary agency workers may be considered natural because of the agency industry's strong regulation. The union's effort to transfer agency workers to client organization employees is bounded legally. The unions' argument for restricting the use of agency workers is not to safeguard the client organization employees, but results from their negative attitude to agency work. According to the union, agency workers are treated badly and should be protected. This reflects what Heery (2004) calls 'replacement', referring to the transition from being an agency worker to a client organization employee. As illustrated, access to collective voice for agency workers at the client organization was crucial for this transition and the opportunity to attain job security.

In contrast, the Swedish agency workers lack collective voice rights at the client organization. According to national regulation (Swedish Code of Statutes, 1974:358), union representation is related to the employer relationship. Although the union at the client organization welcomes agency workers and wants to represent them, this is only possible in issues relating to the management relation. On issues concerning the employment relation including job security, the agency worker has to turn to the union representative at the regional level if, as normal, a local trade union branch is not present at the temporary work agency. However, the regional ombudsman witnesses the difficulties in following the labour law stipulating the tenure principle. The representation structure at client organizations thus restricts the union's strategies independent of their inclusive stance, as they are by law prevented from representing agency workers in issues related to job security. This highlights how job insecurity and representation insecurity are intertwined.

Conversely, in Belgium job insecurity for agency workers is the result of the temporal character of the employment contract regulated by Belgium legislation. This is because of the relatively high level of regulation of the agency industry, which is the result of the law, collective agreements and collective representation rights being guaranteed in the client organization and the agency. The unions' replacement response is functional to the regulatory logic that makes job security for agency workers impossible but promotes transition of employment to client organizations. This is in line with Regalia's (2013) idea on the gradual transfer to a standard employment contract.

Conclusion

Muñoz de Bustillo et al. (2009, 2011) consider employment quality as a multi-dimensional concept that should be measured on the individual level. However, to understand how temporary agency workers' employment quality is produced, we argue that we have to go beyond the individual level and analyse how national and sectoral regulation shapes workplace practices and access to collective voice.

National regulations and collective structures for representation shape the unions' possibilities to represent agency workers and their general approaches towards TAW. Hence, our findings add to the understanding of the conditions contributing to job insecurity and representation insecurity for agency workers. Conversely to Regalia (2013), we found that achieving job security by transforming agency workers to client organization employees is not only about unions building pacts with the employer, but it requires a strong representation structure for the agency workers at the client organization. The comparative findings highlight that this is the case in Belgium but not in Sweden, thereby explaining the differences in employment quality across countries. However, our study also shows that a strong representation structure at the client organization and inclusive attitudes towards agency workers is a prerequisite, but it is not sufficient to guarantee security. This chapter indicates that national regulation granting agency workers on assignment access to collective voice in the client organization is crucial for job security. Thus, this chapter illustrates the multi-dimensionality of employment quality by showing how job security and representation security are intertwined.

References

Aletraris, L. (2010). How satisfied are they and why? A study of job satisfaction, job rewards, gender and temporary agency workers in Australia. *Human Relations*, 63, pp. 1129–1155.

Allvin, M., Jacobsson, A. and Isaksson, K. (2003). *Att avgränsa det gränslösa sjuksköterskearbetet. En intervjustudie om sjuksköterskors villkor och valmöjligheter i bemanningsbranschen*. Solna: Arbetslivsinstitutet.

Arrowsmith, J. (2006). *Temporary Agency Work in an Enlarged European Union*. Available at: www.eurofound.europa.eu/pubdocs/2005/139/en/1/ef05139en.pdf.

Bemanningsföretagen. (2006). *Bemanningsföretagens utveckling, 4:e kvartalet 2005*. Stockholm: Bemanningsföretagen.

Bemanningsföretagen. (2009). *Antal anställda och penetrationsgrad i bemanningsbranschen 2008*. Bemanningsföretagens utveckling. Stockholm: Bemanningsföretagen.

Bemanningsföretagen. (2011). *Antal anställda och penetrationsgrad i bemanningsbranschen 2010*. Stockholm: Bemanningsföretagen.

Bemanningsföretagen. (2012). *Antal anställda och penetrationsgrad i bemanningsbranschen 2011*. Stockholm: Bemanningsföretagen.

Bemanningsföretagen. (2013). *Bemanningsindikatorn Q4 2013*. Stockholm: Bemanningsföretagen.

Bemanningsföretagen. (2014). *Bemanningsindikatorn Q3 2014*. Stockholm: Bemanningsföretagen.

Bemanningsföretagen. (2015). *Bemanningsföretagens årsrapport 2014*. Stockholm: Bemanningsföretagen.

Bemanningsföretagen. (2016). *Bemanningsföretagens årsrapport 2015*. Stockholm: Bemanningsföretagen.

Bemanningsföretagen. (2017). *Bemanningsföretagens årsrapport 2016*. Stockholm: Bemanningsföretagen.

Benassi, C., Doellgast, V. and Sarmiento-Mirwaldt, K. (2016). Institutions and inequality in liberalizing markets: Explaining different trajectories of institutional change in social Europe. *Politics & Society*, 44(1), pp. 117–142.

Bergström, O. and Storrie, D. (Eds.) (2003). *Contingent Employment in Europe and the United States*. Cheltenham: Edward Elgar Publishing.

Bergström, O. and Styhre, A. (2010). Irish butchers rather than Irish meat: Trade union responses to agency work in Sweden. *Journal of Industrial Relations*, 52(4), pp. 477–490.

Björkemarken, M. (2012). *Bemanningsbranschen i Västsverige – Fackliga Erfarenheter* [The Staffing Industry in Western Sweden – Trade Union Experiences]. Göteborg: Swedish Trade Union Confederation, LO-distriktet i Västsverige.

Burroni, L. and Carrieri, M. (2011). *Bargaining for Social Rights (BARSORI) Country Report Italy*. Available at: http://uva-aias.net/uploaded_files/regular/BarsoriReport-Italy.pdf.

Chung, H. (2016). Dualization and subjective employment insecurity: Explaining the subjective employment insecurity divide between permanent and temporary workers across 23 European countries. *Economic and Industrial Democracy* [online]. Available at: http://dx.doi.org/10.1177/0143831X16656411.

Ciett. (2013). *The Agency Work Industry Around the World. Economic Report*. Brussels: Ciett.

Ciett. (2014). *Economic Report. 2014 Edition*. Brussels: Ciett.

Clauwaert, S. (2000). *Survey of Legislation on Temporary Agency Work*. Brussels: European Trade Union Institute (ETUI). Available at: http://library.fes.de/pdf-files/gurn/00326.pdf.

Croucher, R. and Brewster, C. (1998). Flexible working practices and trade unions. *Employee Relations*, 20(5), pp. 443–452.

Davidsson, J. B. and Emmenegger, P. (2013). Defending the organization, not the members: Unions and the reform of job security legislation in Western Europe. *European Journal of Political Research*, 52(3), pp. 339–363.

De Cuyper, N., Notelaers, G. and De Witte, H. (2009). Job insecurity and employability in fixed-term contractors, agency workers, and permanent workers: Associations with job satisfaction and affective organizational commitment. *Journal of Occupational Health Psychology*, 14(2), pp. 193–205.

De Graaf-Zijl, M. (2012). Job satisfaction and contingent employment. *Economist-Netherlands*, 160, pp. 197–218.

Delbar, C. and Léonard, E. (2002). *Le travail intérimaire*. Courrier hebdomadaire no. 1778. Bruxelles: Centre de Recherche et d'Information Socio-Politiques (CRISP).

Doerflinger, N. and Pulignano, V. (2015). Temporary agency work and trade unions in comparative perspective: A mixed blessing? *Journal of Workplace Rights*, 5(2), pp. 1–10.

Eisenhardt, K. (1989). Building theories from case study research. *Academy of Management Review*, 14(4), pp. 532–550.

Elcioglu, E. (2010). Producing precarity: The temporary staffing agency in the labour market. *Qualitative Sociology*, 33(2), pp. 117–136.

Emmenegger, P., Häusermann, S. and Palier, B. (2012). *The Age of Dualization: The Changing Face of Inequality in Deindustrializing Societies*. Oxford: Oxford University Press.

Forde, C. and Slater, G. (2005). Agency working in Britain: Character, consequences and regulation. *British Journal of Industrial Relations*, 43(2), pp. 249–271.

Gazier, B. (2007). 'Making transitions pay': The 'transitional labour markets' approach to 'flexicurity'. In Jörgensen, H. and Kungshøj Madsen, P. (Eds.) *Flexicurity and Beyond: Finding a New Agenda for the European Social Model*. Copenhagen: DJØF Publishing.

Håkansson, K. and Isidorsson, T. (2014). Trade union response to agency labour in Sweden. *Industrial Relations Journal*, 45(1), pp. 22–38.

Håkansson, K. and Isidorsson, T. (2015). Temporary agency workers–precarious workers? Perceived job security and employability for temporary agency workers and client organization employees at a Swedish manufacturing plant. *Nordic Journal of Working Life Studies*, 5(4), pp. 3–22.

Håkansson, K., Isidorsson, T. and Kantelius, H. (2012). Temporary agency work as means of achieving flexicurity? *Nordic Journal for Working Life Studies*, 2(4), pp. 153–169.

Håkansson, K., Isidorsson, T. and Strauss-Raats, P. (2013). *Arbetsmiljö för hyresarbetskraft – inhyrdas fysiska och psykosociala arbetsmiljö*. Stockholm: Arbetsmiljöverket.

Hall, R. (2006). Temporary agency work and HRM in Australia. *Personnel Review*, 35(2), pp. 158–174.

Heery, E. (2004). The trade union response to agency labour in Britain. *Industrial Relations Journal*, 35(5), pp. 434–450.
Holst, H., Aust, A. and Pernicka, S. (2008). Kollektive Interessensvertretung im strategischen Dilemma – Atypisch Beschäftigte und die 'dreifache Krise' der Gewerkschaften. *Zeitschrift für Soziologie*, 37(2), pp. 158–176.
Holst, H., Nachtwey, O. and Dörre, K. (2010). The strategic use of temporary agency work: Functional change of a non-standard form of employment. *International Journal of Action Research*, 6, pp. 108–138.
Houwing, H. and Vandaele, K. (2011). Liberal convergence, growing outcome divergence? Institutional continuity and changing trajectories in the 'low countries'. In Becker, U. (Ed.) *The Changing Political Economies of Small West European Countries*. Amsterdam: Amsterdam University Press, pp. 125–148.
Kalleberg, A. (2009). Precarious work, insecure workers: Employment relations in transition. *American Sociological Review*, 74(1), pp. 1–22.
Kalleberg, A. and Marsden, P. (2005). Externalizing organizational activities: Where and how US establishments use employment intermediaries. *Socio-Economic Review*, 3(3), pp. 389–416.
Kjellberg, A. (2011). The decline in Swedish union density since 2007. *Nordic Journal of Working Life Studies*, 1(1), pp. 67–93.
Kjellberg, A. (2016). Parternas organisationsgrad och kollektivavtalens utbredning. In Andersson, B. (Ed.) *Avtalsrörelsen och lönebildningen*. Stockholm: Medlingsinstitutet, pp. 42–48.
Leschke, J., Schmid, G. and Griga. D. (2007). On the marriage of flexibility and security: Lessons from the Hartz-reforms in Germany. In Jörgensen, H. and Kungshøj Madsen, P. (Eds.) *Flexicurity and Beyond: Finding a New Agenda for the European Social Model*. Copenhagen: DJØF Publishing.
McKenzie, R., Forde, C., Robinson, A., Cook, H., Eriksson, B., Larsson, P. and Bergman, A. (2010). Contingent work in the UK and Sweden: Evidence from the construction industry. *Industrial Relation Journal*, 41(6), pp. 603–621.
Morris, J. A. (1999). Injury experience of temporary workers in a manufacturing setting. Factors that increase vulnerability. *AAOHN Journal*, 47, pp. 470–478.
Muñoz de Bustillo, R. M., Fernández-Macías, E., Antón, J.-I. and Esteve, F. (2011). E pluribus unum? A critical survey of job quality indicators. *Socio-Economic Review*, 9, pp. 447–475. doi:10.1093/ser/mwr005.
Muñoz de Bustillo, R. M., Fernández-Macías, E., Esteve, F. and Antón, J. I. (2009). *Indicators of Job Quality in the European Union: Employment and Social Affairs*. Brussels: European Parliament, IP/A/EMPL/ST/2008-09 PE 429.972.
OECD. (2013). *OECD Employment Outlook 2013*. Paris: OECD Publishing. Available at: http://dx.doi.org/10.1787/empl_outlook-2013-en.
Olsen, K. (2005). Unions' dilemma when firms use employment intermediaries. *European Sociological Review*, 21(3), pp. 289–300.
Pulignano, V. and Doerflinger, N. (2013). A head with two tales? Trade unions' influence on addressing temporary agency workers security while enhancing flexibility in Belgian and German workplaces. *International Journal of Human Resource Management*, 24(22), pp. 4149–4165.
Pulignano, V. and Doerflinger, N. (2017). Changing labour markets and solidarity: Comparing local unions' responses to management flexibility strategies in the German and Belgian metalworking and chemical industries. In Doellgast, V., Lilie, N. and Pulignano, V. (Eds.) *Reconstructing Solidarity: Labour Unions, Precarious*

Work, and the Politics of Institutional Change in Europe. Oxford: Oxford University Press.

Pulignano, V. and Signoretti, A. (2016). Union strategies, national institutions and the use of temporary labour in Italian and US plants. *British Journal of Industrial Relations*, 54(3), pp. 574–596.

Purcell, J., Purcell, K. and Tailby, S. (2004). Temporary work agencies: Here today, gone tomorrow? *British Journal of Industrial Relations*, 42(4), pp. 705–725.

Regalia, I. (2013). Regional and local experiments for labor market policy in Europe. In Stone, K. and Arthurs, H. (Eds.) *Rethinking Workplace Regulation: Beyond the Standard Contract of Employment*. New York, NY: Russell Sage Foundation.

SCB. (2014). *Statistisk årsbok 2013*. Statistiska centralbyrån. Stockholm: SCB, Statistics Sweden.

Schmitter, P. C. and Streeck, W. (1999). *The Organization of Business Interests: Studying the Associative Action of Business in Advanced Industrial Societies*. MPIfG Discussion Paper, 1999/1.

Sheikh, A. Z. (2017). Political economy of agency work. Flexibility or exploitation? *World Review of Political Economy*, 8(2), pp. 162–189.

Staffing Agreement. (2016). Arbetare. Avtal för Bemanningsföretag. Avtal Tecknat 2016 Giltighetstid: 2016-05-01-2017-04-30, Bemanningsföretagen, Fastighetsanställdas Förbund, GS – Facket för skogs, trä- och grafisk bransch, Handelsanställdas förbund, Hotell och Restaurang Facket, IF Metall, SEKO – Service och Kommunikationsfacket, Svenska Byggnadsarbetareförbundet, Svenska Elektrikerförbundet, Svenska Kommunalarbetareförbundet, Svenska Livsmedelsarbetareförbundet, Svenska Musikerförbundet, Svenska Målareförbundet, Svenska Pappersindustriarbetarförbundet, Svenska Transportarbetarförbunder (Collective Agreement for Blue-collar workers working for staffing agencies from 1 May 2016–30 April 2017, Swedish Staffing Agencies, and 14 Blue-collar Trade Unions within the Swedish Trade Union Confederation), Stockholm.

Standing, G. (2011). *The Precariat: The New Dangerous Class*. London: Bloomsbury Academic.

Storrie, D. (2007). Temporary agency work in the European Union: Economic rationale and equal treatment. In Furåker, B., Håkansson, K. and Karlsson, J. Ch. (Eds.) *Flexibility and Stability in Working Life*. Basingstoke and New York, NY: Palgrave Macmillan.

Swedish Code of Statutes. (1974:358). *Trade Union Representatives' Status at the Workplace Act, No 1974:358*. Stockholm: Swedish Parliament.

Swedish Code of Statutes. (1982:80). *The Employment Protection Act, No. 1982:80*. Stockholm: Swedish Parliament.

Swedish Code of Statutes. (1993:440). *The Private Employment Agencies and Temporary Labour Act, No. 1993:440*. Stockholm: Swedish Parliament.

Swedish Code of Statutes. (2012:854). *The Agency Work Act, No. 2012:854*. Stockholm: Swedish Parliament.

Vandaele, K. (2006). A report from the homeland of the Ghent system: Unemployment and union membership in Belgium. *Transfer*, 13(4), pp. 647–657.

9 Job quality, flexibility and obstacles to collective agency

Pedro Mendonca

Introduction

The impacts of flexible working schemes on job quality and employee well-being have recently become an important topic of debate in both the public and academic spheres (Henly, Shaefer and Waxman, 2006; De Cuyper and Witte, 2007; Kalleberg, 2011; Holman, 2013; Henly and Lambert, 2014). In addition, academics have highlighted the key role that trade unions may have in regulating employers' behaviours over forms of flexible employment (Hoque, Earls, Conway and Bacon, 2014; UNITE, 2016; Simms, 2017). This chapter aims at contributing to this debate by examining the scope that trade unions have in actively addressing issues of job quality. This will enable this chapter to understand how trade unions' action can be strengthened or curtailed in workplaces where flexible working schemes are prevalent.

In Continental Europe, researchers have addressed the extent to which trade unions are capable to positively influence job quality by constraining the usage of flexible working schemes (Hyman, 2001). It is now consensual that unions' effectiveness is in great part dependent on institutional support, which is defined as the norms and rules which shape the interaction of economic and social actors and their associated interests (Rubery, Ward, Grimshaw and Beynon, 2005; Carré, Tilly, Van Klaveren and Voss-Dahm, 2010). In countries where the institutional support is limited, trade unions are only able to exercise influential power to the extent that they are recognised in the workplace. In other words, union's effectiveness is very dependent on the employer's will (Simms, 2017). According to Hyman (2001), the withdrawal of state intervention in the UK was key to weaken trade union presence and influence. For Hyman (2001) it has been left a void within the employment relationship following a series of alterations to the legal framework in 1980s, which involved weakening the legal protections available to individual workers, ending the tradition of trade union "immunities", and imposing complex procedural requirements. This gave the employer increasing discretionary control to determine the terms and conditions of the employment relationship. Currently, in the UK, it has been argued that the number of matters to which trade unions still have a decisive role during negotiations fell over the last years (Marchington, Wilkinson, Ackers and Dundon, 2001). Indeed, increasingly, management regards trade unions as consulting rather than negotiating partners (Danford, Richardson, Stewart, Tailby and Upchurch, 2005). Quantitative studies have also contributed to the debate by providing evidence of declining trade union membership and influence (Bryson and Forth, 2010; BIS, 2014; Waddington, 2016)

Given these concerns, this chapter empirically examines how job quality is an outcome of a dynamic relationship between employer and trade unions. In doing so, the chapter specifically analyses how trade unions are able or unable to influence and regulate flexible working schemes in the workplace in order to improve job quality. A case study involving a bottling hall operating in the Scottish Spirits Industry (SSI), where intense market fluctuations are present, was used for this investigation. The following sections firstly discuss how the context of industrial relations in the UK can give insights into the examination of trade union effectiveness in countering and regulating flexibility in the workplace; secondly, a bottling plant in the SSI will be taken as an example for describing flexible working arrangements and its impact on job quality; thirdly, by analysing the workers' structural and associational power resources in the bottling plant, the chapter discusses the trade union's capacity to influence the employers' behaviour. Lastly, the findings will be discussed taking into consideration the extant literature.

Theoretical framework: trade unions, job quality and flexible work practices

Control over aspects of jobs has been highlighted as one of the main components of good jobs (Holman, 2013), and researchers have emphasised the role of trade unions in enhancing such control by demonstrating the ways in which they can shape and regulate certain dimensions of job quality (Kalleberg, 2012; Simms, 2017). However, such influence is argued to be dependent on three interrelated "powers" which provide trade unions the capacity to constrain employers' harmful actions. Brookes (2013) argues that unions are accrued with three distinct types of power: institutional, associational and structural power. Institutional power is the combination of laws and regulations existing in specific national or regional contexts, which aid in channelling interests from one actor [employee] to the other [employer]. Associational power derives from the workers' capacity to organise themselves into collective bodies such as trade unions and political parties. Structural power comes from the ability for workers and/or trade unions to shape employers' behaviours using the strategic position that they occupy in relation to the economic system. However, structural power can be hindered by high levels of unemployment or underemployment in the labour market, or because the required skills to perform the job are not very complex or rare. In Brookes' (2013) account, these power resources can be used by workers and trade unions in order to effectively disrupt employers' actions that potentially curtail job quality.

It has been demonstrated that institutional power has been key for trade unions across Europe (but not in the UK) to exercise some type of regulatory constraint of flexible working practices (Hyman, 2001). The established "standard employment" and "standard working week" typically illustrate trade union action in most Continental European countries (Hyman, 2001). Indeed, research has demonstrated positive effects on job quality resulting from trade unions constraining management-led flexible working arrangements (Carré et al., 2010; Holman, 2013). For instance, Holman (2013) reports that unions will be more effective in positively influencing job quality in countries where they have institutional support. Holman (2013) highlights countries such as Germany, Belgium and Nordic as those with better outcomes. In a similar vein, other researchers have argued that in coordinated market economies, where trade unions are strongly backed by institutional support, higher levels of job quality are more prevalent (Esser and Olsen, 2012; Green et al., 2013). Hoque et al. (2014) add to this discussion by demonstrating that such outcomes are a result of institutional support aimed at enabling workers' and unions' involvement in organisational decision-making.

However, in the context relevant to this chapter it is important to consider that the industrial relations debate in the UK points to the withdrawal of institutional support, erosion of collective action, and declining influence of trade unions in the workplace since the 1970s (Waddington, 2016). It has been argued that nowadays trade unions are only able to exercise some influential power insofar as they are recognised in the workplace (Simms, 2017). Even when that is the case, some studies have suggested that trade unions experience various constraints. For instance, Hoque et al. (2014) highlight that workers' voice is highly dependable on managers' motivation to respond constructively to workers concerns. Similarly, it has been argued that even in workplaces where trade unions are recognised their power is diminutive (Kersley et al., 2006). These accounts are sound when one considers that private sector unions and collective bargaining covers only 17 per cent of the workplace in the UK (BIS, 2014, p. 31). In addition, Bryson and Forth (2010) report that the percentage of union representatives involved in collective disputes declined from 29 per cent in 1980 to 18 per cent in 2004. Indeed, union density and bargaining coverage in the UK has been reported to be at an all-time low (see Waddington, 2016).

Moreover, researchers suggest that low levels of institutional support and union density have been coupled with processes of workforce fragmentation due to the ever-more usage of flexible contract arrangements. This is problematic for trade union because, as Haidinger and Flecker (2015) argue, workforce fragmentation is an effective divide-and-rule strategy that weakens labour by inhibiting solidarity. Similarly, Doellgast and Greer (2007) contend that the workforce fragmentation on the one hand makes it easy for employers to introduce variation in working conditions for different groups of workers; and, on the other hand, makes it more difficult for trade unions to coordinate and organise different groups of workers who hold different and often conflictual interests. These aspects entail that trade unions in the UK are constrained in both their institutional and associational powers. Furthermore, Selwyn (2013, pp. 78–79) suggests that intensification of market pressures, internationalisation of product markets, and contemporary forms of production rooted in highly pressured workplaces have all challenged trade union structural and associational power. In the context of the withdrawal of institutional support and low levels of associational power within the UK, employers gain increasingly greater latitude to unilaterally implement flexible working practices and negatively influence job quality.

Thus, lacking the institutional support of their continental counter-parts, coupled with low levels of union density and bargaining power, unions in the UK have been increasingly pushed into adopting partnership agreements[1] with employers (Danford, Richardson, Stewart, Tailby and Upchurch, 2008, 2009). According to Danford et al. (2008), the partnership model is to a large extent a process of weakening trade unions, where the union is closer to management and further from the real problems of the shop floor. Typically, this is because trade unions engage in concessions related to productivity, which results in managers gaining control over workers (Stewart and Matinez Lucio, 1998). Furthermore, for Kelly (2004), the partnership outcomes are in many ways dependent on strong or weak bargaining power, i.e. the balance of power in the workplace determines which side is most favoured in partnership deals. Kelly (2004) argues that partnership deals usually contribute to the reinforcement of common interests between the employer and trade union in benefit of the former, which weakens the union's capacity to influence the employer's behaviours. Thus, a trade union in a partnership agreement combined with low levels of institutional support is unlikely to positively influence job quality. Given this context, the research question of this chapter is to examine the extent to which a trade union is able or unable to influence and regulate flexible working schemes in the workplace in order to improve job quality.

Research methods

This chapter draws on research evidence from one case study, a large bottling hall involved in the process of bottling and packaging of spirit. The case study organisation is located in Glasgow, Scotland and it is referred to as SpiritsCo. SpiritsCo is part of a large Scottish spirits manufacturer, involved in production, bottling and packaging of spirit. The company has recently increased their market-share with a series of mergers and acquisitions, which has resulted in an increase of production and sales worldwide. This has led to a closer relationship and dependency with supermarkets, in order to sell their products. In turn, the company has been going through a process of change by focusing on flexibilisation of the workforce, such as new highly flexible contractual arrangements, adopting three 8-hours shifts, and other practices that involve availability for work, overtime, discretion over shift pattern change, annualised hours and termination of contract. Arguably, it is through these practices that the company is able to adjust labour costs to market demands and fluctuations. Nevertheless, the company is considered to be a good employer, as it is able to provide good wages and generally good terms and conditions in an area of Glasgow where employment is limited. This research study focuses particularly on one production site – the bottling hall. This workplace has a varying workforce throughout the year, ranging from around 130 to 220 workers. It is a unionised workplace, where the union has a strong presence.

Although the process of bottling and packing spirit is highly automated, the work tasks are typically physically and mentally draining. Individuals undertake their work in teams and have a specific assembly line to which they are assigned. The work tasks involve repetitive movements, such as placing cartons into the machines, picking up bottles, packing bottles into boxes, quality check and loading and unloading storage in the required amounts. Depending on their level of skills, workers can perform different but limited working tasks.

Qualitative research data was gathered during the course of one year (from July 2014 to September 2015) using semi-structured interviews, focus groups, and numerous hours of observation. Overall, research included 28 semi-structured interviews and three focus groups with a total number of 17 participants. The participants included workers (permanent full-time, permanent core-flexi and temporary workers), managers and line managers, and union representatives. The interviews were in general 45 minutes to one hour long and were conducted within the premises of the workplace, whereas the focus groups varied between one and one and one-half hours. In addition, a number of organisational documents were analysed, coupled with long hours of observation.

By adopting a qualitative research the sample in this study was not aimed at making it statistically significant; rather it was aimed at discussing in a comprehensive way the theoretical aspects using a multilevel analysis (Ackroyd, 2004). This is accomplished when the collection of new data no longer helps furthering the understanding of the studied social phenomenon. Thus, the sampling is driven by theoretical assumptions. Lastly, the gathered data was coded and analysed using NVivo, which enabled a systematic theoretical coding of the data (Bazeley and Jackson, 2013).

The research evidence is presented in two segments. The first examines managerial intents to organise labour and the labour process in response to market derivatives, and in which ways this can curtail job quality. This first segment is important in order to comprehensively frame the trade union's role within the studied context. Therefore, the second segment explores by what processes the trade union is able or unable to influence flexible working schemes and improve job quality.

Findings

Management's role in shaping job security and flexible work practices

The bottling hall staffing levels, as stated in the methodology, varied throughout the year from 130 during periods of low market demand to 220 in "rush periods". Managers reported that SpiritsCo was using three types of contracts to cover their labour needs in the bottling hall – permanent full-time contracts, permanent core-flexi contracts and temporary contracts. The first is a standard contract of employment, whereas the second and third contract types entail certain flexible aspects. One HR member of staff reported a rising trend in flexible contracts, which resulted from a policy that blocked hiring workers on full-time contracts, allowing only the recruitment of individuals on flexible contracts. As Figure 9.1 indicates, such policy resulted in a sharp decrease of permanent full-time workers over the years. This illustrates the importance of flexible forms of contracts for SpiritsCo.

The flexible contracts have risen over the years to a level that dominated the bottling hall shop floor, and all interviewees consistently stated that this was due to one main purpose: to effectively adjust labour costs to sales demands.

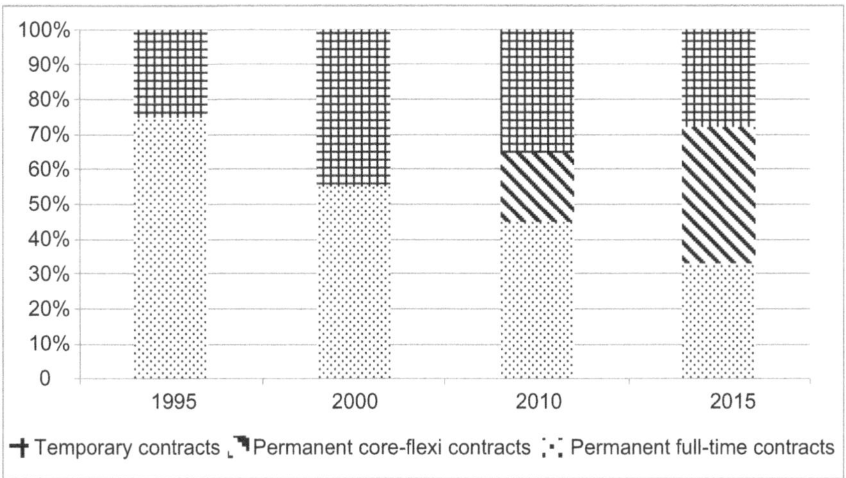

Figure 9.1 Development of ratio over the years (1995–2015) between different types of contracts used in SpiritsCo bottling hall

The permanent full-time workers were considered by management as part of the core workforce, and the majority had been working for the company for 15 years or more. Most managerial staff argued that full-time workers did not have the "right attitude", and were averse to change and flexible working schemes. In terms of working time, interviewees referred that full-time workers were employed on fixed 38 weekly hours with overtime being voluntary and upon an increased hourly rate. Moreover, the bottling hall managers mentioned that the present collective agreement granted full-time workers the choice on which shift to work, and whenever the night-shift came on they were given prerogative. The night-shift was appealing to workers due to its enhanced "shift allowance", where workers would get an extra one pound and half an hour compared to other shifts. Although management reported ways in which they could circumvent these constrains, these rules generally protected full-time workers from the maximisation of flexible working schemes.

In relation to the two types of flexible contracts, SpiritsCo management consistently mentioned that its *raison d'etre* was to adjust labour costs to market demands. Both temporary and core-flexi contracts entailed different levels of flexibility, which allowed management to adjust manning numbers in the shop floor in different ways.

Specifically relating to temporary workers, the way in which management controlled labour costs was two-fold: firstly, by breaking service; and, secondly, through variations in working time. Relating to the first aspect, breaking service meant the company could avoid costs with pensions, holidays and statutory compensation fees. Although management had to mandatorily give one-week notice to lay off temporary workers, it was reported that this had a collateral effect: temporary workers were being laid off, and brought back in for very short periods of contract, so that management could maximise the flexibility from these contracts. One line manager illustrates how this process obeys to market imperatives:

> When they're brought in here [we] give them 2 week contracts, and then again 2 weeks and then we look at the business, like how is it going to progress over the year.
>
> (Line Manager 1)

Despite this system of uncertainty, most of the temporary workers would come back to SpiritsCo "year in, year out" (Bottling Hall site manager). The company, due to the previously outlined financial gains, fostered this type of relationship. However, it was also welcomed by the workers, due to the lack of labour market alternatives in the area. Illustrative of this returning dynamics is that from the interviews made to temporary workers, the majority of them had more than 10 years of (broken) service with the company.

In relation to working time, it was reported that management had total control over individuals' shift patterns and overtime work. Managerial staff and workers consistently reported that the control was attained through the power imbalances between management and temporary workers. For instance, one HR member of staff reported that power imbalances were nurtured right from the recruiting process: management would only hire individuals that showed the most availability to work in the three different shifts. By confirming this level of compliance, the bottling hall manager stated that workers showing greater availability for the day-shift would have less probabilities of being hired. This was because the company's needs lay primarily on the twilight and night shifts.

The core-flexi contractual scheme was fairly new to the organisation and was aimed at bringing further flexibility to the workplace. This was particularly acute in terms of working time, as this group of workers was employed on "annualised hours". There were two important working time features within this contract. Firstly, despite the permanent nature of their contracts, individuals' working hours were reviewed on a yearly basis to adjust to sales forecasts. As a result, these could increase or decrease depending on market demands. Secondly, the flexible nature of the core-flexi contract allowed management to adjust staffing levels to market demands on a daily and hourly basis. Overall, managers considered this contract to be highly valuable in the day-to-day run of the business:

> [N]ow with this system of the flexi it all changed . . . because now we have a lot more flexibility. We don't have to use the full workforce at all times, we just put them at home when there is not enough demand and we bring them when needed.
>
> (Line Manager 4)

The real value of core-flexi contracts lies in the capacity it provided management to adjust the individuals' working hours by the minute. Workers could be brought to work and sent home in the same day, depending on the supply needs of the business. Most managers, and particularly line managers, emphasised that the nature of this contract was purely based on the sales and production needs of the company. Core-flexi workers are contracted on annualised hours that are not set. The flexible nature of annualised hours contracts allowed management to keep core-flexi workers sitting at home during the periods of less production demand, and bring them back to the bottling hall in "rush periods", where they have to make up for the hours that they did not work when sitting at home.

In sum, the SpiritsCo's attempt to maximise flexibility in the workplace is clear by this evidence. The flexibility brought clear divisions and different managerial treatment between groups of workers with different contracts. This data also emphasise that the site's flexibility was not limited to flexible forms of employment contracts, but also to the various types of working time schemes.

Trade union's prospects in influencing flexible working schemes

The aim of the chapter was to examine the ways in which the union is able or not to regulate flexible working schemes in order to shape job quality. As outlined previously, flexible working schemes in SpiritsCo were to some extent under the regulation of collective agreement, which aimed at placing a number of constraints on managerial action. This collective agreement had been an outcome of a partnership deal between SpiritsCo and the trade union present in the workplace. However, the union's capacity to improve job quality conditions was highly constrained by two interrelated emerging themes. The first relates to the internalisation of market pressures rhetoric into the trade union's discourse. The second relates to the lack of capacity to harmonise the different interests existing in the three-tiered workforce.

Relating to the first theme, union representatives frequently legitimised management drive to introduce flexible practices by claiming: "it's the nature of business" (Union Representative 1). It was consistently reported by union representatives that the fluctuation of market demands was an imperative to which the company could not run away from, and thus had to adjust to. While interviewing one of the union representatives, it was clear the assimilation of the company's logic by emphasising organisational objectives:

> We've got to be part of the company structure, we're not self-sufficient . . . hmm [we] can't influence everything, we don't have a say on everything because in the end of the day the company has to be profitable.
>
> (Union Representative 2)

This approach was present in the other union representatives' narratives, where it was emphasised that the company has to move forward and "keep up with the challenges of the current economy" (Union Representative 1). In turn, the various flexible practices were accepted by the union as an inevitable response to the vagary of the market. This vision was clearly present in union representatives' interviews:

> [I]f the business requires core-flexis to work more [hours] than they are expected to understand that . . . we as representatives have to understand that.
>
> (Union Representative 1)

This approach directly clashed with flexible workers' interests. Illustrative of this was the general idea that the union was more of a "business partner, than protecting workers' interests" (Permanent Employee 1). This acceptance of market derivatives intersects with the second identified theme – the union's lack of capacity to bring together the different interests showed by

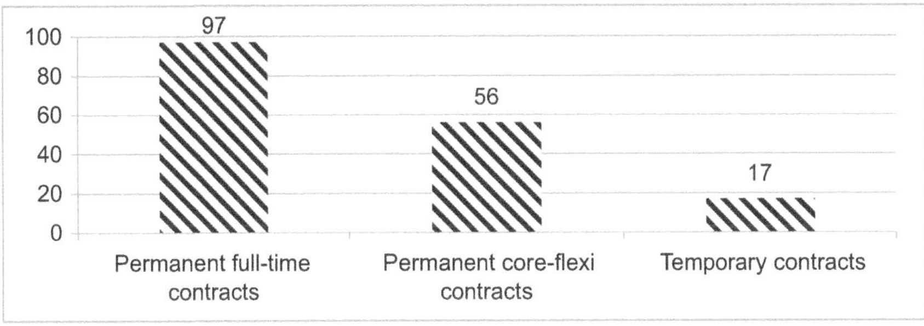

Figure 9.2 Union membership per type of contract at SpiritsCo bottling hall

the three-tier workforce. Considering Figure 9.2, a clear division of union membership rates between groups of workers can be seen: the membership amongst permanent full-time workers is close to maximum (97 per cent), whereas for the other two groups of workers the percentages are significantly lower.

These figures partly illustrate the fragmented workplace, which impacts on the union's strategy in bringing together the divergent, and often conflictual, interests of different groups of workers. The union's capacity to regulate flexible working schemes and harmonise workers' interests was constrained differently in relation to temporary and core-flexi workers.

Regarding temporary workers, interviewees explained that the short-term nature of the contracts and the victimisation and vulnerability of these individuals hampered the union's capacity to get involved and workers' willingness to become involved with the union. One union representative argued that flexible contracts naturally hindered the capacity for the union to systematically defend individuals' rights, as he explains:

> Relationship can be slightly stranded, and lot of it comes down to the fact that these temporary workers when they come back, they are in here for short[er] periods of time . . . it is difficult to engage with these people to become part of the union. The union struggles a wee bit with that.
>
> (Union Representative 3)

Moreover, interviewees further discussed that managerial intimidation relating to job security resulted in temporary workers feeling vulnerable and fearful of taking a more militant stance by engaging with the union. This perception was consistently reported by all interviewed union representatives and the majority of workers. One union representative justified this because temporary workers were highly dependent on SpiritsCo "to boost their finances from the wages they get in here, even for a short period of the year" (Union Representative 2). Temporary workers who highlighted subtle threats by management supported this:

> [Y]ou are often told that we get much better conditions than in other bonds . . . people with zero hour contracts and employed through agencies. . . . we get told "wake up and smell the coffee".
>
> (Temporary Worker 3)

The vulnerable employment situation of temporary workers meant that changes in working time patterns were seldom challenged by individuals. Although temporary workers showed an overall dissatisfaction with the regime in place, they were unlikely to voice it or to get involved with the union.

Regarding the core-flexi workers, contrary to the temporary workers, the union was able to maintain and defend many of the pay-related benefits such as yearly bonuses and pay increases. This was crucial for the union to maintain a significant membership rate amongst core-flexi workers. However, interviewees explained that the nature of the core-flexi contract constrained the union's capacity to oppose flexible working practices. The union's inability was also predicated in its internalisation of management's needs for flexibility. For instance, the acceptance of the newly implemented core-flexi contracts is a strikingly illustrative example of the union's approach to flexible working practices. One of the measures taken to reduce temporary contracts was to allow SpiritsCo to implement the recent core-flexi contracts. The union representative mentioned that these contracts were allowed by the union because they recognised the company's needs to maintain levels of flexibility, but at the same time could also meet the needs of individuals by offering more stable contracts. Despite the union's good intentions, this practice furthered divisions and fragmentation amongst the workforce. However, the workers' view was that the union used flexible workers as a bargaining ship to maintain some terms and conditions for the full-timers. In turn, the union had become innocuous in preventing and regulating management's abuse in the usage of these contracts:

> Since the new model [core-flexi contracts] come in, 5 or 6 years ago with the increase of business orders an' all that, all of that has escalated and now flexi contracts seems to be the norm.
>
> (Union Representative 2)

Furthermore, interviewees referred to two main barriers to the union's capacity to provide effective support to core-flexi workers in relation to changes in working time patters. Firstly, workers reported that union representatives often legitimised management drive in using core-flexi contracts flexibility to its maximum extent. Union representatives argued that flexibility was established contractually and thus it was within management's scope to use it. Secondly, union representatives mentioned that most core-flexi workers overlooked union's involvement when contractual changes were being negotiated. Similarly to temporary workers, the core-flexi workers recognised that they were highly reliant on getting enough annual working hours (and consequently weekly wages) for their livelihoods and frequently reported lack of bargaining power and capacity to challenge the employer's flexible practices. This aspect was also referred by one union representative who discussed workers' fear and vulnerability:

> [I]t is not as easy to stop all the changes that are going on in here. Most of them [core-flexi workers] are dead scared. . . . I mean, they don't stand up to management. . . . So they sometimes agree with things and now they are being pushed all over, and they can be called the day before to come to work often 10 or 12 hours in the following day . . . so then you have people working here 50 or sometimes 60 hours and people here dragging themselves at work.
>
> (Union Representative 2)

It was clear the union had not made a successful transition from representing a largely integrated workforce (Figure 9.1) to adopt new strategies that protected individuals from being used as part of a process of labour flexibilisation. Not only the union in the bottling hall failed to find an effective way of regulating and moving towards harmonisation across the three-tier workforce, but also so did assimilated management's viewpoints and perceptions relating to the need of flexibility in the workplace.

Discussion and conclusion

The main aim of this chapter was to examine the extent to which a trade union has the ability or not to influence flexible working schemes and improve job quality.

The first contribution of this chapter relates to the fact that this data clearly demonstrates company-level practices and dynamics influenced by market pressures, which resulted in negatively affecting job quality. Although this was not the main aim of this paper, we consider that this is particularly important in order to comprehensively frame the trade union's role within the studied context. The inclusion of management's account allows this study to examine the reasons for the usage of flexible working practices related to job security and working time. It was clearly evidenced that management's motivation stemmed from the company's requirement to exactly match labour costs to the market demands. In this way, this chapter supports existing evidence that managerial action is partly driven by a wider political-economic framework, which in this case comes from market pressures (Kalleberg, 2011). However, it was also these market interferences that negatively influenced the trade union's ability to shape job quality in the workplace. This finding gives weight to the account that pressures rooted in the market are key determinants of change in job quality standards. It was clearly evidenced how the trade union assimilated the market values, and the way in which it constrained and hindered their capacity to oppose harmful flexible working schemes. The most striking evidence relates to agreement between the union and management, which resulted in the implementation of the new core-flexi contract based on annualised hours. This finding is also important as it addresses the problematic of job quality macroeconomic studies giving little attention to the role of the trade union in shaping job quality. In doing so, this chapter contributes to the extant literature not only by arguing that trade union are key actors in shaping (even if negatively) job quality (Hoque et al., 2014; Simms, 2017), but also by conceptualising and contextualising the driving forces that constrain the trade union's role.

The second contribution is interlinked with the latter, and relates to the union's ineffectiveness in regulating the employer's HR practices that aimed for the maximisation of labour flexibilisation. Previous studies in Continental Europe indicating that institutional power is a key determinant for trade unions to effectively constrain flexible working schemes may help understand this outcome (Carré et al., 2010; Holman, 2013). Nevertheless, taking into consideration this case study's union's associational power, where the membership is relatively high (especially for full-time and core-flexi workers), the finding is in this way surprising. There are two main reasons that help explain this finding – the first relates to the partnership deal; the second relates to the market pressures and consequent workforce fragmentation.

Firstly, by referencing Danford et al.'s (2008) conceptualisation of partnership agreements, the evidence previously outlined shows that the agreement between SpiritsCo and the trade union was employer-dominated, where the trade union defended its membership's interests, but mostly disregarded the interests of flexible workers (core-flexi and temporary workers). For instance, it was clear that the union accepted the implementation of various flexible working practices and a new form of contractual arrangement, which clearly impacted job quality for the flexible workers. Kelly (2004) argues that the results of partnership agreements are in many ways dependent on strong or weak bargaining power. The data presented in this chapter show that the union had very limited scope for bargaining, whereby SpiritsCo was able to implement practices and policies considered to be the most appropriate to adapt to market constraints and fluctuations. The findings evidenced that the union tended to frame flexible working arrangements as intrinsic and necessary in the overall running of the business. This finding shows why the union did not attempt to forcefully contest the flexible working schemes used by the employer. Thus, in addition to this finding contributing to support Danford et al.'s (2008) argument that partnership deals are to a large extent a process of weakening trade unions, it also gives weight to Kelly's (2004) findings in which partnership deals usually result in employer and trade union sharing common interests. This study contributes to the extant literature arguing that sharing interests produces negative outcomes in terms of job quality.

In relation to the second point made relating to the union's ineffectiveness in regulating the employer's behaviour, there are important considerations to highlight. Despite the union having a relatively high membership density compared to the rest of the union density in the private sector – 17 per cent (BIS, 2014), it was not enough to counter SpiritsCo's willpower. This can be explained by Brookes' (2013) power resources. As argued throughout the theoretical framework, the trade unions' capacity to constrain employers' actions relates not only on membership numbers and density, but also to the union's capacity to enhance and take advantage of its structural power (Brookes, 2013). The research evidence from this study suggests that the underlying cause for the union's lack of structural power were the market pressures. The response of management to the vagary of the market was to produce a highly fragmented workforce, which progressively resulted in increasing dissimilar interests amongst the workers. In addition, this was amplified by workers' feeling of insecurity and by the lack of viable labour market opportunities. Despite the relative high percentage of union membership, it was this phenomena that lead to the union's lack of capacity to regulate the employer's actions. On the one hand, the disparate interests meant the union was unable to speak for the whole workforce. On the other hand, the evidence showed that workers were fearful in joining the union. It was these two interrelated factors that impacted the union's structural power. As a result, the union was easily manipulated to comply with management's desire for increased flexibility in the bottling hall. Thus, although some researchers have argued that low levels of union density have been an outcome of processes of workforce fragmentation (Doellgast and Greer, 2007; Haidinger and Flecker, 2015), this chapter suggests that fragmented workforces have also an important role in weakening trade union's structural power. This case illustrates how multiple lines of fragmentation and tiering can be seen as weakening labour's influence and capacity to counter, regulate and shape job quality. This is particularly acute where pressures stemming from the market are accepted not only by management but are also assimilated by the trade union. In this way, this contribution empirically supports Selwyn's (2013) view that the intensification of market pressures undermines union's structural power.

As noted earlier, trade unions in the UK lack institutional support (particularly when they are compared with trade unions operating in Continental Europe). Although this research study shows a trade union with relatively high levels of associational power, the lack of institutional and structural powers hinders the union's capacity to disrupt production, and consequently constrains agency in improving job quality standards for the majority of workers in this specific workplace. These findings are important because they can help lead the job quality literature away from the static analysis (Gallie, 2013) to an understanding of how distinct social actors and their different interests at workplace level influence job quality.

Note

1 Trade unions may attempt to develop working relationships with employers, which can take the form of a partnership agreement. Within this agreement both parties identify and work for common interests and objectives. The principles of partnership were incorporated into the Trade Union Congress's [TUC] New Unionism project in the aftermath of the 1997 general election in the UK. The New Labour government provided an important impetus for this development, by emphasising the "modernisation" of employment relations (Danford et al., 2009).

References

Ackroyd, S. (2004). Methodology for management and organisations studies: Some implications of critical realism. In Fleetwood, S. and Ackroyd, S. (Eds.) *Critical Realist Applications in Organisation and Management Studies* (1st ed.). London: Routledge, pp. 137–163.

Bazeley, P. and Jackson, K. (2013). *Qualitative Data Analysis With NVivo*. London: Sage Publications.

BIS (Department of Business Skills and Innovation). (2014). *Trade Union Membership 2013: Statistical Bulletin*. London: Department of Business Skills and Innovation.

Brookes, M. (2013). Varieties of power in transnational labor alliances: An analysis of workers' structural, institutional, and coalitional power in the global economy. *Labor Studies Journal*, 38(3), pp. 181–200.

Bryson, A. and Forth, J. (2010). *Trade Union Membership and Influence 1999–2009*. National Institute of Economic and Social Research.

Carré, F., Tilly, C., Van Klaveren, M. and Voss-Dahm, D. (2010). Retail jobs in a comparative perspective. In Gautié, J. and Schmitt, J. (Eds.) *Low-Wage Work in the Wealthy World* (1st ed.). New York, NY: Russell Sage Foundation, pp. 211–268.

Danford, A., Richardson, M., Stewart, P., Tailby, S. and Upchurch, M. (2005). Workplace partnership and employee voice in the UK: Comparative case studies of union strategy and worker experience. *Economic and Industrial Democracy*, 26(4), pp. 593–620.

Danford, A., Richardson, M., Stewart, P., Tailby, S. and Upchurch, M. (2008). Partnership, high performance work systems and quality of working life. *New Technology, Work and Employment*, 23(3), pp. 151–166.

Danford, A., Richardson, M., Stewart, P., Tailby, S. and Upchurch, M. (2009). Union organizing and partnership in manufacturing, finance and public services in Britain. In Gregor, G. (Ed.) *Union Revitalization in Advanced Economies: Assessing the Contribution of Union Organising* (1st ed.). Basingstoke: Palgrave Macmillan, pp. 56–82.

De Cuyper, N. and De Witte, H. (2007). Job insecurity in temporary versus permanent workers: Associations with attitudes, well-being, and behaviour. *Work & Stress*, 21(1), pp. 65–84.

Doellgast, V. and Greer, I. (2007). Vertical disintegration and the disorganization of German industrial relations. *British Journal of Industrial Relations*, 45(1), pp. 55–76.

Esser, I. and Olsen, K. (2012). Perceived job quality: Autonomy and job security within a multi-level framework. *European Sociological Review*, 28(4), pp. 443–454.

Gallie, D. (2013). *Economic Crisis, Quality of Work, and Social Integration: The European Experience*. Oxford: Oxford University Press.

Green, F., Mostafa, T., Parent-Thirion, A., Vermeylen, G., Van Houten, G., Biletta, I. and Lyly-Yrjanainen, M. (2013). Is job quality becoming more unequal? *Industrial & Labor Relations Review*, 66(4), pp. 753–784.

Haidinger, B. and Flecker, J. (2015). Positioning labour in service value chains and networks: The case of parcel delivery. In Newsome, K., Taylor, P. and Bair, J. (Eds.) *Putting Labour in Its Place: Labour Process Analysis and Global Value Chains* (1st ed.). New York, NY: Palgrave Macmillan, pp. 64–82.

Henly, J. and Lambert, S. (2014). Unpredictable work timing in retail jobs: Implications for employee work–life conflict. *ILR Review*, 67(3), pp. 986–1016.

Henly, J., Shaefer, H. and Waxman, E. (2006). Nonstandard work schedules: Employer-and employee-driven flexibility in retail jobs. *Social Service Review*, 80(4), pp. 609–634.

Holman, D. (2013). An explanation of cross-national variation in call centre job quality using institutional theory. *Work, Employment and Society*, 27(1), pp. 21–38.

Hoque, K., Earls, J., Conway, N. and Bacon, N. (2014). Union representation, collective voice and job quality: An analysis of a survey of union members in the UK finance sector. *Economic and Industrial Democracy*, 38(1), pp. 27–50.

Hyman, R. (2001). *Understanding European Trade Unionism: Between Market, Class and Society*. London: Sage Publications.

Kalleberg, A. (2011). *Good Jobs, Bad Jobs: The Rise of Polarized and Precarious Employment Systems in the United States, 1970s to 2000s*. New York, NY: Russell Sage Foundation.

Kalleberg, A. (2012). Job quality and precarious work: Clarifications, controversies and challenges. *Work and Occupations*, 39(4), pp. 427–448.

Kelly, J. (2004). Social partnership agreements in Britain: Labour co-operation and compliance. *Industrial Relations*, 43(1), pp. 267–292.

Kersley, B., Alpin, C., Forth, J., Bryson, A., Bewley, H., Dix, G. and Oxenbridge, S. (2006). *Inside the Workplace: Findings From the 2004 Workplace Employment Relations Survey*. London: Routledge.

Marchington, M., Wilkinson, A., Ackers, P. and Dundon, T. (2001). *Management Choice and Employee Voice*. London: Chartered Institute of Personnel and Development.

Rubery, J., Ward, K., Grimshaw, D. and Beynon, H. (2005). Working time, industrial relations and the employment relationship. *Time and Society*, 14(1), pp. 89–110.

Selwyn, B. (2013). Social upgrading and labour in global production networks: A critique and an alternative conception. *Competition & Change*, 17(1), pp. 75–90.

Simms, M. (2017). Unions and job quality in the UK: Extending representation within regulation institutions. *Work and Occupations*, 44(1), pp. 47–67.

Stewart, P. and Matinez Lucio, M. (1998). Renewal and tradition in the new politics of production. In Thompson, P. and Warhurst, C. (Eds.) *Workplaces of the Future* (1st ed.). London: Palgrave Macmillan, pp. 65–83.

Unite. (2016). *Unite Secures Minimum Wage Victory for Sports Direct Workers* [online]. Available at: www.unitetheunion.org/news/unite-secures-minimum-wage-victory-for-sports-direct-workers/ [Accessed 2 October 2016].

Waddington, J. (2016). Employment relations in the United Kingdom. In Bamber, G., Lansbury, R., Wailes, N. and Wright, C. (Eds.) *International and Comparative Employment Relations: National Regulation, Global Changes*. London: Sage Publications, pp. 20–46.

10 Job quality for temporary agency workers and client organization employees at a Swedish manufacturing plant

Kristina Håkansson and Tommy Isidorsson

Introduction

This chapter deals with job quality in terms of job security and employability in workplaces using temporary agency workers. Statistics show an increase in the number of temporary agency workers across Europe, often interpreted as an increased demand for flexibility in the labour market. However, it is important to note that this flexibility is gaining the client organizations hiring agency workers who can adjust the number of staff. From the perspective of the temporary agency worker, this flexible staffing might imply insecurity in employment (Jonsson, 2007; Håkansson and Isidorsson, 2007). Job security and employability are important aspects of job quality (Kalleberg, 2013; Muñoz de Bustillo, Fernández-Macías, Esteve, and Antón, 2009; Muñoz de Bustillo, Fernández-Macías, Antón, and Esteve, 2011; Stier, 2015); a crucial issue is of course how job security could be achieved for those workers who are believed to be most exposed to flexible staffing strategies. Standing (2009, 2011) argues that insecurity is becoming more diffused in society and also concerns several dimensions. According to Standing the precariat is a new emerging class consisting of people facing insecurity in several aspects, among them employment security and future career development. The precariat is not a homogenous group but includes temporary agency workers, who are the focus of this study. This study takes its start from temporary agency workers as their labour market situation in a clear way illuminates the job security and employment security aspects of job quality.

In order to better understand temporary agency work, it is essential to understand the concept of flexibility, and especially numerical flexibility. There is a strong conception of temporary agency workers being used in order to achieve numerical flexibility (Atkinson, 1984; Houseman, 2001; Kalleberg, 2001; Kalleberg, Reynolds, and Marsden, 2003, see also Introduction in this volume). Hence, these workers are used only in times of peak demand, and it is easy for the client organization to terminate contracts when demand slackens. There is a built-in logic in this kind of use of temporary agency workers: Since they are envisaged as staying for only a limited period of time, they are given work tasks with brief initial on-the-job training and no access to the internal labour market at the client organization (Kantelius, 2010). This use entails a division of the workforce into core and periphery, with the temporary agency workers constituting the peripheral workforce. There is a large body of research confirming that temporary agency workers have unfavourable working conditions compared with those of client organization employees; they are less secure, and they experience lower job quality and job satisfaction (Wagenaar et al., 2012; Paoli and Merllié, 2001; Nienhüser and Matiaske, 2006). These results are strongly associated with numerical flexibility. However, a new way of using temporary agency workers has recently emerged: that of strategic use, in which such workers constitute a quasi-permanent part of the client organization's staff (Håkansson, Isidorsson, and Strauss-Raats, 2013; Holst, Nachtwey, and Dörre, 2010; Vidal and Tigges, 2009). This strategic use of temporary agency workers is long-term and interweaves the temporary agency workers with the client organization employees within the work organization. Accordingly, there is no obvious segmentation into core and periphery, as is the case when temporary agency workers are used in order to achieve numerical flexibility. Rather, the border between the client organization's insiders, or core workers, and the outsiders, or peripheral workers, is somewhat blurred (Håkansson et al., 2013; Holst et al., 2010; Olsen, 2006).

Swedish temporary agency workers' job security, by that also the job quality, might be seen as an exception since they can obtain open-ended contracts and receive pay between assignments. In cases where temporary agency workers are used long-term, are integrated into the work organization of the client organization, and perform the same work tasks, their working conditions seem to be fairly equal to those of the other employees.

The aim of this chapter is to empirically elucidate and explain how job quality expressed as job security and employability is perceived in Swedish workplaces using temporary agency workers. To do this, we have selected a 'best case' situation involving Swedish temporary agency workers who share the same work tasks as user firm employees and who are highly integrated within the work organization.

In the following sections, we describe the triangular relationship in the staffing industry and put our study into a theoretical framework including a review of previous research, and then present the Swedish context for temporary agency work. Next, we discuss the aim and elaborate the research questions for this study. Subsequent sections outline our methods, results, discussion, and conclusion.

Previous research and theoretical framework

As described in the introductory Chapter 1 of this volume, job quality is a multi-dimensional concept that consists of two major aspects, the employment quality and the work quality. The employment quality refers to aspects of the employment relationship such as employment contract and remuneration (Muñoz de Bustillo et al., 2009, p. 14, 2011, pp. 455–457). Work quality refers to the activity of work itself. According to the same model, skill development and also participation can influence both work quality and employment quality. Skill development can be obtained via formal training but also via on-the-job training. This chapter focuses on job quality for temporary agency workers from an organizational perspective in order to understand how managerial practices affect individuals' job quality. First we have to understand the relations within the staffing industry. Temporary agency work can be described as a triangular relationship (Bergström, 2003, p. 9; Storrie, 2007, p. 106). There is an employment relationship between the temporary agency worker and the agency, a management relationship between the temporary agency worker and the client organization, and a business relationship between the client organization and the temporary work agency. Figure 10.1 illustrates this triangular relationship.

From the perspective of a temporary agency worker, there is a dual relationship: an employment and a management relationship. The employment relationship deals with employment conditions such as type of employment contract and wages. The management relationship concerns factors in the day-to-day working situation, cf. Figure 10.1.

The dual employment and management relationships are interesting from a theoretical perspective. Most research on job quality departs from a single relationship in which the employer is responsible for both the employment and management relationship. However, for temporary agency workers employment quality, including job security, refers to the agency (the employer), while the work quality refers to the client organizations (the manager). A study of temporary agency work gives us the opportunity to separate the employment relationship and the management relationship. Furthermore, studying temporary agency workers that are integrated in the work organization sharing the daily work tasks with the client organization employees makes it possible for us to investigate the importance of differences in employment relations for job quality.

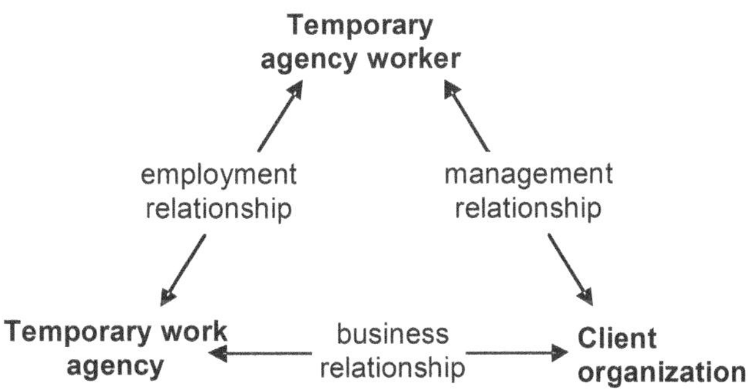

Figure 10.1 The triangular relationship in the staffing industry

There is a long-standing literature that empirically analyses the working conditions for temporary agency workers. Wilkin (2013) shows in a meta-study that job satisfaction is significant lower among temporary agency workers compared with permanent workers and temporary employees. One important explanation for lower job satisfaction among temporary agency workers is the lack of job security. Leschke, Schmid, and Griga (2007, p. 340) define job security as 'the certainty of retaining a specific job with a specific employer.' Gazier (2007, p. 102) draws on the definition by Leschke et al., but formulates it as 'granting the continuation of the same job.' Accordingly, job security connects to the actual employer and the possibility of remaining in the job with that employer. Job security is thus also connected to the regulation of employment protection. A large number of studies show that temporary agency workers experience lower job security compared to workers in other types of employment when age, gender, educational level, and occupational group are also taken into account (Aletraris, 2010, p. 1144; Håkansson, Isidorsson, and Kantelius, 2012; De Cuyper, Notelaers, and De Witte, 2009; de Graaf-Zijl, 2012; Forde and Slater, 2005; Morris, 1999). Also in line with these results is a study by Hall (2006), showing that temporary agency workers are less satisfied with job security than are employees with traditional contracts. Results from another study show that type of employment contract, age, and training have a significant impact on perceived job security (Håkansson et al., 2012). However, according to Standing (2009, 2011), precarious workers are not only those on temporary contracts, but also include employees with open-ended contracts. The point is that the precariat faces insecurity and unpredictability in several different dimensions. In addition, results from an extensive research review of agency work and occupational health and safety indicate job insecurity as a major psychosocial issue in the temporary agency work industry compared with traditional forms of employment (Håkansson et al., 2013, pp. 19–27). Although these results were conclusive, nurses were one group that was not found to perceive job insecurity, indicating that the labour market situation is an important consideration in understanding job insecurity (Allvin, Jacobson, and Isaksson, 2003).

Another aspect of job quality is employment security or employability, which is the possibility of remaining in a paid job. Employability is not connected to one specific job or one specific employer, but to the security that is associated with staying in employment in the labour market (Wilthagen and Tros, 2004). Muñoz de Bustillo et al.'s (2011; see also Chapter 1 in this volume) use 'skill development' which is connected to this concept and includes both on-the-job-training and formal training. Employability can thus derive from both the employment relationship and the management relationship (see Figure 10.1). Work experiences gained from working in client organizations can improve their skill development and by that their employability and chances of staying in a paid job. Also, the temporary work agency can also offer training, increasing agency workers' employability. Wagenaar et al. (2012) investigate perceived employability using data from the Netherlands Working Conditions Survey 2008. They compare temporary agency workers with workers having four other types of employment contract, and find that temporary agency workers have the lowest values when it comes to perceived employability.

On the individual level, employability can be seen as a person's own responsibility to increase his or her qualifications in order to become more employable (Smith, 2010). In this context, employability refers to different kinds of educational achievements on the individual level (Campbell, 2000; Gazier, 1998; McQuaid and Lindsay, 2005). Fugate, Kinicki, and Ashforth (2004, pp. 15–16) argue for a more complex view of employability as a psychosocial phenomenon in which the individual has to 'acquire the knowledge, skills, abilities, and other characteristics (KSAOs) valued by current and prospective employers'. Thus, Fugate et al. (2004) include the individual's behaviour, experiences, abilities, feelings, motivation, and attitudes. Employability, in this case, is intertwined with personal characteristics and is not easily changed.

Employability can also be understood as an organizational responsibility. De Vos, De Hauw, and Van der Heijden (2011) found that the employer's support for skill development enhances the worker's perceived employability. Thus, employability is not merely an individual's ability to achieve continuous learning, but also the employer's, or the client organization's in the case of agency workers as in this study, ability to offer skill development and to support such development. Kirves, De Cuyper, Kinnunen, and Nätti (2011, p. 900) argue that employability is more important to temporary workers than to permanent employees. This argument can be understood from an exchange relation perspective. In exchange for the insecurity of their employment, temporary workers may expect training and opportunities to learn new things and, in doing so, to increase their employability. In addition, employability can be seen as a coping strategy for the insecure labour position of temporary workers; thus, it can be viewed as an alternative to the job security that is achieved by tenure (McQuaid and Lindsay, 2005, p. 202).

While job security can be strengthened by tenure due to the employment regulation of 'last to hire – first to fire'. Employability, i.e. employment security, seems to be weakened by tenure. Furåker, Nergaard, and Saloniemi (2014) found that perceived employment security depends on age, tenure, and health. Older workers perceive fewer possibilities of getting a new job, and the same holds true for people with long tenure or poor health.

Previous research has shown differences between the employability of client organization employees and that of temporary agency workers (Kantelius, 2010). The former group perceives higher employability due to better possibilities of skill development. Temporary agency workers can obtain skill development from both the client organization and from the agency, that is, the employer. However, there is an in-built logic in the hiring of personnel that hinders skill development. The client organization does not invest any more skill in the temporary agency worker than is required for performing the assignment. The temporary work agency does not offer skill development to temporary agency workers who are currently on assignment, as this would jeopardize the business contract with the client organization (see the triangular relationships within the staffing industry shown in Figure 10.1). Hence, temporary agency workers on long-term assignments have difficulty accessing skill development (Kantelius, 2010).

To summarize, the general picture from previous research is that temporary agency workers have lower job quality due to a more insecure position compared to workers in other types of employment relations, including client organization employees. However, most studies are done in contexts where the agency workers have temporary contracts lasting for the time of the assignment or lack the rights to pay in-between assignments. There is a need for studies that scrutinize job security and employability for temporary agency workers when their working conditions are equal to that of user firm employees.

Temporary agency work in Sweden

Sweden is characterized in rather liberal terms in its regulation of agency work (Arrowsmith, 2006). Prior to the Temporary Work Agency Act of 1993, it was illegal to run private work agencies for the purpose of making a profit (Berg, 2008, p. 106). There is no specific legislation governing the staffing industry in Sweden. Temporary work agencies are treated like any other business and labour laws are the same for both temporary agency workers and other workers. This lack of specific legislation is in line with Swedish labour market practice, with the social partners being given the responsibility to regulate via collective agreements. Collective agreements covering temporary agency workers have emerged for both white- and blue-collar occupations. Even though there has been some discussion within the trade unions about conditions concerning the use of temporary agency workers (Håkansson and Isidorsson, 2014), agency work can be described as an integral part of the Swedish labour market (Bergström, Håkansson, Isidorsson, and Walter, 2007).

According to the Swedish Employment Protection Act, there are two principal types of employment contracts: open-ended and limited duration (Swedish Code of Statutes, 1982:80). These two types are usually referred to as permanent and temporary contracts. Since Swedish temporary work agencies are treated like any other kind of business, the normal employment contract for a temporary agency worker should be open-ended. According to the Act, the principle of 'last to hire, first to fire' should apply if there is any downsizing. However, in negotiations with the local trade union it is possible for the employer to make exceptions from this rule. Few countries stipulate a certain type of contract for temporary agency workers in their legislation. Open-ended contracts are possible in a little more than half of all European countries (OECD, 2013, p. 89).

The directive on temporary agency work lays down the principles of equal treatment for temporary agency workers and client organization employees (European Commission, 2008). These principles are also stated in the Swedish Agency Work Act, which explicitly stresses that temporary agency workers must have the same conditions as those who are directly employed by the client organization (Swedish Code of Statutes, 2012:854, Section 6). According to the collective agreement between Swedish Staffing Agencies and the blue-collar unions of the Swedish Trade Union Confederation, temporary agency workers must have an hourly wage corresponding to the average hourly wage at the client organization or, as expressed in the collective agreement, 'the average earning position . . . for comparable groups at the client' (Staffing Agreement, 2016, Section 4, Subsection 2). The collective agreements also provide employees with the right to a wage during periods when they are not on assignment, which is known as the guaranteed wage. In the collective agreement for blue-collar workers, the guaranteed wage is SEK 104.50 (€ 10.7) or SEK 110.50 (€ 11.3) per hour (Staffing Agreement, 2016, Section 5). Even though there are examples of deregulation, the trend is for legislation and regulation to be increased, with the aim of reducing social dumping; the EU directive 2008/104/EC constitutes an example of such legislation (Arrowsmith, 2008). However, even though many countries have a regulation guaranteeing equal pay, such a regulation does not describe the whole truth of the situation. In the UK, for example, it takes 12 weeks for an agency worker at the same assignment to 'qualify' for equal treatment (OECD, 2013, p. 91). In some countries, such as Australia, Iceland, Japan, and Switzerland, the guaranteed pay only refers to the minimum standards (OECD, 2013, p. 91).

In sum, Sweden distinguishes itself as the country with the best prerequisites regarding equal treatment for temporary agency workers' wages and employability. Temporary agency workers have the same opportunity for open-ended contracts as other employees, and for blue-collar temporary agency workers, pay is in accordance with the average pay at the workplace. In addition, having guaranteed wages between assignments adds to the security net.

Aim and research questions

The aim of this chapter is to empirically elucidate and explain how job quality, expressed as job security and employability, is perceived in Swedish workplaces using temporary agency workers.

For the purpose of isolating the effects of the dual employer and management relationships for temporary agency workers, we have selected a case where the temporary agency workers share the same work tasks and are highly integrated with client organization employees.

We examine our aim through the following research questions:

1. Where is the border line between temporary agency workers and client organization employees when it comes to job quality if both groups share the same work tasks and are highly integrated?
2. Is there any difference in job security satisfaction between temporary agency workers and client organization employees? In other words, is a permanent employment contract with a temporary work agency valued equally with a permanent contract with a client organization?
3. Is there any difference in the perception of employment security, i.e. employability, between temporary agency workers and client organization employees?
4. What factors from the employment relationship and the management relationship impact workers' job security satisfaction and perception of employability?

Method

This chapter is based on a survey of both client organization employees and temporary agency workers at a manufacturing plant in Sweden. This workplace constitutes one case in a broader research project on agency work and the work environment. We have previously conducted several studies of the workplace between 2008 and 2011 (Håkansson et al., 2013), from an organizational perspective. The workplace is a medium-sized production unit with day-to-day operations consisting of both assembly work and R&D. The production unit, which is the focus in this study, is staffed by skilled blue-collar workers. Work tasks there require two to three months of training and the cycle time is 1 hour. Temporary agency workers periodically constitute up to 30 per cent of the production staff.

The case

The plant has been using temporary agency workers for blue-collar work since 2004. Prior to that date, the client organization experienced a decline in demand and reduced its employees accordingly, laying off a large number of employees in 2003. When demand increased in 2004 due to a large order, the client organization decided to use temporary agency workers since the increased need for staff was thought to be temporary. Although the use of temporary agency workers thus began as a temporary solution for a large order, with no intention on the part of the client organization to continue the hiring of personnel after this peak, the plant has been using temporary agency workers on a fairly regular basis ever since. Most assignments have been staffed by the same agency workers for a considerable period of time, exceeding 2 years in some cases. Both the human resources manager and the production manager described the use of temporary workers as a means of achieving numerical flexibility.

In the wake of the financial crisis, the corporate executive board required local plants to provide for 30 per cent flexibility. Thus, this new use of temporary agency workers is not directly linked to an increase in orders, but rather to a strategic management decision. This decision is in line with the strategic use of workers that is distinguished by Holst et al. (2010). With the new staffing strategy, management at the client organization considered how temporary agency workers could be integrated into the work organization more efficiently than before – a reorganization that is an important part of the shift towards long-term strategic use.

According to the managers, all staff – temporary agency workers and client organization employees alike – are treated equally. The temporary agency workers are now used in the same way as client organization employees: They get on-the-job-training and participate in job rotation.

Design

In this chapter we use the longitudinal case study design where information derives from interviews with the local union representative, HR manager, and production manager as background. A questionnaire given to all staff at the workplace investigates how the two groups, that is, client organization employees and temporary agency workers under contract to this workplace, perceive their work.

The questionnaire was distributed at the workplace during a monthly production stop and staff meeting. The production stop lasted for 60 minutes and gave us a total time of 30 minutes to inform the workers about the survey and to have the workers fill in the questionnaire. Hence, everybody at the workplace that day had the opportunity to participate in the survey. This arrangement required our access to the company's ordinary meeting time, so the questionnaire had to be distributed and collected in one day. The response rate among the staff was extremely high, with only a few workers not handing in their questionnaires. However, the single-day distribution meant that absent employees could not participate. If the staff on sick-leave and on business trips were to be taken into account, the total response rate for blue and white-collar workers would be 80 per cent. The survey was distributed to all staff members at the plant. However, as the strategic use of temporary agency workers at this plant only concerns production, this chapter restricts itself to an analysis of blue-collar workers. White-collar temporary agency workers were not integrated with client organization employees in this work organization. By excluding white-collar workers from our study, we are able to restrict the study to a 'best case' scenario in which we expect no differences between temporary agency workers and client organization employees.

In total, 139 blue-collar employees at the client organization and 30 temporary agency workers returned the questionnaire. The proportion of temporary agency workers of the total workforce at the plant at the time of the survey was 18 per cent.

The questionnaires given to client organization employees and temporary agency workers were almost identical, although some wording was adapted in order to apply to the two different groups of respondents. The questions cover job characteristics, working conditions, and individual background data.

Operationalizations and data analysis

The dependent variables in this study are the two kinds of security: job security and employment security. Job security, that is, the certainty of being retained by the current employer, is measured using the question, 'How satisfied are you with your job security?' The response alternatives were: very satisfied, slightly satisfied, neither satisfied nor dissatisfied, slightly dissatisfied, and very dissatisfied. As the dependent variable is on the ordinal level of measurement, we have dichotomized the variable in order to be able to use logistic regressions. Satisfaction with job security was dichotomized into 'satisfied with job security' (very and slightly satisfied) and 'not satisfied' (others). This dichotomization implies a strict interpretation of job security, so that those responding as neither satisfied nor dissatisfied are coded as dissatisfied. The question does not measure objective job security, but rather how satisfied the respondent is. In general, job security is seen as important by a large majority of employees (Furåker, 2005, p. 151); thus, it is very likely that people who perceive low job security are dissatisfied in this regard. Our wording of the question is the same as that used in the European Community Household Panel Questionnaire, which makes it possible to compare our results with those of other studies.

A fruitful way of studying employability is, according to Berntson (2008), to focus on employees' perceived employability. In this study we have used Berntson's definition 'employability refers to an individual's perception of his or her possibilities of getting new, equal, or better employment' (Berntson, 2008, p. 15).We asked both temporary agency workers and client organization employees if they were obtaining skills that would be useful for future work at other companies. We used the question, 'How do you perceive your possibilities of getting a similar or better job in this or another sector?' The possible responses were: very high, rather high, neither high nor low, rather low, and very low. In order to be able to use logistic regression, we had to dichotomize this variable as well. In the analysis, we want to distinguish those who perceive high employability, so for that reason we only included the response alternatives for high and rather high possibilities in the category 'high employability.' Other responses are coded as 'low employability.'

Independent variables include: position as client organization employee or temporary agency worker, job tenure, training, skill development, work content, age, and education.

Previous research has shown overwhelming evidence for temporary agency workers' poor situation. In our study, we selected temporary agency workers experiencing the best conditions. Furthermore, from interviews we have the information that they share the same working conditions as their workmates employed by the client organization. The outcomes in job security and employability are therefore not self-evident. In a Swedish context, which includes employment protection legislation with the 'last to hire, first to fire' principle, tenure is important for job security. The average tenure for the client organization employees is 21 years. For the temporary agency workers, the mean tenure is slightly over 2.5 years. It is important to bear in mind that the two groups have different employers. Accordingly, it is not possible to compare tenure in absolute terms. To capture the employees at risk of being 'first out,' we used job tenure in relative terms. Client organization employees with less than 14 years' tenure were coded as short tenure, those with 14–24 years were coded as medium, and those with more than 24 years were coded as long tenure. For temporary agency workers, the corresponding periods were less than 16 months, 16–24 months, and more than 24 months.

Previous research also shows that training and development can increase employability. For temporary agency workers, both the employer (i.e. the agency) and the client organization can contribute in this regard. The employer can offer skill development and annual progress interviews. We measured skill development using the question, 'How satisfied are you with skill development provided by your employer?' We measured progress interviews using a question that asked whether or not the respondent had had a progress interview during the last 12 months.

Issues with work quality refer to the relationship with management, that is, the client organization (see Figure 10.1). These include having opportunities to decide how to perform work tasks, participating in change projects at the client organization, and learning new things. The latter refers to on-the-job-training. In the questionnaire, these questions are relational: Temporary agency workers are asked whether their opportunities are equal to, better than, or worse than those of client organization employees. Client organization employees are asked whether their opportunities are equal to, better than, or worse than those of temporary agency workers.

Methodological discussion

Since the workplace we investigated uses temporary agency workers who are fully integrated into production, and who perform the same work tasks as regular employees and participate in the same work rotation, this case gives us a unique opportunity to compare perceived job security and employment security among client organization employees and temporary agency workers. Furthermore, it is also possible to control for type of employment contract, since both groups have open-ended contracts. Because our selection of the workplace and the individuals studied is not random, it is impossible to generalize the responses to the labour market. Rather, this study can be seen as a best or unique case scenario, since we have selected a workplace with a staffing strategy that is characterized by the strategic long-term use of temporary agency workers and that offers them the best possible opportunities to achieve work development and to learn new skills – thus improving their employability and job security. According to Yin (2003, p. 40), this case study can be regarded as a critical case, that is, a case that tests a theory or a hypothesis. That is, if this best case of temporary agency workers do not have or perceive job security or employability, it is not likely that other groups of agency workers perceive job security or employability.

Results

Temporary agency workers constitute a stable proportion of the staff at the client organization studied. According to our survey the majority of these blue/collar agency workers, 57 per cent, entered into an employment relationship with the temporary work agency because they had no other choice – it was the only work they could get. Age, educational level, and tenure differ greatly between the two groups of workers at the plant. The mean ages of the client organization employees and the temporary agency workers are 48 and 29, respectively. Almost all temporary agency workers have attended upper secondary school, while one third of client organization employees have only 9 years of compulsory schooling. This difference can mainly be explained by the age differences. In general, today's younger generation has attended upper secondary school, and this level of education is usually a requirement for any employment. The investigated workplace is male-dominated, with about 90 per cent of both client organization employees and temporary agency workers being men. The bulk (93 per cent) of the temporary agency workers have been assigned to the client organization for more than 1 year. There are no differences between client organization employees and temporary agency workers concerning type of contract; all but one worker have open-ended contracts. Our analyses include only employees with open-ended contracts. Table 10.1 shows the background variables for the respondents.

Even though there are some differences in individual background, the blue-collar agency workers have been assigned to the workplace for long enough to learn the work tasks, and they take part in job rotation along with the client organization employees. The managers claim that both the employees and the temporary agency workers are treated equally. This claim seems to be valid when it comes to performing daily work tasks. Bivariate cross-tables show that there are no significant differences between client organization employees and temporary agency workers in work quality

Table 10.1 Background variables for respondents (per cent and numbers)

	Client organization employees	*Temporary agency workers*
Age (mean)	48 (SD 9.2)	29 (SD 6.5)
Education (%)		
Compulsory	32	3
Upper secondary school	48	93
Post-secondary	21	3
Total	100	100
Number	136	30
Sex (%)		
Male	89	93
Female	11	7
Total	100	100
Number	133	30
Tenure (%)		
Less than 14 years	24	
14–24 years	38	
More than 24 years	38	
Total	100	
Number	136	
Less than 16 months		30
16–24 months		40
More than 24 months		30
Total		100
Number		30
Length of assignment (%)		
Less than 7 months		0
7–12 months		7
More than 12 months		93
Total		100
Number		30

factors such as deciding how to execute their work tasks, learning new things, using their own skills, or having access to information or support. The majorities of both groups perceive their possibilities as being at least equal. There is no significant difference between the two groups in terms of satisfaction with the training provided by the employer.

However, there is a large difference in the occurrence of progress interviews. About 30 per cent of the temporary agency workers reported such talks, while the corresponding share of client organization employees was

60 per cent. Furthermore, opportunities to take part in change projects or development work seemed to be mainly intended for client organization employees. Almost half of the temporary agency workers estimated their possibilities as worse than those of the client organization employees in this regard, as shown in Table 10.2. Taking part in this kind of activity indicates a more lasting relationship, since experience with change projects or development work is seen as valuable, both to the company and with regard to the future. The border line between temporary agency workers and client organization employees thus lies in the client organization's investment in their skills and knowledge. The equal treatment and the integration within the work organization refer only to the daily work.

Our analysis shows that 69 per cent of client organization employees are satisfied with their job security, as shown in Table 10.3. This value can be compared to the Swedish labour market as a whole, where 70 per cent of employees are satisfied with their job security (Furåker and Berglund, 2014, p. 175). It should be noted that Furåker and Berglund's data includes

Table 10.2 Opportunity for client organization employees and temporary agency workers to take part in change projects or development work in relation to each other (per cent)

	Client organization employees	*Temporary agency workers*
Equal or better opportunity	90	52
Worse	10	48
Total	100	100
N	135	27

Sign. $p < 0.001$

Table 10.3 Satisfaction with job security for client organization employees and temporary agency workers (per cent)

Satisfaction with job security	*Client organization employees*	*Temporary agency workers*
Very satisfied	15	10
Slightly satisfied	54	33
Neither satisfied nor dissatisfied	21	17
Slightly dissatisfied	8	23
Very dissatisfied	2	17
Total	100	100
N	136	30

Sign. $p < 0.001$

employees on both permanent and temporary contracts, with 10 per cent of their sample having temporary contracts, while the client organization employees in our study are all on permanent employment contracts. A significantly lower share of the temporary agency workers in our study, 43 per cent, is satisfied with job security. Given that these workers have the same employment status, that is, permanent contracts, there is a considerable difference between the two groups.

Even though satisfaction with job security turned out to be less likely among temporary agency workers on permanent contracts compared with client organization employees, temporary agency workers may still experience employment security – i.e. employability. In our questionnaire, employability is captured by a question on the level of confidence of getting another job that is equivalent to or better than the present one. There were no statistically significant differences in perceived employability. In total, slightly more than one fourth of client organization employees think that they have a good chance of finding another (equivalent or better) job, as opposed to one third of temporary agency workers, as shown in Table 10.4. However, as mentioned before, these differences in employability between client organization employees and temporary agency workers are not statistically significant. Age and tenure have a significant impact on the perception of employability. Client organization employees are generally older and have longer (actual and relative) tenure. Therefore this result can be understood from a locked-in perspective (Furåker et al., 2014).

Our research review shows that several conditions can strengthen temporary agency workers' satisfaction with job security. Job security is connected with the employer relationship (see Figure 10.1). However, workers' current job at the client organization might impact their satisfaction with job security. That is, parts of the management relation such as the client organization's investment in the temporary agency worker's skill may spill over to

Table 10.4 Perceived employability for client organization employees and temporary agency workers (per cent)

Possibility of finding another equivalent or better job	*Client organization employees*	*Temporary agency workers*
Very high	1	10
Rather high	25	23
Neither high nor low	41	40
Rather low	22	20
Very low	11	7
Total	100	100
N	137	30

Not significant

impact the employment relationship. In Table 10.5, we analyse satisfaction with job security and the impact of training from the employer, a progress interview with the employer, the client organization's investment in skill such as participating in change projects or development work, and tenure. The control variables are age and education. In the logistic regression, we

Table 10.5 Factors impacting satisfaction with job security for client organization employees and temporary agency workers[1] (odds ratios, logistic regression)

	Satisfied with job security (odds ratio)	*Numbers*
Employer		
Client organization	4.33+	121
Temporary work agency (ref)	1	27
Skill development offered by the employer		
Satisfied	12***	54
Not satisfied (ref)	1	94
Progress interview with employer		
Yes	0.76 n.s.	83
No (ref)	1	65
Job tenure (relative measure)		
Short (ref)	1	39
Medium	1.75 n.s.	54
Long	1.55 n.s.	55
Participation in change project or development work		
Better opportunities	0.79 n.s.	59
Equal opportunities	0.89 n.s.	65
Worse opportunities (ref)	1	24
Education		
Upper secondary school or compulsory school (ref)	1	121
Post-secondary school	0.95 n.s.	27
Age		
<30 (ref)	1	
30–45	0.98 n.s.	22
46–65	0.59 n.s.	57
Constant	0.33	69
Nagelkerke	0.31	

Note: n.s. = not significant, + $p < 0.1$, * $p < 0.05$, ** $p < 0.01$, *** $p < 0.001$.

1 Only blue-collar temporary agency workers on permanent contract and client organization employees on permanent contract are included in the analyses.

have to use the dichotomized version of job security where answers 'very satisfied' and 'slightly satisfied' with job security denotes job security. The coefficients in the regression are to be interpreted as odds ratios.

Despite both groups having permanent contracts, the logistic regression shows that it is 4.3 times more likely for client organization employees to be satisfied with job security than for temporary agency workers to be satisfied. This result is significant at the 90 per cent level. According to employment protection legislation, temporary agency workers may have permanent contracts with their temporary work agencies independently if their assignment is limited in time or is terminated by the client organization. However, despite the temporary agency workers having permanent employment contracts at the temporary work agency, they do not experience job security to the same degree as client organization employees. Furthermore, the occurrence of progress interviews with employers does not seem to have any effect on workers' satisfaction with job security, while skill development being offered by the employer has an extremely large effect. It is important to note that, in the case of temporary agency workers, skill development as offered by the employer involves the temporary work agencies. Employees who are satisfied with the skill development offered by their respective employer are 12 times more likely to experience job security. The large difference between temporary agency workers and client organization employees in opportunities to participate in change project as presented in Table 10.2, did not show any significant effect on job security when adding 'satisfaction with skill development offered by the employer' into the analysis.

As shown in Table 10.4, there were no significant differences between client organization employees and temporary agency workers concerning the perception of employability. In addition to the factors included in the analysis of job security, we also analysed possibilities of learning new things and skill development by the client organization. These can be seen as indicators of skill development, which is crucial for employability.

However, a logistic regression of the factors impacting employability did not reveal any factors significantly impacting perceived employability. We also performed logistic regressions separately for client organization employees and temporary agency workers in order to find out whether different factors could explain the perceived employability, but found no differences. It seems that the client organization's management strategy of equal treatment levels out differences in employability – both client organization employees and agency workers perceive rather similar possibilities of finding another job.

Discussion

According to previous research on job quality, one important aspect is type of employment contract (Muñoz de Bustillo et al., 2011). Previous research has also shown that agency workers experience lower job security compared to workers in other types of employment (Aletraris, 2010, p. 1144; Håkansson et al., 2012; De Cuyper et al., 2009; de Graaf-Zijl, 2012; Forde and Slater, 2005; Morris, 1999) However, research shows this insecurity is affected by the temporary nature of the employment contract. In Sweden, where temporary agency workers have access to permanent employment contracts in the same way as other employees, and where the same employment protection legislation is valid for temporary agency workers as for other groups of employees, we might expect to find a different picture. In this chapter, we focused on a group of temporary agency workers who, in many important respects, have the same working conditions as client organization employees and who are integrated within the work organization. These workers have permanent employment contracts with the work agency and, according to management and union representatives at the client organization, are treated like client organization employees. At the client organization studied, the temporary agency workers form part of a strategic staffing buffer, which is labelled as 'strategic use' in previous research (Håkansson et al., 2013; Holst et al., 2010). Accordingly, we have chosen a critical case (Yin, 2003) that we consider to be very likely to contradict existing statements regarding temporary agency workers' precariousness when it comes to job quality.

Our analysis of this best case shows that temporary agency workers can overcome some of the features of its precariousness. In this case, agency workers are integrated into the work organization and there is no difference between their relationship with management and that of the client organization employees. Furthermore, our analysis shows that the border line that differentiates job security between agency workers and client organization employees does not merely lie between different kinds of employment contracts. Previous research has shown that type of contract has an impact on perceived job security. In this study agency workers not only share the same working conditions, both groups also have permanent contracts. This is supporting Standing's (2009, 2011) view that not only type of contract is important to take into account when discussing different groups' precariousness. Rather, the border line is caused by the client organization's different skill investments in temporary agency workers and in client organization employees. Thus, this border line between the two groups is not visible in daily work tasks.

However, even though the temporary agency workers and client organization employees have permanent contracts and share the same work tasks, they value their employment relationships differently. A permanent contract with a temporary work agency does not seem to entail job security to the same degree as a permanent contract does for client organization employees. Client organization employees are 4.33 times more likely to be satisfied with job security compared with temporary agency workers (Table 10.5). Even though both sets of workers fall under the same employment protection legislation, they perceive differences in job protection practices. The most important explanatory factor regarding the lower level of satisfaction with job security among temporary agency workers is their lack of satisfaction with skill development offered by their employer – that is, the temporary work agency. Previous research has highlighted the importance of training in relation to temporary agency workers' employability (Kirves et al., 2011). Our study shows that employers' investment in skill development has a direct effect on perceived job security. It is important for temporary agency workers to keep their competencies up to date, as this is necessary for new assignments. Skill development offered by the client organization satisfies the need for that particular assignment, but does not necessarily contribute to new assignments at other client organizations.

It has been argued that employability is more important than job security to temporary agency workers (Kirves et al., 2011). Employability can be achieved by formal training and on-the-job training, cf. Muñoz de Bustillo's skill development. In this case study, the temporary agency workers have the same general opportunities to skill development in their daily work as do the client organization employees. Even though there is a significant difference in the opportunities to participate in change projects or development work, this difference does not seem to have any impact on perceived employability. The management strategy of equal treatment in daily work seems to level out the differences in the perceived employability of the two groups.

Conclusion

This study contributes to a nuanced picture for some dimensions of temporary agency workers' job quality. Temporary agency workers and client organization employees sharing the same work conditions show both differences and similarities in job quality. Our analysis shows no difference concerning perceived employability, the equal treatment in daily work seems to level out the differences in the perceived employability of the two groups. However, they differ in job security, one of the dimensions of job quality. The most important explanation for temporary agency workers' lack of job security is the lack of skill development offered by their employer, i.e. the temporary work agency. In this regard, client organization employees are much better off. It seems that temporary agency workers on long-term assignment are trapped in a vicious circle. The agency does not have its workers interrupt their ongoing assignment at the client organization for skill development at the agency, since this interruption would jeopardize the business relationship between the client organization and the agency (see Figure 10.1). From the client organization, temporary agency workers only receive the skill development that is required for the specific assignment at the client organization. This means that even though the temporary agency workers are integrated into the work organization at the client organization, and perform the same daily work tasks as client organization employees, the client organization has no incentive to invest in any more than the required skills, because the temporary agency workers constitute only a 'buffer' in case of downturns. We argue that it is the temporary workers' position as a buffer that results in a lack of job security. Our results also show that the temporary agency workers' job security could be increased if their temporary agencies were to invest in skill development for their employees, thus overcoming the agency workers' vulnerability in constituting a buffer. In this way, skill development would balance the client organizations' flexibility in staffing. Job quality in terms of job security and employability would thus increase for temporary agency workers.

References

Aletraris, L. (2010). How satisfied are they and why? A study of job satisfaction, job rewards, gender and temporary agency workers in Australia. *Human Relations*, 63(8), pp. 1129–1155. doi:10.1177/0018726709354131.

Allvin, M., Jacobson, A. and Isaksson, K. (2003). *Att avgränsa det gränslösa sjuksköterskearbetet. En intervjustudie om sjuksköterskors villkor och valmöjligheter i bemanningsbranschen*. Solna: Arbetslivsinstitutet.

Arrowsmith, J. (2006). *Temporary Agency Work in an Enlarged European Union*. Dublin: European Foundation for the Improvement of Living and Working Conditions.

Arrowsmith, J. (2008). *Temporary Agency Work and Collective Bargaining in the EU*. Dublin: European Foundation for the Improvement of Living and Working Conditions.

Atkinson, J. (1984, August). Manpower strategies for flexible organisation. *Personnel Management*, 15(8), pp. 28–31.

Berg, A. (2008). *Bemanningsarbete, flexibilitet och lokalbehandling. En studie av svensk rätt och kollektivavtalsreglering med komparativa inslag* [Temporary Agency Work, Flexibility and Equal Treatment. A Study of Swedish Law and Collective Agreements Containing Comparative Elements]. Lund: Juristförlaget i Lund.

Bergström, O. (2003). Introduction. In Bergström, O. and Storrie, D. (Eds.) *Contingent Employment in Europe and the United States*. Cheltenham: Edward Elgar Publishing.

Bergström, O., Håkansson, K., Isidorsson, T. and Walter, L. (2007). *Den nya arbetsmarknaden. Bemanningsbranschens etablering i Sverige* [The New Labour Market. The Establishment of the Staffing Industry in Sweden]. Lund: Academia Adacta.

Berntson, E. (2008). *Employability Perceptions. Nature, Determinants, and Implications for Health and Well-Being*. Diss., Psykologiska institutionen, Stockholms universitet.

Campbell, M. (2000). Employability, adaptability and flexibility: Changing labour market prospects. *Regional Studies*, 34, pp. 655–668.

De Cuyper, N., Notelaers, G. and De Witte, H. (2009). Job insecurity and employability in fixed-term contractors, agency workers, and permanent workers: Associations with job satisfaction and affective organizational commitment. *Journal of Occupational Health Psychology*, 14(2), pp. 193–205. doi:10.1037/a0014603.

de Graaf-Zijl, M. (2012). Job satisfaction and contingent employment. *De Economist*, 160(2), pp. 197–218. doi:10.1007/s10645-011-9180-7.

De Vos, A., De Hauw, S. and Van der Heijden, B. I. J. M. (2011). Competency development and career success: The mediating role of employability. *Journal of Vocational Behaviour*, 79(2), pp. 438–447. doi:10.1016/j.jvb.2011.05.010.

European Commission. (2008). Directive on Temporary Agency Work 2008/104/EC of the European Parliament and of the Council. *Official Journal of the European Union*. Available at: https://eur-lex.europa.eu/legal-content/EN/ALL/?uri=celex%3A32008L0104

Forde, C. and Slater, G. (2005). Agency working in Britain: Character, consequences and regulation. *British Journal of Industrial Relations*, 43, pp. 249–271.

Fugate, M., Kinicki, A. J. and Ashforth, B. E. (2004). Employability: A psycho-social construct, its dimensions, and applications. *Journal of Vocational Behaviour*, 65(1), pp. 14–38. doi:10.1016/j.jvb.2003.10.005.

Furåker, B. (2005). Flexibilitet på arbetsmarknaden [Flexibility in the Labour Market]. In Fjaestad, B. and Wolvén, L.-E. (Eds.) *Arbetsliv och samhällsförändringar*[Working Life and Societal Changes]. Studentlitteratur.

Furåker, B. and Berglund, T. (2014). Job insecurity and organizational commitment. *Revista Internacional de Organizaciones*. Tarragona: Universitat Rovira i Virgili.

Furåker, B., Nergaard, K. and Saloniemi, A. (2014). Lock-in patterns among employees: A Nordic comparison. *The International Journal of Comparative Labour Law and Industrial Relations*, 30(4), pp. 435–458.

Gazier, B. (Ed.) (1998). *Employability: Concepts and Policies*. Berlin: European Employment Observatory.

Gazier, B. (2007). 'Making transitions pay': The 'transitional labour markets' approach to 'flexicurity'. In Jörgensen, H. and Kungshøj Madsen, P. (Eds.) *Flexicurity and Beyond: Finding a New Agenda for the European Social Model*. Copenhagen: DJØF Publishing.

Håkansson, K. and Isidorsson, T. (2007). Flexibility, stability and agency work. In Furåker, B., Håkansson, K. and Karlsson, J. Ch. (Eds.) *Flexibility and Stability in Working Life*. Basingstoke: Palgrave Macmillan.

Håkansson, K. and Isidorsson, T. (2015, December). Temporary agency workers – precarious workers? Perceived job security and employability for temporary agency workers and client organization employees at a Swedish manufacturing plant. *Nordic Journal of Working Life Studies*, 5(4), pp. 3–22.

Håkansson, K., Isidorsson, T. and Kantelius, H. (2012). Temporary agency work as a means of achieving flexicurity? *Nordic Journal of Working Life Studies*, 2(4), pp. 153–169. doi:10.1688/1861-9916_IJAR_2013_03_Hakansson.

Håkansson, K., Isidorsson, T. and Strauss-Raats, P. (2013). *Arbetsmiljö för hyresarbetskraft. En kunskapsöversikt om inhyrdas fysiska och psykoso-ciala arbetsmiljö* [Occupational Health and Safety for Temporary Agency Workers – Agency Workers Physical and Psychosocial Working Conditions]. Rapport 2013:10. Stockholm: Arbetsmiljöverket.

Hall, R. (2006). Temporary agency work and HRM in Australia. *Personnel Review*, 35(2), pp. 158–174. doi:10.1108/00483480610645803.

Holst, H., Nachtwey, O. and Dörre, K. (2010). The strategic use of temporary agency work: Functional change of a non-standard form of employment. *International Journal of Action Research*, 6, pp. 108–138.

Houseman, S. N. (2001). Why employers use flexible staffing arrangements: Evidence from an establishment survey. *Industrial and Labor Relations Review*, 55(1).

Jonsson, D. (2007). Flexibility, stability and related concepts. In Furåker, B., Håkansson, K. and Karlsson, J. Ch. (Eds.) *Flexibility and Stability in Working Life*. Basingstoke: Palgrave Macmillan.

Kalleberg, A. L. (2001). Organizing flexibility: The flexible firm in a new century. *British Journal of Industrial Relations*, 39, pp. 479–504.

Kalleberg, A. L. (2013). *Globalization and Precarious Work* (vol. 42). Los Angeles, CA: Sage Publications.

Kalleberg, A. L., Reynolds, J. and Marsden, P. V. (2003). Externalizing employment: Flexible staffing arrangements in US organizations. *Social Science Research*, 32, pp. 525–552.

Kantelius, H. (2010). Inhyrningens logik. Långtidsinhyrda arbetare och tjänstemäns utvecklingsmöjligheter och upplevda anställningsbarhet [The logic of temporary agency work. Learning opportunities and on the job-training of blue-collar and white-collar agency workers on long-duration assignments and the effect on their perceived employability], *Arbete och Hälsa*, 44(10). Gothenburg: Arbets-och miljömedicin, Göteborgs universitet.

Kirves, K., De Cuyper, N., Kinnunen, U. and Nätti, J. (2011). Perceived job insecurity and perceived employability in relation to temporary and permanent workers' psychological symptoms: A two sample study. *International Archives of Occupational and Environmental Health*, 84(8), pp. 899–909. doi:10.1007/s00420-011-0630-y.

Leschke, J., Schmid, G. and Griga, D. (2007). On the marriage of flexibility and security: Lessons from the Hartz-reforms in Germany. In Jörgensen, H. and Kongshøj Madsen, P. (Eds.) *Flexicurity and Beyond: Finding a New Agenda for the European Social Model*. Copenhagen: DJØF Publishing.

McQuaid, R. W. and Lindsay, C. (2005, February). The concept of employability. *Urban Studies*, 42(2), pp. 197–219.

Morris, J. A. (1999). Injury experience of temporary workers in a manufacturing setting. Factors that increase vulnerability. *AAOHN Journal*, 47, pp. 470–478.

Muñoz de Bustillo, R., Fernández-Macías, E., Antón, J. I. and Esteve, F. (2011). E pluribus unum? A critical survey of job quality indicators. *Socio-Economic Review*, 9, pp. 447–475.

Muñoz de Bustillo, R., Fernández-Macías, E., Esteve, F. and Antón, J. I. (2009). *Indicators of Job Quality in the European Union*. Directorate General for Internal Policies, Employment and Social Affairs, European Parliament, IP/A/EMPL/ST/2008-09 PE 429.972.

Nienhüser, W. and Matiaske, W. (2006). Effects of the 'principle of non-discrimination' on temporary agency work: Compensation and working conditions of temporary agency work in 15 European countries. *Industrial Relations Journal*, 37(1), pp. 64–77.

OECD. (2013). *OECD Employment Outlook 2013*. Paris: OECD Publishing. doi:10.1787/empl_outlook-2013-en.

Olsen, K. (2006). The role of nonstandard workers in client-organizations. *Industrial Relations*, 61(1).

Paoli, P. and Merllié, D. (2001). *Third European Survey on Working Conditions 2000*. Dublin: European Foundation for the Improvement of Living and Working

Conditions. Available at: www.eurofound.europa.eu/sites/default/files/ef_publication/field_ef_document/ef0121en.pdf

Smith, V. (2010). Enhancing employability: Human, cultural, and social capital in an era of turbulent unpredictability. *Human Relations*, 63(2), pp. 279–303.

Staffing Agreement. (2016). *Bemanningsavtalet. Kollektivavtal mellan Bemanningsföretagen och samtliga förbund inom LO och som gäller för företag som bedriver verksamhet inom dessa förbunds verksamhetsområden. 2016-05-01-2017-04-30* [Collective agreement for blue-collar workers working for staffing agencies from 1 May 2016–30 April 2017, Swedish Staffing Agencies, and trade unions within the Swedish Trade Union Confederation].

Standing, G. (2009). *Work After Globalization: Building Occupational Citizenship*. Cheltenham: Edward Elgar Publishing.

Standing, G. (2011). *The Precariat: The New Dangerous Class*. London: Bloomsbury Academic.

Stier, H. (2015). The skill-divide in job quality: A cross-national analysis of 28 countries. *Social Science Research*, 49, pp. 70–80. doi:10.1016/j.ssresearch.2014.07.008.

Storrie, D. (2007). Temporary agency work in the European Union: Economic rationale and equal treatment. In Furåker, B., Håkansson, K. and Karlsson, J. Ch. (Eds.) *Flexibility and Stability in Working Life*. Basingstoke: Palgrave Macmillan, pp. 103–122.

Swedish Code of Statutes. (1982:80). *Lag om anställningsskydd*. Svensk författningssamling [Employment Protection Act].

Swedish Code of Statutes. (2012:854). *Lag om uthyrning av arbetare*. Svensk författningssamling [The Agency Work Act].

Vidal, M. and Tigges, L. M. (2009). Temporary employment and strategic staffing in the manufacturing sector. *Industrial Relations*, 48(1). Oxford, UK: Blackwell Publishing, Inc.

Wagenaar, A. F., Kompier, M. A. J., Houtman, I. L. D., van den Bossche, S., Smulders, P. and Taris, T. W. (2012). Can labour contract differences in health and work-related attitudes be explained by quality of working life and job insecurity? *International Archives of Occupational and Environmental Health*, 85, pp. 763–773. doi:10.1007/s00420-011-0718-4.

Wilkin, C. L. (2013). I can't get no satisfaction: Meta-analysis comparing permanent and contingent workers. *Journal of Occupational Behaviour*, 34.

Wilthagen, T. and Tros, F. (2004). The concept of 'flexicurity': A new approach to regulating employment and labour markets. *Transfer*, 2(4), pp. 166–186.

Yin, R. K. (2003). *Case Study Research: Design and Methods* (3rd ed.). Thousand Oaks, CA: Sage Publications.

11 The social dimension of job quality

Perceived social support in contrasting regulatory contexts for temporary agency work

Pille Strauss-Raats

Introduction

Modern work is increasingly reliant on social relationships, illustrated by rising proportion of service sector jobs, workers adding to their income through 'gigs' in sharing economy and other innovative work practices (Eurofound, 2015). Organizational striving for flexibility places permanent full-time employees side-by-side with temporary workers, independent contractors and agency employees. As formal relationships between employers, employees and workplace communities loosen, workers are increasingly faced with the necessity to adapt to new contexts of work. Changing workplaces, tasks and colleagues present inherent risk of instability (Jonsson, 2007) for social relationships based on identity, trust and mutuality (Thoits, 2011). In contemporary western societies, satisfaction with one's social relations contributes more to well-being than increasing income (Lane, 2000), and the negative health effect of social isolation has been found to be comparable to these of the modern epidemics of obesity and smoking (House, Umberson and Landis, 1988). At workplaces, satisfaction with social relationships is positively associated with organizational commitment (Humphrey, Nahrgang and Morgeson, 2007), resilience and positive mood (Ryan and Deci, 2001). Social support at the workplace has a critical role in alleviating work-related stress (House, 1981). In a study based on the European Working Conditions Survey, Tangian (2007) identifies social climate as the third most influential aspect of job quality in terms of its effect on employee well-being (only job security and workload having stronger associations to well-being outcomes).

Temporary agency work (TAW) is a flexible work form where an employee is hired by one company but dispatched to work in either one or a series of other companies, called user firms. Research finds employees in this sector most often in peripheral positions of a segmented workforce (Atkinson, 1984; Doeringer and Piore, 1985), at high risk for low job quality, with particular challenges in the social context of work (Byoung-Hoon and Frenkel, 2004; Håkansson, Isidorsson and Strauss-Raats, 2013; Isaksson and Bellaagh, 1999; Kompier, Ybema, Janssen and Taris, 2009).

However, as the practice of TAW varies significantly between and within national institutional, sectoral and organizational contexts (Schömann and Guedes, 2012; Grimshaw, Ward, Rubery and Beynon, 2001; Håkansson and Isidorsson, 2012), its job quality is likely to vary greatly (Muñoz de Bustillo, Fernández-Macías, Antón and Esteve, 2011). At the same time there is notable shortage of research exploring the impact of these contextual differences, especially in a comparative perspective. Considering the interrelationships and trade-offs between job quality dimensions and their context-specificity (Muñoz de Bustillo et al., 2011), a better understanding of both of micro-level mechanisms and macro level factors shaping jobs at workplaces would be relevant for facilitating efficient interventions at different levels of impact.

The aim of the current multi-method comparative case study is to address this gap and explore how differences in the practice of TAW affect the social dimension of job quality in user firms within different national regulatory contexts. The social dimension of job quality is understood here as a multi-faceted sub-dimension of overall job quality, capturing characteristics of interpersonal relationships such as social inclusion, community membership, social support and so on. By using quantitative survey data along with qualitative evidence collected within one multinational company (MNC) with comparable manufacturing facilities in contrasting regulatory regimes, this chapter compares individual experiences of perceived social support for temporary agency workers and their direct-hired counterparts in two contexts. Acknowledging that job quality aspects tend to be interconnected (Muñoz de Bustillo et al., 2011), the study accounts for workload, skill development and social integration in explaining perceived social support from the supervisor and co-workers in relation to employment contract type.

The chapter will first present a theoretical framework, touching upon workforce segmentation theories that explain relative differences in quality of jobs for different employee groups, followed by an overview of the social dimension of job quality in existing job quality frameworks. Social support as a critical dimension for employee well-being will be discussed along with an overview of existing literature in the context of TAW. An overview of regulatory regimes of TAW in Sweden and Poland is followed by a methodological section describing the study design and presenting the two organizational cases. Empirical results will be followed by a discussion and concluding remarks.

Theoretical framework and previous research

Flexible work practices and workforce segmentation

Following from Mandelbaum's (1978) definition of flexibility as an ability to effectively respond to changing circumstances, Jonsson (2007) elaborates the concept as a continuous context-dependent process for achieving a desired variation in response to change. As described in the introductory chapter of this book, desirability of variation is grounded in a particular perspective depending on the combination of actor's capabilities, motivations and variation in environment. Employer's flexibility in quickly changing workforce levels by using temporary or outsourced workforce may thus be perceived by employees as instability of jobs or workplaces. In the context of work, preconditions for flexibility are largely shaped by (but not limited to) employment regulations and the larger institutional context, conditioning not only the motivation and capabilities of actors but also the inclusion of particular actors within a certain context in the first place. In allowing for flexibility in the mix of workforce, triangular TAW thus extends potentially diverging perspectives from employer-employee to the user firm and its direct-hired workers. Depending on the legal framework, agency workers can be tied to several agencies across time or be bound to one agency over a long term; they can be facing daily re-assignments or spend years at a user's workplace; there can be provisions for financial support between assignments or exposure to financial insecurity when not in work, with all of these provisions shaping the capabilities and motivations for the actors involved.

Workforce segmentation theories describe the division of labour markets into the core of secure good quality jobs and periphery of insecure low quality employment (Doeringer and Piore, 1985), with agency workers commonly categorized into periphery (Giesecke, 2009; Smith, 1998; Standing, 2009). This is often related to use of TAW for numerical flexibility in adapting workforce levels to demands (Atkinson, 1984). However, an increasing body of literature points to more complex patterns (Allvin, Jacobson, and Isaksson, 2003; Geary, 1992; Grimshaw et al., 2001; Smith, 1998). Håkansson and Isidorsson (2012) in describing how using TAW in a long-term perspective leads to strategic use not only for numerical but also functional flexibility. This can result in inclusion of agency workers in the workforce 'core' of skill discretion along with direct-hired workers, impacting not only tasks and skills but also managers' and user firm employees' attitudes towards the 'separate workforce'.

The social dimension of job quality

Social relationships in job quality frameworks

Acknowledging that job quality is a multi-dimensional concept with interconnections and trade-offs among its facets, Muñoz de Bustillo et al. (2009, 2011) limit the dimensions relevant for its understanding to 'those aspects of jobs that have a clear and direct impact on the well-being of workers' (Muñoz de Bustillo, Fernández-Macías, Esteve and Antón, 2009, p. 14). While they emphasize the value of particular job characteristics as outcome measures of job quality (Muñoz de Bustillo et al., 2011), the processes set up to achieve these outcomes can be used as procedural job quality measures with significance for evidence-based interventions.

Most job quality frameworks that pay attention to its social dimension focus on outcomes, referring to the availability of help and support from supervisors and co-workers, having friends at work and being part of a workplace community. Differences in precise operationalization illustrate the variety of understandings, levels of analysis, data availability as well as context-specificity. Muñoz de Bustillo et al. (2009) use the concept of social working environment to cover collegial support and workplace friendships, while alternative frameworks name social support (McClelland and Holman, 2015), comradeship (Green, 2006), collegiality (Tangian, 2007), interpersonal relationships (Clark, 2005) and social connections (Stiglitz, Sen and Fitoussi, 2009). The flip side of social strain (Rook, 1990) is mentioned as intimidation and discrimination at work (OECD, 2014).

The current study follows the procedure-outcome model by Muñoz de Bustillo et al. (2009) by focusing on perceived social support as the main outcome while accounting for both contextual and procedural factors that are relevant in shaping the need for support as well as facilitating its availability at the workplace.

Social support in the context of temporary agency work

The pathway from support as positively intended social interactions to well-being is commonly divided into two. Thoits (2011) describes these as emotional sustenance and instrumental coping assistance. This mirrors a widely used classification by House and colleagues (House, 1981; House and Kahn, 1985), distinguishing between emotional support based on encouragement and sympathy along with informational and instrumental support of advice and assistance. While emotional support can enhance overall resilience, coping assistance acts through matching help to particular situational demands. Exposure to demanding job characteristics at work can thus increase support levels through a heightened need for assistance while its availability is either facilitated or restricted by one's integration in relevant social networks (Brissette, Cohen and Seeman, 2000; Thoits, 2011).

Characteristics of TAW along with previous literature in the field suggest that while fragmented or time-limited presence and outsider status challenge access to support, it is also a context with heightened support needs for coping with insecurities, learning new tasks and managing a tough workload (Bosmans, De Cuyper, Hardonk and Vanroelen, 2015; Isaksson and Bellaagh, 1999; Smith, 1998; Voss, 2015). Formal exclusionary practices have been exemplified in policies restricting agency workers' access to social events and physical space or more subtly by task distribution and visual distinctions such as uniforms and badges (Byoung-Hoon and Frenkel, 2004; Smith, 1998; Winkler and Mahmood, 2015). These in turn can inhibit informal social cohesion by reinforcing conflicting power relations (Bosmans et al., 2015; Smith, 1998; Voss, 2015), with several studies illustrating exclusion by co-workers through various forms of stigmatization and conflict (Boyce, Ryan, Imus and Morgeson, 2007; Byoung-Hoon and Frenkel, 2004;

Chattopadhyay and George, 2001; Olofsdotter and Augustsson, 2008). Conversely, organizational exclusion can also lead to higher dependence on informal networks, increasing agency workers' motivation to form personal connections (Bosmans et al., 2015; Vajen, 2014), especially where there is a chance for future employment (Smith, 1998; Purcell, Brook and Lucas, 2011). Agency workers' accounts of how just being recognized and talked to at workplaces illustrate the human need to connect to others (Voss, 2015).

While the previous illustrates the dominant discourse of social relations in TAW in general, few studies operationalize this through the particular dimension of social support. Qualitative accounts from Sweden have described how agency workers in certain contexts do perceive supportive relationships within user firms (Kantelius, 2012; Voss, 2015) while others describe how discontinuity of assignments hinders supportive relations (Garsten, 2008; Isaksson and Bellaagh, 1999). However, these studies do not include comparison to user's employees. Quantitative studies that do include a comparative aspect have reported either no differences among employment groups (Kompier et al., 2009) or lower perceived support for agency workers (Paoli and Merllié, 2001), though not accounting for variance in job characteristics.

Aim and research questions

The aim of this study is to explore how differences in the practice of temporary agency work affect the social dimension of job quality for agency workers as well as their direct-hired counterparts in different national institutional regimes. Research questions guiding this exploration are following:

> *What are the differences and similarities in perceived social support for temporary agency workers and user firm direct-hired employees in different regulatory regimes?*
>
> *How can the outcomes in perceived social support be understood and explained?*

Regulation of temporary agency work in Sweden and Poland

Muñoz de Bustillo et al. (2011) emphasize the institutional impact on job quality mainly through welfare systems that interact with job characteristics in conditioning employee well-being. However, the institutional context through employment regulation also shapes employers' capabilities and motivations in if and how to use particular employment practices. In restricting TAW in certain jobs, allowing for fixed-term or open-ended contracts, mandating access to user's facilities or facilitating collective bargaining in setting independent standards, differences in contexts can shape the need for as well as availability of social support for agency workers in particular contexts. Sweden and Poland provide contrasting examples of TAW regulation under the common 'umbrella' of EU agency work directive 2008/104/EC.

TAW in Poland is shaped by a restrictive legal framework in the Act of 9 July 2003 on the Employment of Temporary Workers, limiting when, how and where TAW can be used. Polish TAW is characterized by the word *fixed-term*, as agency contracts can only be signed for a specific fixed-term assignment period and consecutive contracts are limited. In Sweden the situation is the opposite – with relaxed statutory regulation, TAW relies on sectoral self-regulation ensuring the norm of *open-ended* contracts with a work agency for blue-collar agency employees after an initial probationary period (Ahlberg et al., 2008). This difference can have implications for the social working environment through facilitating either short-term or long-term presence of agency workers at user firms but also shaping the contact between worker and agency. Even when carrying general employer responsibilities, the role of a work agency in Poland after job placement is secondary to the user firm (Table 11.1). In Sweden the agency carries

Table 11.1 Differences in regulatory contexts of temporary agency work in Sweden and Poland

	Sweden	*Poland*
TAW contracts	No restrictions in statutory law. The norm of open-ended contracts with work agency after initial 6 months negotiated in sectoral collective agreement.	Fixed-term contracts with work agency for duration of assignment in statutory law. Contracts limited to 18 months and consecutive contracts with one agency limited to 3.
TAW assignments	Not regulated, option for unlimited re-assignments.	Tied to particular employment contract.
Equal treatment and inclusionary work practices	General provision for non-discrimination.	Legal prohibition of unfavourable treatment in terms of work environment and employment conditions. User firm must provide work clothing and training if contract exceeds 6 weeks.
Collective bargaining	Sectoral collective agreements for white-collar and blue-collar TAW. Agency workers can join professional unions but cannot be represented in general employment matters by union organization at user firm.	Collective bargaining most active at workplace level where representative unions exist. Agency workers not unionized.

employer responsibilities in a more traditional sense, with open-ended contracts ensuring a level of continuity in supervisory and collegial relations at the agency even when daily work and supervision are at different users – assignment changes are unrestricted.

While agency and user firm employees can be members of the same trade union in Sweden, their representation is arranged through different organizational units – a user firm-based club for user's workers and a regional organization for agency workers with no union club at an agency (Håkansson et al., 2009). Collective representation is based on the employer also in Poland, where unions have difficulties in organizing agency employees and user firm unions cannot represent agency workers (Sula, 2008).

As seen, opportunities and constraints to take advantage of flexibility of TAW differ greatly in these two EU member states, shaping time frames and employer roles. However, both cases expose agency workers to a risk of structural exclusion.

Method and data

Multi-method comparative case study

As the case study method is particularly suitable for exploring pathways of impact in contemporary phenomena in their real-life contexts (Yin, 2014), a comparative multi-method case study design was chosen to better understand the social work environment as an outcome of organizational decisions embedded in their wider institutional settings. The cases of social work environment are investigated by sequentially integrating qualitative and quantitative evidence from interviews, observations and employee surveys (Seawright, 2016). Final inferences rely on quantitative survey results while qualitative methods are used to guide survey development (selecting variables, adjusting measurement scales), as well as support the analysis of quantitative outcomes.

Considering that the standards and practices of TAW vary within and between countries (Watts, 2013; Håkansson and Isidorsson, 2012), the study applies controlled comparison with most similar case design (George and Bennett, 2005). The two cases of social work environment in the context of TAW use are matched by their similarity in company-level characteristics while reflecting maximum variation at the national level.

Access to the MNC with comparable production facilities in both Sweden and Poland was negotiated through the HR department, but research was independent both in terms of funding and research focus. Empirical data collection began with a qualitative stage where organizational level practices regarding TAW use and social integration were explored through semi-structured interviews with the employer and employee representatives (Table 11.2), complemented by on-site observations.

Table 11.2 List of interviewees and interview languages in the two organizational cases

	Poland	*Sweden*
HR manager/specialist	2 (English)	1 (English)
Line/production manager	2 (English)	1 (English)
Head of local trade union	1 (Polish, interpreted into English)	1 (English)
Trade union head safety rep	1 (Polish, interpreted into English)	1 (English)
Company safety rep	1 (English)	*No comparable function*
Total interviewed	7	4

Interviewees were purposefully selected based on their professional status, with the aim to cover main functions relevant for the work environment and TAW use. Both employer and employee perspectives were included to cross-check information and balance response bias (Silverman, 2013).

Organizational context: two cases of temporary agency work

The MNC accessed for this study is a large manufacturing company operating the same type of production process using the same production system and following the same global HR policies both in Sweden and Poland. The MNC positions itself at the 'high-road' strategy in both product quality and employee relations.

In both cases nearly all blue-collar hiring is mediated by work agencies. In the Swedish site agency work is contracted in a long-term strategic partnership with one work agency, with the agency coordinator present at the user firm on a daily basis. In the Polish site the agency workforce is contracted through 2–3 different agencies, with very limited contact between the agency and its employees after the initial placement stage. This places all tasks related to daily supervision to user firm supervisors.

At both sites direct-hired employees and agency workers work in mixed teams of skilled and semi-skilled workers, rotating between stations based on skill levels. At the Swedish site TAW is used for both numerical and functional flexibility with full integration of agency workers in terms of participation opportunities in meetings and trainings but also on-the-job skill development. In the Polish site where the presence of agency workers is restricted in time, TAW is used for numerical flexibility only, with agency workers segregated into low-skilled jobs and excluded from company meetings and trainings. All workers use the same workplace facilities such as changing rooms and canteens at both sites.

Table 11.3 Organizational practices of temporary agency work at organizational level

	Swedish case	*Polish case*
Stability of employment: contracts and tenure	Open-ended TAW contracts after 6 months of probationary period. Tenure with agency and the user for up to 8 years.	Fixed-term TAW contracts with work agency ranging from few months to 18 months. Three consecutive contracts commonly used.
Stability of assignment	Long-term assignments in user firm but can be fragmented by assignments in other user firms according to user's production needs.	Short-term assignments in line with contracts with particular user firm, no transfers between assignments for the duration of contract period.
Integration in work organization: tasks, access and visual identity	Agency clothing. Inclusion in user firm's meetings and trainings. Skill development opportunities through on the job training. Equal access to user's facilities and social events. Additional social events arranged for TAW community by the agency.	User firm clothing but different colour of access badge. Exclusion from user firm's meetings and trainings. Equal access to user's facilities and informal social events. Segregation into low-skilled jobs. Limited contact with work agency and its colleagues, no social activities arranged by agency.

Company level unions aim to support agency workers informally at both sites, though in neither case are agency workers part of their local organizations. In the Polish site the local agreement between user and its trade union organization foresees that some agency workers must be offered direct-hired temporary contracts when a threshold of 15% for agency work is exceeded. In the Swedish site the increasing use of agency work over the years was accompanied by a stop on direct hiring, broken only recently when a few agency workers were hired on user firm permanent contracts. With open-ended agency contracts, assignments in this user firm are long. However, as the need for workforce fluctuates, so do assignments, it being not unusual to work half a week at the MNC and the other half at another client.

Table 11.3 gives an overview of organizational practices, understood here as procedural elements of the social dimension of job quality, with the following sections based on quantitative employee survey data exploring if and how contextual differences are reflected in employee perceptions of their social work environment.

Survey sample and data collection

The quantitative survey sample included all blue-collar workers at the two sites, both direct-hired and agency workers. At the Polish site, supervisors distributed questionnaires during working time, to be filled in at home and placed in locked return boxes at the workplace. Each questionnaire was accompanied by a cover letter explaining the purpose of research, ethical considerations, contacts for additional inquiries and also a small incentive – a coupon that could be exchanged for a chocolate bar in the factory canteen. Two researchers were at the factory to answer questions regarding the project. At the end of the 2-week response period, 498 responses were collected out of the 1215 questionnaires distributed (RR = 40.1%). Twenty-five respondents had not marked their type of employment contract, leaving 475 usable questionnaires.

At the Swedish site research assistants distributed the questionnaires to all production workers during monthly departmental meetings. They also provided a short introduction and collected completed questionnaires at the end of the meeting. The questionnaire included a cover letter with relevant details on the purpose, ethical considerations and contact details for further questions. Of the 209 questionnaires distributed, 202 were collected back (RR = 97%). Agency workers on temporary probationary contracts and trainees were excluded from further analysis due to low numbers in these categories, leaving the final sample size of 176.

Survey measures

Survey questionnaire included measures to capture a variety of aspects of job quality, adapted to the context of TAW. The measures were used in two languages, Swedish and Polish, respectively. Items and scales from pre-adapted tools were used to the extent possible but for self-developed items two-way translation by qualified professionals was used to ensure the correct meaning was conveyed (Hambleton, 2005). In order not to procedurally emphasize group membership based on employment contract, the same version of questionnaire was distributed to all workers, with a few specifying questions aimed only at agency employees.

Dependent variables: supervisor and co-worker support

Social support from supervisor and co-workers was both measured by a 4-item self-constructed scale to capture dimensions of perceived emotional (*Considers how I am feeling at work, Is easy to talk to when I need to discuss important personal matters*), informational (*Gives me advice on how to handle things when I need it*) and instrumental support (*Helps me out when things get tough*) (House and Kahn, 1985). Perceived social support as a generalized belief that support is there when needed was chosen for its strong association to mental health and well-being (Uchino, 2004). The wording explicitly distinguished colleagues and supervisors employed by user firm to avoid misconceptions about which employee group or supervisor to consider (Gallagher and Parks, 2001). Response scales differed slightly in the two countries, with 5-point Likert scales used in Poland and

4-point scales in Sweden, ranging from Always to Never and Often to Never respectively. Cronbach's alpha for the supervisor support scale was .93 in both countries and for co-worker support .94 in Poland and .90 in Sweden. For comparability, the scales were converted into a standardized 0–100-range scale.

Independent variables and controls

The main independent variable *employment contract type* had two categories in Sweden: user firm permanent (0) and agency permanent (1) employee. In Poland there were three groups: user firm permanent (0) and dummy variables (1) for user firm temporary and temporary agency workers.

Control variables included four job characteristics that were expected to condition the need for perceived social support in the context of TAW. A *Skill development* measure was modified from the *Skill discretion* scale of the Copenhagen Psychosocial Questionnaire COPSOQ II (Kristensen, Hannerz, Høgh and Borg, 2005) and included three items reflecting work that enabled on-the-job learning and taking initiative (α = .735 in Poland and α = .695 in Sweden). *Workload* measure was modified from the *Quantitative demands* subscale of COPSOQ II and included three items on excessive quantitative workload (α = .627 in Poland and α = .535 in Sweden). Job and assignment insecurity were measured by single follow-up questions to 'How much do you agree or disagree with the following statements describing some aspects of your job?', with job insecurity captured by 'I might lose my job in the next 6 months' and assignment insecurity by 'I might be transferred to another job against my will'. Response scales again differed slightly in the two countries, with a 5-point Likert scale in Poland and 4-point scale in Sweden. For skill development and insecurity in Poland, the response options ranged from 'To a very large extent' to 'To a very small extent' and for workload measure from 'Always' to 'Never'. In Sweden the range was from 'To a large extent' to 'To a very small extent' and 'Often' to 'Never' respectively. All scales were converted into standardized 0–100-range.

Social integration in the user firm that potentially facilitates access to support through connections in social networks (Thoits, 2011) was addressed by two self-developed context-specific measures. Formal social integration index listed three types of social occasions with access formally determined by user firm policies (meetings, trainings and company celebrations) and informal social integration measure listed three types of social occasions with unsanctioned access (coffee breaks, lunches or celebrations with colleagues). Response options to each item ranged: 1 = never, 2 = occasionally and 3 = often. For both subscales, responses from the three items were summarized, resulting in scales ranging from 3 to 9.

Additional controls included variables with likely impact on the need for and availability of social support. Gender and age can capture potential homophily effects (McPherson, Smith-Lovin and Cook, 2001) but also differences in roles and life stages. However, gender was excluded from final analysis due to the low number of females in the sample (see Table 11.4 for descriptive statistics). Age was measured in years. Previous literature suggests that tenure can have a strong association to workplace social relationships. Here tenure was excluded from among controls due to its high correlation to contract type – user firm employees belonged to high tenure categories while agency workers were almost exclusively short tenured. Trade union membership and participation in a job rotation scheme were first considered due to their potential role in facilitating access to supportive relationships through frequency of contact across diverse contexts. Finally, to control for differences across departments with their particular tasks and supervisory styles of managers, group dummies were used to account for departmental fixed effects.

Statistical methods

Bivariate correlations between all variables were studied as the first step of analysis. Control variables for job rotation and union membership were removed from further analyses as they showed no significant association with any of the dependent or independent variables (Agresti and Finlay, 2013).

Ordinary least squares regression (OLS) in a stepwise manner was used to assess the extent to which employment contract type, job characteristics and social integration explain perceived social support from user firm supervisors and co-workers.

Results

This section will describe the observed differences and significant associations predicting perceived support from user firm supervisor and co-workers for employees on different employment contracts whereas discussion section will further elaborate the results in a comparative context and the impact of different regulatory regimes. Descriptive characteristics of the survey sample and survey measures are provided in Table 11.4.

The share of agency workers within the sample is higher at the Swedish site, reflecting higher use of unrestricted TAW. At the Polish site where use of TAW is locally restricted to 15% and monitored quarterly, the share of 11% of agency workers within the sample suggests this group is somewhat underrepresented. Employees on temporary user firm contracts at the Polish site have been previously working in the user firm as temporary agency workers. At both sites, user firm permanent workers tend to be considerably older than their temporary counterparts, with the difference particularly

Table 11.4 Descriptive statistics of sample and survey measures

	Polish site				*Swedish site*		
	User firm permanent contract	*User firm temporary contract*	*Temporary agency workers*	*Total*	*User firm permanent contract*	*Permanent temporary agency workers*	*Total*
N	394	30	50	474	118	58	176
Per cent	(83%)	(6%)	(11%)	(100%)	(63%)	(31%)	(100%)
Age (M, SD)	45.07 (10.06)	39.93 (11.56)	36.72 (12.2)	43.88 (10.79)	44.87 (10.74)	28.44 (6.66)	38.80 (12.33)
Females	10%	7%	12%	10%	15%	16%	15%
User firm tenure							
Up to 1 year	1.03%	31.03%	46.94%	7.69%	3.54%	37.93%	15.2%
1–3 years	2.31%	58.62%	51.02%	10.9%	5.31%	29.31%	13.45%
3–10 years	46.41%	10.34%	2.04%	39.53%	5.31%	31.03%	14.04%
Over 10 years	50.26%	0%	0%	41.88%	85.84%	1.72%	57.31%
Rotating between different tasks	58%	73%	67%	60%	61%	57%	60%
Union membership	51%	31%	0%	44%	98%	88%	95%
Skill development *scale 0–100* (M, SD)	58.17 (21.31)	65.28 (17.10)	57.00 (18.47)	58.63 (20.60)	61.36 (23.25)	67.83 (18.11)	63.53 (21.83)
Work demands *scale 0–100* (M, SD)	56.41 (16.75)	55.36 (19.01)	48.13 (18.42)	55.26 (17.19)	66.96 (17.47)	61.08 (18.74)	65.04 (18.05)
Job insecurity *scale 0–100* (M, SD)	45.91 (26.60)	65.52 (21.56)	81.50 (28.49)	51.20 (28.68)	41.88 (31.01)	84.48 (28.08)	55.00 (36.11)
Assignment insecurity *scale 0–100* (M, SD)	55.97 (28.02)	56.03 (28.08)	66.00 (28.91)	56.82 (27.96)	69.52 (27.89)	86.78 (22.46)	75.24 (27.39)
Formal social integration *scale 3–9* (M, SD)	5.65 (1.40)	5.63 (1.22)	4.92 (1.23)	5.55 (1.39)	5.68 (1.28)	6.11 (1.36)	5.82 (1.32)
Informal social integration *scale 3–9* (M, SD)	5.18 (1.53)	5.47 (1.50)	5.38 (1.30)	5.20 (1.50)	5.95 (1.20)	6.31 (1.29)	6.07 (1.24)

notable in Sweden. The high tenure of user firm employees in both countries but especially in Sweden reflects low employee turnover. The data shows a 'breaking point' for tenure in Poland at 3 years, reflecting regulatory restriction to long-term and recurring temporary contracts. At the Swedish site the divisive point is at around 10 years – tenure distribution between contracts suggests very few new permanent contracts after TAW was introduced. The majority of all employees at both sites rotate between tasks, though the measure does not differentiate between low-skilled or high-skilled tasks. As can be expected, large differences are found in union membership at the Polish site with agency workers exclusively non-unionized while union membership is high for all employees at the Swedish site.

OLS regression models and outcomes for perceived social support are presented in Table 11.5 (user firm supervisor support) and Table 11.6 (user firm co-worker support). The significance threshold was set at .05. Based on previous research and theoretical framework, it was expected that perceived supervisor and co-worker support will be lower for agency workers but the effect is partly mediated by job characteristics shaping the need for support as well as social integration facilitating access to support. Results however reflect the opposite pattern where work on a temporary agency contract predicts significantly higher perceived support from both sources in both cases, though contrasting between-country differences emerge when job characteristics and social integration are controlled for.

Perceived social support from user firm supervisor

Employment contract alone explains only about 2–3% variation in perceived supervisory support in both cases, but this rises to 26–27% after accounting for the four additional job characteristics and age. Including the social integration measure adds another 4% and controlling for departmental fixed effects raises the variation explained by the models to 38% for the Swedish and 33% for the Polish case.

Without controlling for other job factors, agency workers at the Swedish site report 9.23 points higher supervisory support from their user firm supervisors than user firm own employees on a 100-point scale. However, the 'Job characteristics' model indicates that contract effect is fully mediated by other dimensions of job quality, with employees who report higher skill development perceiving higher supervisory support, those under excessive workload perceiving lower support and employees who think it likely that they will be reassigned to another job against their will also reporting low support from their supervisors. Controlling for social integration does not significantly change the effect of skill development and workload but reduces the effect of assignment insecurity while significantly increasing the effect of job insecurity.

Employees working on temporary agency contracts perceive significantly higher supervisory support when compared to both permanent

Table 11.5 OLS regression: effect of contract type, job characteristics and organizational integration practices on perceived supervisor support

	Perceived supervisor support in Sweden				*Perceived supervisor support in Poland*			
	Employment contract	*Job characteristics*	*Social integration*	*Social integration*	*Employment contract*	*Job characteristics*	*Social integration*	*Social integration*
Independent variables								
Temporary agency contract[a]	9.23 (4.31)*	1.08 (5.82)	1.30 (5.76)	.46 (5.71)	11.84 (4.20)**	16.88 (4.38)***	19.31 (4.35)***	19.01 (4.34)***
User firm temporary contract[a]					4.86 (5.25)	2.36 (5.51)	2.83 (5.30)	1.81 (5.37)
Control variables								
Skill development		.48 (.10)***	.46 (.11)***	.47 (.11)***		.48 (.06)***	.40 (.07)***	.39 (.07)***
Work demands		–.24 (.11)*	–.29 (.11)**	–.31 (.11)**		–.37 (.07)***	–.33 (.07)***	–.34 (.07)***
Job insecurity		.09 (.07)	.16 (.08)*	.21 (.08)**		–.06 (.05)	–.06 (.05)	–.07 (.05)
Assignment insecurity		–.16 (.08)*	–.09 (.08)	–.09 (.08)		–.16 (.05)***	–.12 (.05)**	–.11 (.05)*
Formal social integration			3.51 (1.87)	3.11 (1.87)			3.54 (1.13)**	3.40 (1.33)**
Informal social integration			–.75 (1.82)	–.08 (1.83)			.54 (1.02)	.59 (1.03)
Age in years		–.08 (.22)	.21 (.23)	.32 (.24)		.29 (.12)*	.27 (.12)*	.25 (.13)*
Departmental fixed effects	No	No	No	Yes	No	No	No	Yes
Constant	60.80 (2.48)	58.42 (15.66)	27.27 (18.29)	24.53 (20.71)	47.85 (1.41)	39.57 (7.74)	18.28 (9.10)	26.39 (10.60)
R^2	.03	.26	.30	.38	.02	.27	.31	.33
Observations	172	140	126	126	465	382	363	363

*p < .05; **p < .01, ***p < .001.
a- reference – user firm permanent contract

Table 11.6 OLS regression: effect of contract type, job characteristics and organizational integration practices on perceived user firm co-worker support

	Perceived social support from user firm co-workers. Sweden.				*Perceived social support from user firm co-workers. Poland.*			
	Employment contract	*Job characteristics*	*Social integration*	*Social integration*	*Employment contract*	*Job characteristics*	*Social integration*	*Social integration*
Independent variable								
Temporary agency contract[a]	8.11 (3.43)*	−1.93 (4.93)	−5.74 (4.74)	−4.65 (4.83)	10.09 (3.89)**	12.24 (4.41)**	11.25 (4.16)**	11.16 (4.16)**
User firm temporary contract[a]					13.57 (5.10)**	7.76 (5.57)	4.91 (5.07)	3.91 (5.14)
Control variables								
Skill development		.27 (.08)***	.17 (.08)*	.18 (.08)*		.44 (.06)***	.24 (.07)***	.22 (.07)***
Work demands		−.18 (.10)	−.12 (.09)	−.12 (.10)		−.26 (.07)***	−.18 (.07)**	−.21 (.07)**
Job insecurity		−.01 (.06)	.01 (.06)	.02 (.06)		−.05 (.05)	−.01 (.05)	−.02 (.05)
Assignment insecurity		−.01 (.07)	.05 (.07)	.08 (.07)		−.05 (.05)	−.04 (.04)	−.04 (.04)
Formal social integration			−1.42 (1.50)	−1.95 (1.53)			1.95 (1.08)	2.17 (1.09)*
Informal social integration			5.72 (1.49)***	5.88 (1.55)***			5.50 (0.98)***	5.50 (0.98)***
Age		−.30 (.19)	−.46 (.18)**	−.37 (.20)		.04 (.12)	.09 (.12)	.09 (.12)
Department fixed effects	No	No	No	Yes	No	No	No	Yes
Constant	69.24 (1.96)	80.66 (13.24)	58.49 (14.64)	51.90 (17.07)	49.86 (1.31)	46.82 (7.79)	6.64 (8.71)	8.33 (10.16)
R^2	.03	.17	.25	.29	.03	.20	.30	.31
Observations	174	143	131	131	469	379	360	360

*p < .05; **p < .01, ***p < .001.
a- reference – user firm permanent contract

and temporary user firm employees also at the Polish site, with the effect strengthening when controls of job characteristics and organizational integration are added. On the 100-point support scale, agency workers' perceived support from their user firm supervisors is 11.84 points higher than that of user's permanent employees. Controlling for both job characteristics and social integration, agency worker's predicted perceived support from their user firm supervisor rises to 19.01 points higher than that perceived by the user firm's permanent employees.

Of other job characteristics, higher skill development is associated with higher support and high work demands with lower perceived supervisor support. All else being equal, employees who consider it likely that they will be reassigned against their will report lower support from supervisor while participation in formal workplace social activities such as meetings and trainings is associated with higher perceived support levels. Age does not have a significant effect in the Swedish case but in the Polish case perceived supervisory support increases by .25 points for each one-year increase in employee age.

Perceived social support from user firm co-workers

The variance of perceived social support from user firm co-workers explained by contract type alone at 3% in both countries was comparable to that for supervisor support. Job characteristics increase the explained variance to 17% in Sweden and 20% in Poland, with social integration in combination with departmental fixed effects adding another 12% in Sweden and 11% in Poland, resulting in a model explaining 29% of the variance in perceived co-worker support in Sweden and 31% in Poland. Comparing the models for supervisor and co-worker support indicates that job characteristics contribute relatively more to explaining perceived supervisor support while social integration variables add more to explaining co-worker support.

As for supervisor support, agency workers report higher co-worker support from user firm colleagues in the Swedish case, with the difference of 8.11 points on a 100-point scale. Controlling for job characteristics indicates that this relationship is mediated by skill development, with workers in jobs providing opportunities for learning reporting significantly higher support. Further the 'Social integration' model indicates that in addition to skill development, co-worker support in the Swedish case also is predicted by participation in informal social events with colleagues as well as age, with perceived co-worker support decreasing by .46 points for each one-year increase in employee's age.

In the Polish case the lowest co-worker support is reported by user firm employees working on standard permanent contracts – on the 100-point support scale agency workers report 10.09 points higher and user firm temporary workers 13.57 points higher levels of co-worker support when compared to the permanent workforce. Controlling for job characteristics, the effect of user firm temporary contract disappears but agency contract remains a significant positive predictor for higher support levels. As for supervisor support, with other factors kept constant employees perceiving higher skill development also report higher co-worker support while excessive work demands predict lower support from colleagues. Including social integration to the model does not change this pattern significantly, but does show that informal socialization with colleagues also predicts higher levels of co-worker support. Controlling for departmental fixed effects adds also formal participation among significant predictors for higher collegial support, though the effect size is smaller than that for informal socialization.

Discussion

The aim of this chapter was to explore how differences in the practice of TAW affect the social dimension of job quality for agency workers as well as their direct-hired colleagues in user firms. The first research question guiding this investigation focused on the differences in patterns of perceived social support from user firm supervisor and co-workers for temporary agency workers and user's direct-hired employees, with the second aiming to understand and explain the outcomes in the two cases in the frames of their regulatory contexts.

At both the Swedish and Polish sites of the high-road manufacturing MNC accessed for this study, it was found that temporary agency workers perceive higher support from their user firm supervisor and co-workers than user's direct-hired employees. However, differences reflecting the two regulatory contexts emerged after controlling for job characteristics and social integration.

Use of TAW within the two cases reflects all-core (Sweden) and core-periphery (Poland) work organizational outcomes in terms of task distribution and skill development (Håkansson and Isidorsson, 2012), with agency workers included into user firm skill development schemes as well as integrated into social activities along with their user firm colleagues in Sweden while being segregated both in term of work tasks and social events in Poland. This is mirrored in social support patterns, though with an unexpected twist. In the Swedish case the initial positive association between TAW contract and higher perceived social support disappears after controlling for job characteristics such as skill development, workload and insecurity, indicating that besides similar opportunities for development in high-skilled tasks, the employees on different contracts can also be said to belong to same 'core' of social support. In contrast to the numerous accounts of problematic social work environment (Bosmans et al., 2015; Byoung-Hoon and Frenkel, 2004; Isaksson and Bellaagh, 1999; Olofsdotter and Augustsson, 2008; Smith, 1998) suggesting also deficient social support, the current case illustrates how long-term full integration of TAW can create conditions for social integration where perceived support is associated to job characteristics and not to a particular contract type.

The Polish case in contrast matches the core-periphery of work organization with interview data indicating that short-term use of TAW induces the user firm to segregate agency workers into simple jobs that are learned fast and also to exclude them from user firm meetings and trainings. Controlling for other job characteristics further strengthens the contract effect in the Polish case, suggesting that as the higher perceived support by agency workers does not match higher learning or is explained by workload and insecurity, there must be unobserved aspects related to the TAW contract to explain this. While segmentation into 'a separate workforce' of different tasks and skill development opportunities as described in Håkansson and Isidorsson (2012) could be interpreted either as direct social exclusion or at least a factor contributing to this, employees' own accounts reflected in survey findings show that subjective perception of social support does not necessarily correspond to exclusionary practices. The unexpected pattern of higher perceived social support in the context of formal segregation and exclusion can have several plausible explanations.

First, the association between segregation and higher perceived support for agency workers may be connected to the degree of being 'new' to the case organization that is not captured by the skill development measure. Considering that half of the agency workforce had spent less than a year at the user firm where direct-hired employees tend to have high tenure, it is plausible that agency workers as relative newcomers need additional support for learning 'the way' of the user firm. As their fellow agency colleagues tend also to have limited experience and there is little contact with the agency supervisor, the task of providing coping assistance to the agency workforce is left to the user firm supervisors and colleagues. This explanation points to an unexpected consequence of TAW segregation done with the purpose of limiting investment in the contracted workforce – even with low induction time and quick use of TAW in production, employees still may need considerable resources in terms of support from the user firm to cope within their user organizations.

Second, as suggested before (Vajen, 2014), cutting off formal sources of information can direct agency workers to alternative channels of information and support. This explanation gets some support from the strengthening of the agency effect when controlling for social integration and the strong positive association between formal social integration and supervisor support – as agency workers are excluded from formalized support sources, they may rely more on individual contacts. Informal cohesion within user firm support networks may be further enhanced by agency workers' visual integration through user firm uniforms.

The observed pattern of high support in the context of formal segregation and exclusion may be interpreted as evidence of distinctiveness of perceived social support from other aspects of the social work environment such as feelings of being an outsider (Olofsdotter and Augustsson, 2008) or social strain (Rook, 1990). The current study is in line with the view of support as responding to particular needs arising in the work environment (Thoits, 2011), with the matching effect in the TAW context alleviating the factors associated with skill development and perhaps generally orienting oneself at a new workplace. The flip side of supporting those that are learning their skills and 'outsiders' at a workplace seems to be lower support for those burdened with an excessive workload, suggesting the limited nature of support as a resource. The association between high support and high skill development but low work demands in both cases calls for caution in regards to the long-term effects on employee health and well-being (House, 1981; Thoits, 2011).

However, it must be kept in mind that the case organization in this study is not an 'average' temporary agency user firm, but the sites are one of the 'best' workplaces in their respective sectors and regions. Segmentation patterns may thus be strengthened by low voluntary turnover among the user's own workforce – with outcome differences less pronounced in the Swedish context, where also assignments tend to be longer and more prominent in the Polish context of short-term TAW. Additionally, the availability of social support within this MNC may have been facilitated by particular 'high-road' HR policies and practices, prescribed and enforced globally within the MNC.

Conclusion

This chapter aimed to explore how differences in the practice of TAW affect the social dimension of job quality for agency workers as well as their direct-hired colleagues in user firms. Two main contributions have been made to the understanding of the social dimension of job quality in the context of TAW. First, by using a comparative case study design and contrasting case selection, the paper illustrates how job quality at an individual level is shaped by organizational choices within the frames of their wider regulatory contexts. Second, it sheds light on social support as a critical dimension of job quality, drawing attention to how its need and availability are shaped by other job characteristics in the particular context of TAW.

This study illustrates how employer's opportunities to achieve flexibility through TAW use are shaped by employment regulation and how the flexibility practices in turn shape job quality at the individual level. It was shown how the legally enforced short-term or long-term TAW practice mattered for employer motivations and capabilities to use TAW for either numerical flexibility or also functional flexibility. Short-term use of TAW for numerical flexibility led to segmentation of agency workers into the periphery of skills and exclusion from user firm formal social events. The opportunity for long-term TAW assignments induced the integration of agency workers into the core of the workforce alongside the users direct-hired employees in terms of skills but also social integration.

Differences in these segmentation patterns were reflected in social work environment, operationalized through perceived social support from user firm supervisors and co-workers. In contrast to most existing accounts describing strained social relations in TAW, the current findings indicated that temporary agency workers experienced more support from user firm than their direct-hired colleagues. However, in the Swedish case of integration of TAW into the workforce core in skill development and social inclusion, contract differences were fully explained by other job characteristics while in the Polish case of core and periphery of skills and social integration there was also segmentation in social support – with agency contract predicting significantly higher support in the user firm even when accounting for differences in other job characteristics.

This unexpected pattern of higher perceived support for agency workers in the context of short-term TAW use suggests user firm supervisors' and colleagues' response to agency workers' increased need for support to cope in a new work organization. It also calls attention to the multi-dimensional nature of the social dimension of job quality under the overall umbrella of the concept of job quality, indicating that exclusionary practices are not inherently associated with low social support.

The current comparative findings thus illustrate Muñoz de Bustillo et al.'s (2009) conception that job quality should be understood as multi-dimensional as well as context-specific, with social support a critical element for capturing its essence.

References

Agresti, A. and Finlay, B. (2013). *Statistical Methods for the Social Sciences* (4th ed.). Pearson Education Limited.

Ahlberg, K., Bercusson, B., Bruun, N., Kountouros, H., Vigneau, C. and Zappalà, L. (2008). *Transnational Labour Regulation: A Case Study of Temporary Agency Work*. Brussels: Peter Lang.

Allvin, M., Jacobson, A. and Isaksson, K. (2003). Att avgränsa det gränslösa sjuksköterskearbetet: En intervjustudie om sjuksköterskors villkor och valmöjligheter i bemanningsbranschen. *Arbetslivsinstitutet: Arbetsliv i Omvandling*, 12.

Atkinson, J. (1984). Manpower strategies for flexible organisations. *Personnel Management*, 16(8), pp. 28–31.

Bosmans, K., De Cuyper, N., Hardonk, S. and Vanroelen, C. (2015). Temporary agency workers as outsiders: An application of the established-outsider theory on the social relations between temporary agency and permanent workers. *Society, Health & Vulnerability*, 6(1), p. 27848.

Boyce, A. S., Ryan, A. M., Imus, A. L. and Morgeson, F. P. (2007). 'Temporary worker, permanent loser?' A model of the stigmatization of temporary workers. *Journal of Management*, 33(1), pp. 5–29.

Brissette, I., Cohen, S. and Seeman, T. E. (2000). Measuring social integration and social networks. *Social Support Measurement and Intervention: A Guide for Health and Social Scientists*, pp. 53–85.

Byoung-Hoon, L. and Frenkel, S. J. (2004). Divided workers: Social relations between contract and regular workers in a Korean auto company. *Work, Employment and Society*, 18(3), pp. 507–530.

Chattopadhyay, P. and George, E. (2001). Examining the effects of work externalization through the lens of social identity theory. *Journal of Applied Psychology*, 86(4), pp. 781–788.

Clark, A. E. (2005). Your money or your life: Changing job quality in OECD countries. *British Journal of Industrial Relations*, 43(3), pp. 377–400.

Doeringer, P. B. and Piore, M. J. (1985). *Internal Labor Markets and Manpower Analysis*. ME Sharpe.

Eurofound. (2015). *New Forms of Employment*. Luxembourg: Publications Office of the European Union.

Gallagher, D. G. and Parks, J. M. (2001). I pledge thee my troth . . . contingently: Commitment and the contingent work relationship. *Human Resource Management Review*, 11(3), pp. 181–208.

Garsten, C. (2008). *Workplace Vagabonds: Career and Community in Changing Worlds of Work*. Springer International Publishing.

Geary, J. F. (1992). Employment flexibility and human resource management: The case of three American electronics plants. *Work, Employment and Society*, 6(2), pp. 251–270.

George, A. L. and Bennett, A. (2005). *Case Studies and Theory Development in the Social Sciences*. Cambridge, MA: MIT Press.

Giesecke, J. (2009). Socio-economic risks of atypical employment relationships: Evidence from the German labour market. *European Sociological Review*, 25(6), pp. 629–646.

Green, F. (2006). *Demanding Work: The Paradox of Job Quality in the Affluent Economy*. Princeton, NJ: Princeton University Press.

Grimshaw, D., Ward, K. G., Rubery, J. and Beynon, H. (2001). Organisations and the transformation of the internal labour market. *Work, Employment & Society*, 15(1), pp. 25–54.

Håkansson, K. and Isidorsson, T. (2012). Work organizational outcomes of the use of temporary agency workers. *Organization Studies*, 33(4), pp. 487–505.

Håkansson, K., Isidorsson, T., Pond, R., Sol, E., Teissier, C., Unterschütz, J. and Warneck, F. (2009). *Representation of Agency Workers: The Representation of Agency Workers in Europe at National and Local Level in France, Netherlands, Sweden, Poland and the UK*. Final Report 2009. Department for Work Science, University of Gothenburg. Available at: https://gu-se-primo.hosted.exlibrisgroup.com/primo-explore/fulldisplay?docid=46GUB_GUPgup.ub.gu.se%2F108837&context=L&vid=46GUB_VU1&lang=sv_SE&search_scope=default_scope&adaptor=Local%20Search%20Engine&tab=default_tab&query=any,contains,Representation%20of%20Agency%20Workers:%20The%20Representation%20of%20Agency%20Workers%20in%20Europe%20at%20National%20and%20Local%20Level%20in%20France%20%20Netherlands%20%20Sweden%20%20Poland%20and%20the%20UK&sortby=rank

Håkansson, K., Isidorsson, T. and Strauss-Raats, P. (2013). *Arbetsmiljö för hyresarbetskraft. Inhyrdas fysiska och psykosociala arbetsmiljö. Kunskapssammanställning*. Arbetsmiljöverket Rapport 2013:10. Available at: https://www.av.se/globalassets/filer/publikationer/kunskapssammanstallningar/arbetsmiljo-for-hyresarbetskraft-inhyrdas-fysiska-och-psykosociala-arbetsmiljo-kunskapssammanstallningar-rap-2013-10.pdf

Hambleton, R. K. (2005). Issues, designs, and technical guidelines for adapting tests into multiple languages and cultures. *Adapting Educational and Psychological Tests for Cross-cultural Assessment*, 1, pp. 3–38.

House, J. S. (1981). *Work Stress and Social Support*. Addison-Wesley Longman.

House, J. S. and Kahn, R. L. (1985). Measures and concepts of social support. In Cohen, S. and Syme, S. L. (Eds.) *Social Support and Health*. San Diego, CA: Academic Press, pp. 83–108.

House, J. S., Umberson, D. and Landis, K. R. (1988). Structures and processes of social support. *Annual Review of Sociology*, 14(1), pp. 293–318.

Humphrey, S. E., Nahrgang, J. D. and Morgeson, F. P. (2007). Integrating motivational, social, and contextual work design features: A meta-analytic summary and theoretical extension of the work design literature. *Journal of Applied Psychology*, 92(5), pp. 1332–1356.

Isaksson, K. and Bellaagh, K. (1999). Vem stöttar Nisse? Socialt stöd bland uthyrd personal. *Arbetsmarknad & Arbetsliv*, 5(4), pp. 247–258.

Jonsson, D. (2007). Flexibility, stability and related concepts. In Furåker, B., Håkansson, K. and Karlsson, J. Ch. (Eds.) *Flexibility and Stability in Working Life*. Springer International Publishing, pp. 30–41.

Kantelius, H. (2012). *Inhyrningens logik-konsekvenser för individ och organisation*. Diss. Institutionen för sociologi och arbetsvetenskap, Göteborgs universitet. Available at: https://gupea.ub.gu.se/handle/2077/29134

Kompier, M., Ybema, J. F., Janssen, J. and Taris, T. (2009). Employment contracts: Cross-sectional and longitudinal relations with quality of working life, health and well-being. *Journal of Occupational Health*, 51(3), pp. 193–203.

Kristensen, T. S., Hannerz, H., Høgh, A. and Borg, V. (2005). The Copenhagen Psychosocial Questionnaire: A tool for the assessment and improvement of the psychosocial work environment. *Scandinavian Journal of Work, Environment & Health*, pp. 438–449.

Lane, R. E. (2000). *The Loss of Happiness in Market Democracies*. New Haven, CT: Yale University Press.

Mandelbaum, M. (1978). *Flexibility in Decision Making: An Exploration and Unification*. Toronto: Department of Industrial Engineering, University of Toronto.

McClelland, C. and Holman, D. (2015). Examining the quality of jobs amongst vulnerable groups of workers in Europe. In Holtgrewe, U., Ramioul, M. and Kirov, V. (Eds.) *Hard Work in New Jobs: The Quality of Work and Life in European Growth Sectors*. Basingstoke: Palgrave Macmillan, pp. 49–69.

McPherson, M., Smith-Lovin, L. and Cook, J. M. (2001). Birds of a feather: Homophily in social networks. *Annual Review of Sociology*, 27(1), pp. 415–444.

Muñoz de Bustillo, R., Fernández-Macías, E., Esteve, F. and Antón, J. I. (2011). E pluribus unum? A critical survey of job quality indicators. *Socio-Economic Review*, 9(3), pp. 447–475.

Muñoz de Bustillo, R., Fernández-Macías, E., Antón, J.-I. and Esteve, F. (2009). *Indicators of Job Quality in the European Union*. Brussels: European Parliament's Committee on Employment and Social Affairs.

OECD. (2014). How good is your job? Measuring and assessing job quality. In *OECD Employment Outlook 2014*. Paris: OECD Publishing.

Olofsdotter, G. and Augustsson, G. (2008). Uthyrda konsulter från bemanningsföretag: Främling eller outsider? *Arbetsmarknad & Arbetsliv*, 14(4), pp. 11–25.

Paoli, P. and Merllié, D. (2001). *Third European Survey on Working Conditions 2000*. Dublin: European Foundation for the Improvement of Living and Working Conditions.

Purcell, C., Brook, P. and Lucas, R. (2011). Between keeping your head down and trying to get noticed: Agency workers in French car assembly plants. *Management Revue*, pp. 169–187.

Rook, K. S. (1990). Parallels in the study of social support and social strain. *Journal of Social and Clinical Psychology*, 9(1), pp. 118–132.

Ryan, R. M. and Deci, E. L. (2001). On happiness and human potentials: A review of research on hedonic and eudaimonic well-being. *Annual Review of Psychology*, 52(1), pp. 141–166.

Schömann, I. and Guedes, C. (2012). *Temporary Agency Work in the European Union: Implementation of Directive 2008/104/EC in the Member States*. European Trade Union Institute (ETUI).

Seawright, J. (2016). *Multi-Method Social Science: Combining Qualitative and Quantitative Tools*. Strategies for Social Inquiry. Cambridge: Cambridge University Press.

Silverman, D. (2013). *Doing Qualitative Research: A Practical Handbook*. Sage Publications.

Smith, V. (1998). The fractured world of the temporary worker: Power, participation, and fragmentation in the contemporary workplace. *Social Problems*, 45(4), pp. 411–430.

Standing, G. (2009). Work after globalisation. In *Building Occupational Citizenship*. Cheltenham: Edward Elgar Publishing.

Stiglitz, J., Sen, A. and Fitoussi, J. P. (2009). *The Measurement of Economic Performance and Social Progress Revisited. Reflections and Overview*. Paris: Commission on the Measurement of Economic Performance and Social Progress.

Sula, P. (2008). *Poland: Temporary Agency Work and Collective Bargaining in the EU*. EIROnline. Available at: https://www.eurofound.europa.eu/printpdf/observatories/eurwork/comparative-information/national-contributions/poland/poland-temporary-agency-work-and-collective-bargaining-in-the-eu

Tangian, A. (2007). Analysis of the third European survey on working conditions with composite indicators. *European Journal of Operational Research*, 181(1), pp. 468–499.

Thoits, P. A. (2011). Mechanisms linking social ties and support to physical and mental health. *Journal of Health and Social Behavior*, 52(2), pp. 145–161.

Uchino, B. N. (2004). *Social Support and Physical Health: Understanding the Health Consequences of Relationships*. New Haven, CT: Yale University Press.

Vajen, B. (2014). *Social Relations and Temporary Agency Work*. Oldenburg: Jean Monnet Centre for Europeanisation and Transnational Regulations.

Voss, M. (2015). *Gemenskap och utanförskap i bemanningsbranschen En studie om inhyrda arbetstagares psykosociala arbetsmiljö*. Linneuniversitet.

Watts, J. M. (2013). *The Institutional Context for Temporary Staffing: A European Cross-National Comparative Approach*. Manchester: The University of Manchester.

Winkler, I. and Mahmood, M. K. (2015). The liminality of temporary agency work: Exploring the dimensions of Danish temporary agency workers' liminal experience. *Nordic Journal of Working Life Studies*, 5(1), pp. 51–68.

Yin, R. K. (2014). *Case Study Research: Design and Methods*. Sage Publications.

12 Job quality in an era of flexibility

Conclusions and new emerging issues on job quality for research and policy makers

Tommy Isidorsson and Julia Kubisa

Introduction

The objective of this edited volume is to show how job quality is shaped by different kinds of flexibility practices and also show workers' strategies to cope with internal and external pressures for flexibility in workplaces, professions and sectors. The overarching aim is to describe how and explain why job quality is affected or influenced by different strategies for flexibility.

The general research overview on flexibility and job quality presented in the introductory chapter of this volume shows that for several decades we have been experiencing an era of flexibility. The research overview also showed that there are several definitions of the concept of flexibility and that it is important to be aware of whose perspective we are taking when discussing flexibility. First, it is the approach that shows an employer perspective and an employee perspective (Karlsson, 2007). Second, it is the theoretical framework on flexibility that introduces the two dimensions of desirability (yes/no) and variability (yes/no), resulting in a two by two table with the four outcomes of flexibility, inflexibility, stability and instability (Jonsson, 2007). Flexibility implies a situation with variability that also is desirable. A situation where variability is desired but lacking is from an employer perspective an example of inflexibility. Instability is a situation with variability but where variability is undesired, e.g. an employee who has to adapt to extended work during unsocial hours. Last but not least, the fourth outcome stability is a situation without variability and where variability is not desired. From an employee perspective this is predictability in the work situation, e.g. to know whether you work tomorrow or not. In short, there are two important aspects – whose perspective we are taking and if variability is desired to take into account when making conclusions on flexibility. These perspectives have been used in the chapters in this volume and we will come back to this in the section *Main results*.

If we could state that we are experience an era of flexibility, we cannot do the same thing when it comes to job quality. On the contrary, job quality has diminished from the political agenda and discussion in the previous decade as discussed by Bouquin in his chapter on job quality in the European policy discourse. Job quality has its similarities with the flexibility concept in that it does not have a single shared definition. Despite the best efforts of researchers and institutions, the precise definition and the full understanding of job quality are yet to be consensual (Muñoz de Bustillo, Fernández-Macías, Esteve and Antón, 2009; Muñoz de Bustillo, Fernández-Macías, Antón and Esteve, 2011; Carre, Findlay, Tilly and Warhurst, 2012). Analyses of job quality tend to focus on a number of dimensions. Clark (2005) highlights the importance of pay and skills. Other researchers have drawn emphasis to components of job quality such as job security, training, development, work organisation, task discretion, employee voice, job satisfaction, working time and work-life balance (Green, 2006; Gallie, 2007, 2013; Coats, 2009; Kalleberg, 2011). We argue that job quality is best understood by using a multi-dimensional concept that allows the social aspects of contemporary work to be grasped. In this volume we capture and illustrate the variety of job quality through Muñoz de Bustillo et al.'s (2009, 2011; Chapter 1 in this volume) model, consisting of a set of work and employment quality dimensions.

Finally when it comes to job quality in an era of flexibility we discuss if it is possible to combine the two concepts of flexibility and job quality. There have been attempts to combine flexibility with security, thus introducing the concept flexicurity. The name flexicurity was coined by the former Dutch Minister of Social Affairs and Employment in 1995 but later also as a research topic (Jørgensen and Kongshøj Madsen, 2007; Wilthagen and Tros, 2004). The concept flexicurity is intended to achieve flexibility for employer and at the same time attain employment security for employee. The latter aspect makes one of the dimensions of job quality. The flexicurity concept was an idea implemented in the EU Lisbon strategy in March 2000. However, an evaluation by the European Commission in 2013 showed that additional flexibility for employers was obtained but was not compensated by increased security for employees, rather the contrary (Nardo and Rossetti, 2013, p. 3). There is now a growing consensus that institutional changes that have taken place under this policy are biased towards increasing various forms of flexibility for employers with lowering levels of job quality and its polarisation (Gallie, 2013). According to Lörcher and Schömann (2016 p. 6), the balancing of the flexibility part of the flexicurity concept has been hampered by structural reforms of industrial relations systems and the decentralisation of collective bargaining, resulting in too little security for workers.

Job quality is highly influenced by flexibility. Flexibility is understood as a tool for employers to adapt to the fluidity of the market situation, from an employee perspective it is also a way of thinking about the working life itself. For employees it can lead to flexibility, inflexibility, stability or instability, e.g. when it comes to working time, distribution of working hours, if and where to work and the changing nature of employment relations.

Also for employers it can lead to these four outcomes, e.g. to fill up for sick-leave, production hours etc. This is in line with the theoretical model by Jonsson (2007) used in this volume. This volume shows the experiences of tensions between the pursuit for flexibility and the outcomes for job quality within the setting of workplaces and occupations in different European institutional settings. The volume clearly indicates that it is worth a look into what is inside the 'black box' of an organisation or a profession in order to understand workers' everyday experiences of job quality and to see a more detailed picture beyond institutional approach. The contributors looked at workplaces and occupations in order to see how job quality has been affected by different strategies for flexibility and how workers and their representatives have acted to meet the different measures for flexibility.

This concluding chapter is organised as follows: in the section *Main results* we show how the job quality for workers is affected by different flexibility practices in the chapters in this volume. In *Discussion* we extract the commonalities and broad lines from the main results and relate them to previous research. In *Conclusions* we try to draw some general knowledge of job quality in the era of flexibility based on the findings in this volume. Finally in the section *Emerging issues on job quality*, we point at relevant areas for future research and discuss implications for policy makers concerning measures to improve working condition on job quality in an era of flexibility.

Main results: job quality experiences for workers under different flexibility practices

The individual chapters in this volume present everyday life experiences of tensions between job quality and different settings of flexibility practices on the level of workplaces and occupations in the chosen sample of European countries – Belgium, Sweden, Poland and the United Kingdom. By using the examples from countries that vary in terms of employment regimes, we were able to illuminate the complexities of working life realities in four different national employment regimes (Gallie, 2007, 2013; Visser, 2009, pp. 46–52). The chapters cover the job quality dynamics in old and new sectors of labour markets in Europe, bringing in the experiences in manufacturing and various services, with regard to changes in the institutional frameworks and market pressures.

The first chapters of this volume offer an introduction to the research area and a theoretical background. Chapters 2 and 3 offer a macro overview analysis of the discourse of job quality and a macro perspective of deregulation and its effects on job security and employability in the EU countries. These first three chapters provide framing for a better understanding of the following eight case-study chapters that discuss a variety of relations between flexibility and job quality.

The introductory chapter by Kubisa and Mendonca extensively discusses the theoretical framework for job quality, which serves as reference point for the following chapters studying the relation, tensions and impacts between job quality and flexibility.

In the second chapter Bouquin analyses the development of job quality policy discourse in the European Union (EU) between 1995 and 2016, to show a development from more employee focus to an employer focus. His analysis of official EU documents oriented at creation of more jobs reveals that the policies are increasingly focused on restoration of 'the dynamics of labour markets' through encouraging companies' internal flexibility. Bouquin acknowledges that the policy discourse omits the real social dynamics of labour markets such as segmentation, exclusion, downscaling of social standards regarding wages, health and safety or more generally working conditions, especially when there is a shortage of job vacancies regarding the real existing supply of labour. As a consequence, the issue of developing – through coordination, legal regulation, soft law or social dialogue – minimal standards regarding the quality of work or job quality is nowadays fading away in the European official discourse.

In the third chapter Adascalitei and Vegetti describe deregulation of employment protection legislation (EPL) and its effects on job security and employability during the Great Recession in 2008 and the following year. Most of the reforms that occurred have decreased employment protection for workers by making employment contracts less secure, expanding the prevalence of temporary and agency work, as well as reducing the power that trade unions used to enjoy, i.e. facilitated the use of numerical flexibility for employers at the expense of employment security for employees. The authors focus their study on the employment quality aspect of job quality in that they investigate the extent to which deregulation has influenced perceptions of job security and employability of workers. On the basis of the European Social Survey, they conclude that it is not employment protection legislation reforms that changed the perceptions of job security. Instead, unemployment levels and active labour market programs are the only macro level indicators that significantly predict self-perceptions about job security. A host of individual level predictors impacted perceptions about job security: whereas, e.g. age and education lead to higher levels of self-perceived job security, being on a fixed-term contract is associated with lower self-perceived job security.

In the following section eight individual case-study chapters cast a light onto workplaces in various sectors in chosen European countries in order to show variety of experiences and changes of job quality in the context of flexibility practices. It starts with the analysis of the situation of occupational groups – both in public and private sectors that face external pressures, and then moves to the organisational level cases.

In their chapter Scholarios, Hesselgreaves and Pratt show how police officers in the UK experience overflowing of working time, which spills over to their private life. The budget cuts following the 2008–2009 crisis, along with other factors, made employer-led demands for flexibility which require adjustments to employee work schedules more likely, regardless of the consequences for non-work life. These public sector jobs can be described as extreme due to the prolongation of working hours that affect police officers' well-being. The key to understand the outcomes of employer-led flexibility lies in another aspect of job quality – workers' control over their working time. To use Jonsson's (2007) terminology, the shift extensification represents flexibility for the employer but creates instability for the employees. Scholarios et al. show how the unpredictability of shifts deteriorates job quality. Working time quality is here understood beyond the definitions of unsocial working hours because the authors point out the negative effects of unpredictability on the off work activities that are work-related, such as journeys to work or recovery time. This 'silent erosion' of control over work/life balance may have a growing impact on job quality.

Newsome, Moore and Ross use the case of parcel delivery workers to show how supply chain pressures impact on job quality. This segment of labour market is characterised by many flexible solutions, especially forms of contracts that lead to fragmented employment and self-employment. The employer-led flexibility is supported by technological surveillance that deteriorates workers' autonomy and task discretion in terms of choosing the route to a client or the pace of work. The daily metrics which drive the performance of workers contribute to lowering of work quality as workers face more work pressures. The participation dimension of job quality is studied here to show the importance of collective voice in defence of the frontier of control, preservation of aspects of job quality and dignity at work.

The situation of nurses in Poland is shaped by a kind of bogus flexibility, as Kubisa shows. Management in healthcare adopts flexibility practices in order to face change – or rather a set of different changes, some more explicitly defined and some hidden. The flexible practices in forms of various civil contracts were supposed to bring more market mechanisms to the sector and make it more dynamic. In fact they conceal a major change – the decrease of the number of nurses. The approach of job quality shows that the outcome of flexibility practices is instability for all parties, including patients, because in the long-term perspective the flexibility does not serve anyone.

The call centre sector in Poland studied by Zielińska offers fragmented employment. Although workers have certain control over their working hours as they are free to choose how much time they are willing to spend at work, this is not enough to say that it is a desirable flexibility. This can be understood when looking at another dimension of job quality – access to skill development. It is a very low level of skill development at those workplaces, which can serve as an illustration that the character of flexibility is employer-led. This kind of flexibility practice that offers very uneven job quality results in strategies of micro-resistance and exit strategies by individual employees – however those individual strategies do not translate into collective voice and have a rather low impact on shaping job quality in the call centre industry.

Håkansson, Pulignano, Isidorsson and Doerflinger also take up the topic of collective voice and its role in shaping job quality. Their main focus is on job security experienced by temporary agency workers and their opportunities for voice based on two cases in Sweden and Belgium. The temporary agency workers face lack of adequate channels for voice, or as Muñoz de Bustillo et al. puts it, participation, unless there is a legal framework that enables organisation of trade unions for agency workers. Håkansson et al.'s conclusion is that collective voice and support via the local client organisation is a prerequisite, but not sufficient to give agency workers security. It is the macro level regulations that sets the limits for how the agency workers can be represented and execute their voice and thus the macro level regulations have the final influence for agency workers' job security and thus their job quality.

Mendonca shows how management strategies towards the use of working time flexibility and numerical flexibility have affected workers' job quality and what role the union played. This has shaped employment relations in the workplace and affected job quality foremost when it comes to what Muñoz de Bustillos et al. define as employment quality, including all their indicators of type of contract, working hours, distribution of working hours, wages and social benefits but also illustrates a participation dimension, i.e. participation of workers in the decisions affecting working hours. The chapter also shows the fact that trade unions adapt to strategies for flexibility proposed by management and assimilates market values. The case study shows that this has significant implications for the job quality in the workplace. However, the effect in job quality is not evenly distributed. The outcome of employer-implemented flexibility practices was at the expense of instability for not one but two peripheral groups of workers while trade union efforts protected the core workers who experience stability. The results also show that Karlsson's (2007) expression 'flexibility for whom' must not only include the two categories employer and employee, but also has to include different categories or segments of employees at the workplace.

In the chapter on Temporary agency worker   precarious worker, Håkansson and Isidorsson investigate how job quality is perceived by agency workers and client organisation employees in a workplace using temporary agency workers. To do this they select a 'best case' situation, involving Swedish temporary agency workers who share the same work situation as the client organisation's employees and where the agency workers are highly integrated within the work organisation. In this workplace the employer uses agency workers as a long-term buffer in case of a major downturn. From an employer perspective the use of agency workers can be seen as long-term downward numerical flexibility, and it can also be seen as a way of achieving stability, i.e. stability in the sense that the organisation does not need to dismiss their own staff in a downturn. This means stability also for the core workers, that is the staff employed by the client organisation. From an agency worker perspective, the situation can be described as instability if their assignment is terminated. Their analysis shows no difference concerning perceived employability between the two groups of workers. Their equal treatment in work quality seems to level out the differences in the perceived employability. However, the two groups differ when it comes to job quality expressed as job security, despite the fact that both categories of workers have open-ended contracts, agency workers with the work agency and client organisation employees with the client organisation. The analyses of the quantitative data show that the most important explanation for temporary agency workers' lower job quality and lack of job security is the absence of skill development offered by their employer, i.e. the temporary work agency.

Also Strauss-Raats investigates workplaces using agency workers but with the focus on the social dimension of job quality in a comparative cross-national perspective. Plenty of empirical evidence points to the critical role workplace social relations play for employee well-being. Employer practices, such as temporary agency work used for numerical flexibility, entail special vulnerabilities for stable and supportive workplace relations, as groups of workers are excluded from others by more or less visible organisational borders. The study explores social work environment in two contrasting national contexts shaping organisational flexibility practices. Results illustrate how the Swedish unrestricted long-term use of agency work leads to social integration, while the Polish legally enforced short-term approach restricts employer motivation for integrating agency workers, resulting in formal exclusion but increased supervisory and co-worker support as a compensation mechanism. The study illustrates diversity in the sector as well as the critical impact of regulatory frameworks in shaping organisational flexibility practices, conditioning social work environment for agency workers but also their direct-hired counterparts. In Poland, restrictions in time and use of agency work lead to instability with a situation where a constant flow of 'new' employees pass through the workplace affecting also permanent workers' job quality. At the same time, lack of continuity in relationship between worker and agency limits opportunities for support from agency supervisors and coworkers and places the provision of support on the client organisation. In the Swedish case of open-ended contracts and long assignments, agency workers are provided with the same opportunities as user firm employees, reflected also in their full integration in workplace socialisation as well as perceived social support levels. However, this cross-national comparative case-study shows in both cases that the use of agency work seems to be negatively affecting the social dimension of job quality for direct-hired user firm employees.

These results from the eight case-study chapters show that the elaborated flexibility and stability model by Jonsson (2007) used in this volume is helpful in nuancing how flexibility and job quality are interrelated. The results also show that Karlsson's (2007) expression 'flexibility for whom' must not only include the two categories employer and employee, but must also be extended to include several segments of employees at the workplace experiencing job quality differently.

Discussion

In this section we will discuss recurrent themes on job quality in an era of flexibility shown in our case studies. The research presented in this volume provides enough variety of material to seek for significant commonalities in the experiences of different dimensions of job quality in the European context. In this section we will come back to Muñoz de Bustillo et al.'s (2009) job quality index with its 13 different dimensions that construct employment quality and work quality that we use in this volume. In this perspective job quality includes both employment quality and work qualities, where employment quality stands for type of contract, wage, working hours, distribution of working hours and social benefits, and work quality includes physical effort, speed, autonomy, temperature, noise, risk of accidents and social work environment. There are also two dimensions that are linked with both employment and work quality – those are participation and skill development. The latter of the two can consist of on the job training and formal training. While Muñoz de Bustillo et al.'s (2009) quest is to find indexes to measure job quality, the research presented in this volume is in line with what Holman (2013) and Heyman (2016) request, not only to look at macro data but behind and into the organisation's 'black box' and how inter-firm relations influence job polarisation – this approach further nuances the understanding of the phenomenon of job quality. This enabled us to look for a variety of impacts and consequences of flexibility experienced in workplaces and by certain occupational groups.

There are several questions that arise when discussing job quality in an era of flexibility. What are the broad lines between job quality and flexibility in the research presented in this volume? How is job quality affected by flexibility and what dimensions of job quality are most affected by flexibility practices and what are the effects for workers? What is the role of workers' agency in securing job quality in the context of flexibility practices?

We will attempt to answer those questions by discussing the collection of chapters and describing more general common processes that emerge in different workplaces and occupational contexts that we think are significant for understanding what is happening to job quality in an era of flexibility. The results presented in this volume will of course also be discussed in relation to previous research.

The first broad theme that arises from the research in the volume is segmentation. It is worth looking at the debates on dualisation and segmentation of the labour market and job polarisation in order to understand it in a broader context. They are usually focused on macro-developments, such as globalisation, institutional and technological change (Pulignano, Doerflinger and Keune, 2017).

Doeringer and Pioe (1971) use the concepts 'internal and external labour markets' to understand the mechanisms that shape divisions of labour markets. The internal labour markets are characterised by jobs with higher stability, gained both thanks to the rules of internal labour markets of the companies and the position of the workers – who were unionised, and who offered skills that were needed and difficult to replace. Jobs in the internal labour market offer more predictability in terms of career ladders, opportunities for training, development and security, which was also connected to the relatively high wages. Other concepts to describe this are primary labour market or the core. The external labour market was characterised as far more insecure, as it was dependent on the market pressures and lacked the inner stability and norms specific for the core segment. The workers in this external segment had less skill and definitely less chances to improve them. They recruited from the social groups more prone for exclusion on the labour market – women, immigrants and low skilled workers (Doeringer and Piore, 1971). External labour market is also described as the secondary labour market and can also be seen as the periphery in opposition to the core.

In their edited volume 'The Age of Dualism' Emmenegger, Hausermann, Palier and Seeleib-Kaiser (2012a) try to develop the concept of dualisation. They suggest that dualisation can take three different forms: deepening of existing institutional dualism, widening of existing institutional dualism or finally a new institutional dualism 'which we did not witness during the postwar era of economic growth' (Emmenegger, Hausermann, Palier and Seeleib-Kaiser, 2012b, p. 10). However, their focus is primarily the politics of change, and not the outcome of dualism. Standing (2009, 2011, 2014) pays attention to outcomes that current development of flexibilisation, dualisation and segmentation have on today's working life. He argues that insecurity is becoming more diffused in society and also concerns several dimensions. Standing suggests that the precariat as a new emerging class consisting of people facing insecurity in several aspects, among them employment security and future job career. According to the researcher, the precariat is not a homogenous group and includes different types of workers such as temporary employed, agency workers or self-employed.

The debate on dualisation can be sensitised by the approaches of job segmentation and job types. The job segmentation approach goes along with the major core/periphery debate, showing the division of low commitment and high commitment jobs that is growing on contemporary labour markets (Schuler and Jackson, 1987), that differentiate in terms of task discretion, skill requirements, pay, access to training and forms of contract. Segmentation is also discussed by Scott (2014) who distinguishes between four different segments combining the two dimensions of primary vs secondary labour market and internal vs external labour markets, ending up with a two by two table with the four groups of primary internal labour market, primary external labour market, secondary internal labour market and secondary external labour market. In segmentation theories one basic assumption is that there is little movement between the segments. This holds true especially for the movement between the primary and the secondary labour market. Internal and external markets are connected, with movement between them at specified ports of entry and exit. Otherwise jobs in the internal market are for workers who have already gained entry. According to Scott, the secondary external segment provides jobs that are low skilled with low and unstable earnings, little autonomy and responsibility and poor working conditions. The secondary internal sector offers jobs that are generally low grade but with some on-the-job training, security and promotion prospects. The model makes it clear that movement between the secondary external segment and the primary internal segment is more or less impossible. However, there might be movement between adjacent segments, determined by changes in human capital and employers' responses to the changing economic environment.

Another approach named the 'job types approach', is based on the demand and control theory of job design (Karasek and Theorell, 1990) and focused on job demands and task discretion, which when set in various configurations, sums up to four major types of jobs: active jobs, high-strain jobs, passive jobs and low-strain jobs. It is much in line with Gallie's (2013) definition of a good job, which is formulated as combination of job security and autonomy – in other words, how secure a person is in the job and what is the degree of control and influence employees have over their jobs. As Holman (2013) points out, the research on job quality is far more often focused on comparisons of institutional regimes than on the impact of particular institutional arrangements on job quality on organisational or individual levels. The types of jobs approach can serve as a proxy to combine the restraints imposed by institutional regimes with the situation in the particular sectors and organisations that try to react to market pressure, and the workers' agency, experiences and strategies to shape the expression of high- and low- quality jobs within an institutional regime. This volume takes on Holman's request and focuses on job quality on the organisational or individual levels, while including analysis of the institutional context.

Adascalitei and Vegetti in this volume show that the perception of job security was negatively impacted by higher unemployment levels and positively impacted on active labour market policies and GDP growth. These results were in line with previous research. Strangely enough, stricter employment protection legislation has a negative effect on perceived job security. This rather counterintuitive finding might be explained by the fact that their analysis is capturing a labour market segmentation or dualisation effect in which outsiders, that is, workers in the secondary labour market on atypical contracts, do not benefit from employment protection legislation for regular workers. Previous research has also emphasised the negative consequences of job insecurity for employees' physical and mental health (De Cuyper and De Witte, 2007; Vander Elst, Van den Broeck, De Witte and De Cuyper, 2012; Vander Elst, Van den Broeck, De Cuyper and De Witte, 2014). Moreover, Taylor (2013) argues that flexible dynamics lead to fear of losing jobs, which forces individuals to comply with increasingly demanding managerial mechanisms. Several of the chapters in this volume take on this issue and focus on the employment quality dimensions of job quality. Our research shows a very clear link between job quality and job security. One extreme example is Newsome et al.'s chapter on parcel delivery where the self-employed experience a very low job security. Respondents highlighted that failure to deliver the required parcels could result in the immediate removal of work. One important explanation for the poor job quality in this case is the technology that has the capacity to monitor every moment in the driving labour process. Also the case-study by Håkansson and Isidorsson shows that temporary agency workers and client organisation employees sharing the same work conditions and both having permanent contracts with their respective employers still differ in job security, one of the dimensions of job quality. The most important explanation for temporary agency workers' lack of job security is the lack of skill development offered by their employer, i.e. the temporary work agency. The importance of skill development is also evident in Zielińska's chapter on call centre workers where lack of skill development results in exit strategies by individual employees.

The approach of dualisation of the labour market and the expansion of insecurity, along with the job types debate sensitised our approach to segmentation but at the same time showed that they leave out the area of organisational level. Pulignano et al. (2017) stress the importance of investigating the organisational level and under what conditions dualisation is produced within the workplace, which, according to Pulignano et al., is the level at which employment relationships are shaped. Our result is in line with this argument in the way that our findings also indicate the importance of the organisational level to fully understand how segmentation and dualisation occurs.

What seems to be crucial here is that the debate on the importance of job quality and the search for the best fit set of indicators that would qualify jobs in terms of their quality, is still ongoing at the European level. However, the macro level perspective provided by Bouquin's analysis of job quality discourse in Chapter 2 and by Adascalitei and Vegetti's overview of deregulation in Chapter 3 is a good starting point to look at the common consequences of flexibility for job quality. The contributors in this volume look at what is happening to different workplaces and organisations, but it is worth looking at the broader context at first. Flexibility in the form of atypical contracts – non-permanent, fixed-term has spread in Europe. From the employers' point of view the use of atypical contracts is an adaptation to change – from the employees point of view atypical contracts contribute to lower perception of employability. The institutional aspect, studied in the form of active labour market policies (ALMPs), does not play a vital role in individual perceptions of possibilities of stability or control over flexibility. Workers' self-perceptions are therefore more sensitive to macroeconomic changes, such as GDP levels and unemployment. As Bouquin notices, from 2010 the European-level policies present a more integrated approach, combining employee-centred and employer-centred expressions. However, job quality even though frequently quoted, has not much impact on policies, the focus is on the employers' perspective and the institutional solutions such as a flexicurity approach. Therefore it is interesting to see what happens on the workplace and occupational levels, taking into consideration the spread of market pressures and the austerity policies in the public sector in times of weakening of trust in institutional protections.

When looking at the cases on workplace and occupational level, the process of segmentation is much clearer. As the research presented in the book shows, flexibility produces different segments on the workplace level, as well as in certain occupations – which creates different outcomes for job quality. Our results clearly show that a segmentation or dualisation in just two groups is misleading. In all of the case studies of this volume, job quality has been negatively affected in several of the dimensions pointed out by Muñoz de Bustillo et al. (2009) for at least part of the workforce due to the introduction of strategies for flexibility. What is more, in all but one of the chapters (Scholarios et al.) the deterioration in job quality has affected workers differently and thus led to a further stratification of the secondary segment of the workforce. In Mendonca's study the core or the primary internal labour market to use segmentation theory concepts has permanent full-time contracts with good employment conditions while the periphery or the secondary labour market is split into two segments, permanent core-flexi contract employed on annualised working hours and temporary contracts with periods without any job offers. To use segmentation theory concepts, we see that the different groups of workers belong to the primary internal labour market, the secondary internal labour market and the secondary external labour market. All these examples in our volume underline a further workforce fragmentation in the secondary labour market. The core group of employees, i.e. workers in the primary internal labour market, not only kept their employment quality but rather improved it, while the other part of the workers were re-hired into the secondary labour market on either employment contract with annualised hours or on temporary contracts. This case is in line with Heyman's (2016) quantitative research on the polarisation effect within firms and Mendonca further elaborates on these processes and also shows that the primary internal labour market is not a segment with a non-permeable border towards the secondary labour market. In both cases the employment quality is affected via contract type and working time dimensions.

A clear segmentation of the workforce is also seen in the three cases using temporary agency workers (Håkansson et al.; Håkansson & Isidorsson; Strauss-Raats). In all these cases different dimensions of job quality are affected such as contract, social working environment and participation. In Strauss-Raats's chapter the workforce in the Polish case is segmented into three different groups: the core in the primary internal labour market employed on permanent full-time contract and two peripheral groups in the secondary labour market with different employer relations to the user firm – on the one hand, employees with temporary contract and on the other hand, agency workers employed by temporary work agency on assignment in the user firm. To speak with the labour market theorist, the latter two groups belong to the secondary internal labour market and to the secondary external labour market. The situation of employees on temporary contracts and agency workers in the Polish case matches the core-periphery of work organisation by segmentation of work tasks into simple jobs with general skills that are learned fast and also by excluding temporary agency workers from user firm meetings and trainings. These results are in line both with previous research on core-periphery by Atkinson (1984) and segmentation theories described by Scott (2014). However, the picture of core and periphery has been elaborated in later research (Håkansson and Isidorsson, 2012).

Newsome et al.'s chapter illustrates in a clear way that segmentation in the secondary labour market not only includes temporary workers, but also self-employed owner-drivers and home-based courier workers. Concerning the last two groups of the low end of the segmented workforce in the secondary labour market, employers transfer the risk of the social costs of employment onto the individual worker, removing their access to employment rights that affected several dimensions of the job quality such as employment contract, working hours, wages and social benefits. Our case studies cannot say how common this development of a rather extreme form of segmentation is. However, our cases cover a wide range of occupations and type of organisations in different archetypal industrial relation countries and by that indicating that the secondary labour market is undergoing a further development with several layers or segments in the lower end of the labour market that it is possible to state that the phenomenon seems to be widespread in the era of flexibility. It seems that there is a deterioration of the job quality in the lower end of the labour market. The upper segment, in a segmentation theory primary internal labour market, is also affected and there is a transit of employees from the primary internal labour market into the secondary internal labour market. Our findings also support and illustrate Standing's (2011, 2014) notion of the precariat represented by several fractions of the dualised and segmented labour market.

Kubisa's research shows how nurses experience segmentation by working in different workplaces on different forms of contracts. They belong to the core group at a hospital, where they have a permanent contract and at the same time they belong to the peripheral group in another workplace due to another form of contract, regulated by civil law. They are less engaged in the social working life at the peripheral workplaces due to fragmentation of their employment. The form of numerical flexibility – creation of numerous part-time positions with the use of flexible civil contracts instead of standard employment that is spreading in the healthcare sector in Poland in order to deal with labour shortages – produces instability both for workers and for the workplaces. Kubisa's chapter on nurses in the healthcare sector and Zielińska's on call centres workers illustrates the segmentation of the workforce on the sector level due to newly introduced employment forms based on the Civil Code in Poland with worse employment quality for the group with this new type of Civil Code employment contracts with less job security and worse benefits.

Segmentation exposes how flexibility affects working time – one of the employment quality aspects. We would like to use the working time dimension as an example of an ambiguous impact of flexibility on job quality and the necessity to study this interrelation with regard to the context of other dimensions. The working time dimension is more evident in five of the cases: Mendonca, Kubisa, Zielińska, Scholarios et al. and Newsome et al.'s chapters. In the bottling industry case by Mendonca both the number of working hours and the distribution of working time over the year are affected, because of the uneven distribution among different groups or segments. Most evident deterioration of employment quality concerning the working time dimension is the so-called core-flexi group of employees with permanent contracts but with annualised working time where working hours were not set in beforehand. In Scholaris et al.'s chapter on the police there is no exposed strategy for flexibility, on the contrary ad hoc solutions occur with extension of working time in the existing shifts on short notice. This unpredictability, or to speak with Jonsson's (2007) instability for the employees, is richly illuminated in this chapter, giving clear evidence that working time affects employment and job quality. Kubisa shows in her chapter on nurses that low staffing levels are compensated with employer-induced working time flexibility low staffing that produces overworked nurses who simply have to work too many hours per month – in the end it is instability for everyone. A commonality between nurses and parcel delivery couriers studied by Newsome et al. is that both groups lose their autonomy and control over working time. In case of couriers it is managers and customers that via ICT monitor their performance. This is a panopticon disguised as ICT under the role of productivity. Interestingly, the only group that can control the working time aspect of job quality are the call centre workers, who may choose when and for how long they would like to work – while other aspects of job quality are deteriorated, also due to employer-led flexibility.

Another common theme that evolves in the case studies presented in this volume is the possibilities for workers to participate via formal and informal channels to exercise their voice. The voice dimension is discussed by Muñoz de Bustillo et al. (2009, p. 134, 2011) as one that applies both to work quality and employment quality. Muñoz de Bustillo et al. (2009) argue that participation and its effect on job quality can be considered to be an important element of job quality. According to Muñoz de Bustillo et al., it can be seen from a procedural perspective where the existence of an open channel for participation should lead to a better position for workers to improve their working conditions and the job quality. It can also be seen that participation itself empower workers to feel like agents in control in their working lives, the sheer participation is then seen as an aspect of job quality. Muñoz de Bustillo et al.'s focus is to investigate opportunities of finding a relevant indicator for participation that could be included in an index for job quality. Their conclusion is that an indicator for participation should be justified from a results rather than a procedural perspective. Voice is part of job quality since it allows workers to actively shape other dimensions of job quality. The authors in this volume looked at trade unions and voice as a form of exercising job quality and showed a variety of models of trade unions activity and attitudes – from actions that reproduce segmentation at the workplace level, to strategic use of regulations to represent different types of workers, to attempts of producing alternative discourse that is linked to job quality.

As already mentioned in Mendonca's case on the bottling industry, the union did participate in the process of introducing flexibility in the workplace; nevertheless they did not represent the workforce equally and quickly took up management's argumentation. Due to the outcome of segmentation at workplace level, part of the workforce, the core, enjoyed the same employment conditions as before the introduction of the flexibility forms, and from a job security perspective even higher employment quality. This was possible since the peripheral workforce functioned as a cushion and by that the core enjoyed better job quality. For the employees hired on temporary contracts and the core-flexi workers, the management strategy for flexibility implied lower employment quality.

A relatively similar situation is described in Newsome et al.'s case, where trade unions represent only workers who are hired directly and part of the internal labour market. Thus, the voice aspect in terms of job quality is executed unevenly because the self-employed workers are not organised. The trade unions can at least try to influence the job quality for all – in this case it is the attempt to limit the scope of surveillance in the case of each group of workers, including the non-organised self-employed. Nevertheless, the case shows exclusion from the possibility to shape job quality that is experienced by non-standard workers, whose form of employment is a result of the numerical flexibility approach.

In the case presented by Kubisa trade unions cannot even organise nurses who are self-employed due to legal regulations. The union's strategy is to create their own discourse to counteract employers' discourse on the positive aspects of flexibility in the form of civic contracts and self-employment. They show the connection between job quality and quality of care that is deteriorated by the use of flexible practices. However, the self-employed nurses cannot exercise voice on their own.

The studies by Zielińska and by Håkansson et al. show that participation as a procedural aspect is important for job quality outcome. Zielińska shows lack of participation and collective voice in forming working lives at call centres. Due to deterioration in several job quality dimensions and the absence of voice, employees choose an exit strategy. This creates a vicious circle with no improvement in the job quality. In the Belgium and Sweden comparison, there was trade union presence in both of the organisations using temporary agency workers. However, due to differences in the regulatory systems in Belgium and Sweden, it was not possible for the local trade union at the client organisation in Swedish workplaces to represent temporary agency workers in an adequate way concerning the employment contract, resulting in lower employment quality for this group.

The cases discussed in these paragraphs underline that participation in the form of procedural rights and possibilities to have voice in issues important for employment and work quality is of importance for workers in achieving fair job quality. These results are contrary to Muñoz de Bustillo et al.'s (2011) conclusion that procedural aspects of participation not should be included in an index on job quality. The bottling case shows that other aspects, e.g. power balance and solidarity, must be included to fully understand the relation between participation and job quality. However, the Belgium – Sweden comparison in this volume shows that a strong representation structure at the client organisation and inclusive attitudes towards all type of workers at the workplace is a prerequisite, but it is not sufficient to guarantee job quality, indicating that national regulation on how voice can be executed is crucial for job quality.

Conclusion

The objective of this edited volume was to show how job quality is shaped by different kinds of flexibility practices and also to show workers' strategies to cope with internal and external pressures for flexibility in workplaces, professions and sectors. This has been illustrated in the different chapters of the volume. The communalities in the individual chapters has been compiled in the previous section and discussed in relation to previous research. By the way of conclusion, we may come back to the questions asked in the previous section: what are the broad lines between job quality and flexibility in the chapters presented in this volume? Which dimensions of job quality are most affected by flexibility practices and what are the effects for workers? What is the role of workers' agency in securing job quality in the context of flexibility practices? The research conducted on the organisational and occupational level shows that the dimensions change in an uneven way. The broad lines between job quality and flexibility can be seen in form of segmentation and segregation of workers on the organisational level that starts with the changes in the employment quality in form of contracts and working time arrangements. This further affects aspects of work quality – the pace of work is intensified, the autonomy and task discretion are limited and the social work environment is hardly integrated. The workers that experience flexibility practices have difficulties in access to skill development – which affects their self-perceived employability.

The questions of roles of parties in shaping job quality are crucial regarding the fact that the era of flexibility somehow obscures the fact that certain solutions, flexibility-informed, are 'for someone' and not necessarily for all. Our use of Jonsson's theoretical model of flexibility and stability has shown to be a useful tool and helped us to elaborate and illuminate different outcomes in job quality for different groups of employees. Increased flexibility on the organisational level, which is desirable for management, which is clear in most of the chapters, has mixed results for different groups or segments of workers. For some workers it is at the expense of increased instability and a deteriorated employment quality. However, for other workers the same strategy implies stability and an increased employment quality. The discursive aspect raised in the research enables us to understand the transparency of segmentation, followed by uneven development or deterioration of job quality dimensions such as autonomy, work pressures, skill development and working time.

The overarching aim for the volume was not only to describe how but also explain *why* job quality is affected or influenced by different strategies for flexibility. One important communality we observe in several of the studies in this volume is the absence or weakening of collective voice. Voice, or to speak with Muños de Bustillos et al.'s view, participation in decisions, is part of job quality dimensions. Absence of voice for workers may lead to employer-led flexibility that affects job quality. In the absence of collective voice and participation, workers can only influence their job quality by individual strategies – using micro-resistance at the workplace or choosing an 'exit strategy' that improves their own situation but does not translate into the improvement of job quality at the workplace. If the exit strategy is performed within the same sector, workers might change their own work quality but the employment quality stays more or less the same.

In several chapters in this volume the role of trade unions in shaping job quality is weak and the role of management increases, indicating an uneven and unbalanced power relation. As shown in this volume, unions do not always represent the voice for all workers in the workplace. This takes its outcome in a segmentation of workers in the same workplace into several separate segments with differences in job quality. This development, where high-skilled workers are those who have access to voice, is similar to what Johnstone and Ackers (2015) discuss in their volume on voice at work. One important conclusion from our research is therefore to increase workers' influence, which can improve both work quality and employment quality. The work quality dimension is more related to the local workplace and voice and representation within the organisation; and employment quality dimension is more, but not entirely, related to voice and representation on a macro level. As shown in this volume, a strong representation structure at the client organisation and inclusive attitudes towards all type of workers at the workplace are prerequisites for improving job quality, but are not sufficient to guarantee job quality – indicating that improvements of the national regulation on how voice can be executed is crucial for improving job quality.

Emerging issues on job quality: opportunities for flexiquality

The collection of chapters provides a rather grim picture of job quality in an era of flexibility. The European experiences show that only where employment regimes still provide some sort of regulations, such as right to organise for temporary agency workers, the dimensions of job quality can be protected when confronted with flexibility practices. Although in some countries such as Belgium the regulations matter, it is clear that regardless of employment regime, flexibility affects working lives, even though differently. The research presented by authors in this volume answers the 'flexibility for whom?' question with the usual answer – employers. This fits the debates from Heery and Salmon (2000) to Kalleberg (2011) that point out that primary internal labour markets no longer protect workers from market forces and that risks are transferred from employers to workers in the form of flexible contracts. At the same time the studies presented in the volume present a much more complex picture of job quality in an era of flexibility as seen from the organisational and occupational perspective, which goes beyond more static approaches to job quality on the aggregated level that allow one to study only numerical flexibility (Howell and Rehm, 2009; Bell and Blanchflower, 2010). Our findings also elaborate on the discussion on segmentation. Originally the segmentation theory states that the segments are separated with no transfer between the primary and secondary labour market (Scott, 2014). Several of the chapters in this volume show a transit from the primary internal labour market to the secondary internal and to the external labour market. Different ports of entry into other segments have been acknowledged previously. However, our cases from different organisations illustrate these processes. The result of these processes is a further segmentation of the lower end of the labour market with poor job quality.

This allows us to formulate a more general conclusion, which is a proposal of new paths for research and policies that start with question – are there any flexibility practices that improve job quality? In other words, how to approach 'flexiquality'?

The research presented in the volume can serve as an inspiration to seek for solutions and mechanisms that would balance the employer-led flexibility. The flexicurity solutions that were promoted to achieve flexibility for employers and security for employees did not succeed in this task. The further segmentation of workers on the organisational level shown in our case studies in countries with different employment regimes makes a significant example.

This critical stance on flexicurity protection serves as a signal for setting new paths for higher job quality in an era of flexibility. Our research shows that deteriorating job quality on the organisational and occupational level is strongly connected to the weakening of collective voice. Results also show that the quality of working experiences and job quality should include studies on the organisational level and within the context of prevailing flexibility. The multi-dimensional approach to job quality helps us to understand the social aspects of contemporary work and in turn to improve job quality.

We suggest that the future research and policy investigation should focus on *flexiquality* – a combination of developed dimensions of job quality that are beneficial for workers within the context of flexibility imposed by managers. Therefore we suggest looking for the meeting points in which aspects of job quality are not deteriorated by flexibility. In order to find flexibility beneficial for both employers *and* employees, such strategies for flexibility must include work quality dimensions and employment quality dimensions. One example of such a model is the multi-dimensional model of job quality presented by Muñoz de Bustillo et al. (2009).

While acknowledging that flexibility always is 'for someone' and job quality is changing in an ongoing manner, our suggestion is to focus further research on the topics of dynamics of change and the variety of stakeholders that shape it, in a form of multilevel analysis taking into consideration aspects on both organisational and societal levels. The research presented in the volume shows that some aspects of job quality are shaped nationally, like the forms of contracts or the working time regulations, while others are negotiated on the workplace level by a variety of actors. These are managers, workers, trade unions but also customers, other participants in the supply chain, clients and temporary work agencies. Each of them has their own agenda that does not necessarily refer to workers' job quality in an explicit way. Nevertheless, they all play a vital role in shaping conditions for job quality. The role of trade unions in shaping job quality is weak and the role of management increases, supported by market pressures in different forms. In case of manufacturing, temporary work agencies become the third party of the job quality dynamics. In case of services – public or private – the clients play a vital role in shaping some of the dimensions of job quality, in different ways. Customers perform additional control that limits autonomy and speeds up the pace of work, which serves as a prolongation of managerial control in the services in the private sector. However, the deterioration of job quality of workers poses a direct threat to the clients of public services. Therefore it is the well-being of clients that can serve as an argument to improve job quality of workers. Inclusion of different actors into the analysis can improve and broaden the understanding of the dynamics of job quality.

This should be followed by the further investigation of the role of voice in shaping job quality in an era of flexibility. The forms of collective organising and strategies that shape dynamics of job quality were revealed as an important and recurring theme in the research presented in this volume. In our view the use of voice and representation could be studied in its variety of forms and methods in order to grasp the potential for achieving flexiquality.

An era of flexibility hereby contextualises new ways that voice can be exercised and different ways it can shape job quality.

To conclude, in this era of flexibility we suggest switching the perspectives; instead of looking at job quality being deteriorated by flexibility, we recommend using aspects of job quality to look at flexibility in order to find flexiquality, a solution that is beneficial both in terms of job quality and flexibility for employers as well as for employees.

References

Atkinson, J. (1984, August). Manpower strategies for flexible organisation. *Personnel Management*, pp. 28–31.

Bell, D. N. and Blanchflower, D. G. (2010). Recession and unemployment in the OECD unemployment crisis. *CESifo Forum: A Quarterly Journal on European Economic Issues* (a joint initiative of Ludwig-Maximilians-Universität and the Ifo Institute), 11(1), pp. 14–22.

Carre, F., Findlay, P., Tilly, C. and Warhurst, C. (2012). Job quality: Scenarios, analysis and interventions. In Warhurst, C., Carre, F., Findlay, P. and Tilly, C. (Eds.) *Are Bad Jobs Inevitable? Trends, Determinants and Responses to Job Quality in the Twenty First Century*. Basingstoke: Palgrave Macmillan.

Clark, A. (2005). What makes a good job? Evidence from OECD countries. In Bazen, S., Lucifora, C. and Salvedra, W. (Eds.) *Job Quality and Employer Behaviour*. Basingstoke: Palgrave Macmillan.

Coats, D. (2009). The sunlit uplands or bleak house? Just how good are today's workplaces? In Bolton, S. and Houlihan, M. (Eds.) *Work Matters: Critical Reflections on Contemporary Work*. Basingstoke: Palgrave Macmillan, pp. 21–37.

De Cuyper, N. and De Witte, H. (2007). Job insecurity in temporary versus permanent workers: Associations with attitudes, well-being, and behaviour. *Work & Stress*, 21(1), pp. 65–84.

Doeringer, P. B. and Piore, M. J. (1971). *Internal Labor Markets and Manpower Analysis*. Lexington, MA: Heath Lexington Books.

Emmenegger, P., Hausermann, S., Palier, B. and Seeleib-Kaiser, M. (2012a) *The Age of Dualization: The Changing Face of Inequality in Deindustrializing Societies*. International Policy Exchange Series. Oxford and New York, NY: Oxford University Press.

Emmenegger, P., Hausermann, S., Palier, B. and Seeleib-Kaiser, M. (2012b) How we grow unequal. In *The Age of Dualization: The Changing Face of Inequality in Deindustrializing Societies*. International Policy Exchange Series. Oxford and New York, NY: Oxford University Press.

Gallie, D. (Ed.) (2007). *Employment Regimes and the Quality of Work*. Oxford: Oxford University Press, pp. 1–33.

Gallie, D. (Ed.). (2013). *Economic Crisis, Quality of Work, and Social Integration: The European Experience*. Oxford: Oxford University Press.

Green, F. (2006). *Demanding Work: The Paradox of Job Quality in the Affluent Economy*. Princeton, NJ: Princeton University Press.

Håkansson, H. and Isidorsson, T. (2012). Work organizational outcomes of the use of temporary agency workers. *Organization Studies*, 33(4), pp. 487–505. doi:10.1177/0170840612443456.

Heery, E. and Salmon, J. (2000). *The Insecure Workforce*. London: Routledge.

Heyman, F. (2016). Job polarization job tasks and the role of firms. *Economics Letters*, 145, pp. 246–251.

Holman, D. (2013). Job types and job quality in Europe. *Human Relations*, 66(4), pp. 475–502.

Howell, D. R. and Rehm, M. (2009). Unemployment compensation and high European unemployment: A reassessment with new benefit indicators. *Oxford Review of Economic Policy*, 25(1), pp. 60–93.

Johnstone, S. and Ackers, P. (2015). Introduction: Employee voice. The key question for contemporary employment relations. In Johnstone, S. and Ackers, P. (Eds.) *Finding a Voice at Work? New Perspectives on Employment Relations* (1st ed.). Oxford: Oxford University Press.

Jonsson, D. (2007). Flexibility, stability and related concepts. In Furåker, B., Håkansson, K. and Karlsson, J. Ch. (Eds.) *Flexibility and Stability in Working Life*. Basingstoke: Palgrave Macmillan.

Jørgensen, H. and Kongshøj Madsen, P. (2007). Flexicurity and beyond: Reflections on nature and future of a political celebrity. In Jørgensen, H. and Kongshøj Madsen, P. (Eds.) *Flexicurity and Beyond: Finding a New Agenda for the European Social Model*. Copenhagen: DJØF Publishing.

Kalleberg, A. (2011). *Good Jobs, Bad Jobs: The Rise of Polarized and Precarious Employment Systems in the United States, 1970 to 2000s*. New York, NY: Russell Sage Foundation.

Karasek, R. and Theorell, T. (1990). *Healthy Work: Stress, Productivity, and the Reconstruction of Working Life*. New York, NY: Basic Books.

Karlsson, J. (2007). For whom is flexibility good and bad? An overview. In Furåker, B., Håkansson, K. and Karlsson, J. Ch. (Eds.) *Flexibility and Stability in Working Life*. Basingstoke: Palgrave Macmillan.

Lörcher, K. and Schömann, I. (2016). *The European Pillar of Social Rights: Critical Legal Analysis and Proposals*. Brussels: European Trade Union Institute.

Muñoz de Bustillo, R. M., Fernández-Macías, E., Antón, J.-I. and Esteve, F. (2011). E pluribus unum? A critical survey of job quality indicators. *Socio-Economic Review*, 9, pp. 447–475.

Muñoz de Bustillo, R. M., Fernández-Macías, E., Esteve, F. and Antón, J. I. (2009). *Indicators of Job Quality in the European Union: Employment and Social Affairs*. Brussels: European Parliament.

Nardo, M. and Rossetti, F. (2013). *Flexicurity in Europe: Administrative Agreement*. European Union.

Pulignano, V., Doerflinger, N. and Keune, M. (2017, August). Re-introducing the company in the analysis of labour market dualisation: Variety of patterns and diversity of outcomes between standard and non-standard workers in multinational subsidiaries in Belgium, Germany and Britain. *Economic and Industrial Democracy*, pp. 1–24. doi:10.1177/0143831X17731610.

Schuler, R. and Jackson, S. (1987, August). Linking competitive strategies with human resource management practices. *The Academy of Management Executive (1987–1989)*, 1(3), pp. 207–219.

Scott, J. (2014). Labour-market segmentation. In *A Dictionary of Sociology* (4th ed. rev. ed.). Oxford: Oxford University Press.

Standing, G. (2009). *Work After Globalization: Building Occupational Citizenship*. Cheltenham: Edward Elgar Publishing.

Standing, G. (2011). *The Precariat: The New Dangerous Class*. London: Bloomsbury Academic.

Standing, G. (2014). *A Precariat Charter: From Denizens to Citizens*. London: Bloomsbury Academic.

Taylor, P. (2013). *Performance Management and the New Workplace Tyranny: A Report for the Scottish Trades Union Congress*. Scottish Trades Union Congress.

Vander Elst, T., Van den Broeck, A., De Cuyper, N. and De Witte, H. (2014). On the reciprocal relationship between job insecurity and employee well-being: Mediation by perceived control? *Journal of Occupational and Organizational Psychology*, 87(4), pp. 671–693.

Vander Elst, T., Van den Broeck, A., De Witte, H. and De Cuyper, N. (2012). The mediating role of frustration of psychological needs in the relationship between job insecurity and work-related well-being. *Work & Stress*, 26(3), pp. 252–271.

Visser, J. (2009). The quality of industrial relations and the Lisbon strategy. In Visser, J. (Ed.) *Industrial Relations in Europe 2008*. Bryssel: European Commission kommissionen. doi:10.2767/54876.

Wilthagen, T. and Tros, F. (2004). The concept of 'flexicurity': A new approach to regulating employment and labour markets. *Transfer: The European Review of Labour and Research; Quarterly Review of the European Trade Union Institute Research Department*, 10(2), pp. 166–186.

Index